THE CONSCIENCE OF EUROPE

Edited by John Coleman

Council of Europe Publishing

All rights reserved. No part of this publication may be reproduced, stored in a retrieval system, or transmitted, in any form or by any means, electronic, mechanical, photocopying, recording or otherwise, without the prior permission of Council of Europe Publishing and New European Publications.

This book is sold subject to the condition that it shall not, by way of trade or otherwise, be lent, re-sold, hired out or otherwise circulated without the publisher's prior consent in any form of binding or cover other than that in which it is published and without a similar condition including this condition being imposed on the subsequent purchaser.

British Library Cataloguing in Publication Data
A full catalogue record for this book is available from the British Library

ISBN 92-871-4030-8 [Council of Europe Publishing]

Copyright © Council of Europe Publishing, October 1999

Published by **Council of Europe Publishing**
F-67075 Strasbourg Cedex

in association with **New European Publications**
14-16 Carroun Road, London SW8 1JT, United Kingdom

Cover design: Graphic Design Workshop, Council of Europe
Printed in Germany

"For myself, I am certain that the good of human life cannot lie in the possession of things which, for one man to possess, is for the rest to lose, but rather in things which all can possess alike, and where one man's wealth promotes his neighbour's."

Spinoza

"The heart of man is deceitful above all things."

Jeremiah

"Whenever a man has cast a long eye on them [offices], a rottenness begins in his conduct."

Thomas Jefferson

Contents

Acknowledgements 9

Part I

1. **Introduction** 13
   John Coleman

2. **A vision of Europe** 19
   John Coleman

   The Second World War and post-war conditions – a historical background and the origins of the spirit of Europe

Part II – Historical emphasis

3. **The first European institution – (post-war)** 37
   Cosmo Russell

   Launch of the Council of Europe – the European Convention on Human Rights – the Assembly – conventions – the Council of Europe and the WEU – the final Assembly – initial trends and evolution – the European Social Charter

4. **Britain and Europe in the post-war period** 43
   Peter Smithers

   France – Italy – Spain – Germany – Britain – the USSR – the European Movement – the Council of Europe – the Treaty of Rome – Britain climbs down – summary

5. **Europe at the collapse of Communism** 53
   Barney Milligan

   The Churches' response to a new political situation – the EECCS – reflection and scope for the Churches – the Conference of European Churches – Central Europe – 1989, its consequences and the Council – ecumenical approaches – decentralisation – NGOs – Eastern Europe – human rights – British attitudes – the USA – Graz 1997 – leadership, East-West relationships – the future of 'Church' and 'nation'

6. **Europe – what Europe? – the future** 79
   Robin Guthrie

   Union/unity: definitions, factual history, routine and powers – power and principles – problems of expansion

Part III – Europe: aims and ideals

7. Dreaming aloud 89

Václav Havel

Personal experiences – Charter 77 – approaches to the Assembly – new structures – bipolarity/multipolarity – Central Europe and the EC – dreaming the seemingly impossible

8. Institutions and inspirations: Europe's pressing needs 97

George Bull

Concepts of Europe – confederation – renewal and creativity – cultural fragmentation

9. Christianity and the new Europe 101

George Carey

Unity and diversity – the role of the Church of England

10. The Union, the Commonwealth and the Council of Europe 113

Emeka Anyaoku

Lessons from previous political ties – shared values and diversity – homogeneity – pluralism – forms of support

11. The end of the noble savage 119

Colin Tudge

Attitudes to the past – disappearing species – worldwide losses – simple versus complex solutions – consequence of hunting

12. The missing heart of Europe 125

Noriko Hama

The EU as a body – the Church of England as heart – sustaining diversity – dangers of size – economics as social question – equality and competitivity – unity – heart and soul

13. Unity of Europe: conscience of Europe 129

Karekin I, Catholicos

Europe seen from Armenia – future partnerships

14. Ten commandments for Europe's renaissance 133

Diana Schumacher

Multilateral responsibility – the dominance of economic progress – challenges and dangers – international crime – manipulation – the

CAP – a return to the wider vision – the danger of centralised economic power – principles for community policies – conservation – appropriate scale – empowerment – evaluation – diversification – co-ordination – social justice – principle of low risk – unity – sustainability

15. **European Muslims and European identity** 153

    Ziauddin Sardar

    Europe and Islam – historical background – need for dialogue – misrepresentation – heterogeneity – modern identity and nationalism – globalisation based on diversity

Part IV – Epilogue and appendices

Epilogue 165

John Coleman

Appendices

A. Europe's spiritual guidelines 175

Cardinal Franz König

B. Scientific method applied to history 179

J. A. Froude

C. The two commonwealths: continental and oceanic 181

Sir John Biggs-Davison

D. A federated Europe 185

Peter Unwin

E. The octopus: Europe in the grip of organised crime................. 189

Brian Freemantle

F. Our moral evasion 195

David Selbourne

G. Regionalism and world peace 199

Ted Dunn

H. Nigeria and Europe: not-so-distant cousins............................. 203

Dele Oguntimoju

I. Karekin I, Catholicos – obituary 209

The Times

Acknowledgements

John Coleman, editor

In a book like this it is difficult to acknowledge sufficiently all those who have contributed to enabling it to arrive at its present form. Nevertheless a few have to be picked out simply because they made the difference between the book not being and being. First in that list has to be Barney Milligan. I recall how we wandered around the various press conferences at the Vienna Summit of the Council of Europe in 1993 agonising about the role of Europe in the world, five years after I had founded and edited the *New European*. One of the very special events of that summit was Václav Havel's press conference which he squeezed in between meetings with the Presidents and Prime Ministers of Europe's member states. Jack Hanning, as the new head of the Press Centre in Strasbourg, also played a vital part in giving both moral and practical support then and ever since. Now as the world approaches the new millennium that conscience which we thought about then seems more than ever desperately necessary. Jeremy Geelan of Adamantine Press read a few chapters of the book at a critical stage and gave me the encouragement I badly needed and Barbara Zatlokal of Council of Europe Publishing expressed wonderful enthusiasm when she read the book in more or less complete form. Helen McPhail, author of *The Long Silence*, also read the book, expressed equally encouraging enthusiasm and made some extremely useful comments. Margaret Allen did much more than just putting the chapters on disk as they came in, and always seemed to play a special role in turning the ideas into reality.

PART I

1. Introduction

John Coleman

On 3 September 1939 the British Prime Minister, Mr Neville Chamberlain, together with the French Prime Minister declared war on Nazi Germany. Chamberlain had been notoriously reluctant, perhaps too reluctant. The British people were also clearly reluctant and a sombre mood had descended on them. You have to know what it was like to be a schoolchild being fitted with a gas mask in an empty London shop, or talking to a group of soldiers with their helmets and equipment on, on a bleak Kent railway station on their way to France. The Great War, as they called it then, was still fresh in the minds of the British people. There was no waving of flags or enthusiasm this time, as there had been on that former occasion. A lightning and brutal attack on Poland had just occurred. It seemed that an essentially moral decision had been taken by the British and French Governments, designed to root out a cancer at the heart of Europe.

I believe that this needs stressing because it was that moral decision, reinforced by the experiences of the war itself, that led to the creation of the Council of Europe and to a double determination that nothing like that war should ever occur again. Both the Council of Europe and the United Nations embodied these aims and hopes. In its origin the Council was about much more than human rights, though this was one, perhaps the most significant, manifestation of the conscience that had grown out of the twentieth century's two terrible wars. It is that conscience that this book is about. It is not a conscience that any one part of the horrors of war can claim exclusively, not even the Holocaust, but it is a universal conscience in which the Jewish nation must share, especially as it is in the unique position of being the only member of the Council of Europe outside Europe itself. That conscience which cannot be exclusive must be universally set against all violence and oppression wherever it manifests itself.

The next aim of this book has been to stress the need to focus on an institution that can provide expression for all those who are specially concerned with giving guidance on the way in which our continent of Europe develops. Its purpose should not be to make laws, nor develop trade, nor create a civil service or bureaucracy, but to provide that subtle authority which leads humanity away from barbarism and towards civilisation. If that authority is not present then the blind are being led by the blind.

Although this book aims to look profoundly into the origin and purpose of the Council, it does not aim primarily to chronicle its history but almost to resuscitate the principle out of which it was born. In doing so it must, of course, place it in the changing contexts of time which must involve a measure of history.

The book is divided into three main parts: an introductory chapter which was sent to those who were invited to contribute; secondly, the contributions – the contributors being clearly divided between those who were directly involved in the work of the Council at the various stages of its development and those concerned with the ideas from the outside; and thirdly, a final chapter which seeks to identify some common threads and some shared conclusions.

The first group of contributors have what, in today's jargon, is called 'hands-on' experience. They include Cosmo Russell, who was with Winston Churchill at the inauguration of the Council, Sir Peter Smithers, who was its Secretary General in the early post-war period and whose strong views are clearly shaped by the experiences of those times, Canon Barney Milligan, who represented the Churches, especially the Church of England, for whom he was also the Council of Europe Chaplain in Strasbourg over the period of the change and collapse of the Soviet Union and finally Dr Robin Guthrie, who was Director of Social and Economic Affairs at the Council of Europe until recently.

Milligan's views, expressed at the crucial time of the collapse of Communism, are of special importance because of the unique opportunity that was missed to reach out and welcome the East European countries back into the European family, something I believe Mr Gorbachev was particularly anxious to achieve. Of course it is pointless to cry over spilt milk but even now lesser opportunities of a similar kind will occur – not least in the Balkans – and should not be overlooked. Milligan speaks of some kind of Marshal Plan for Eastern Europe. This theme seems so important that I decided to include in the appendix an article by Ted Dunn, which appeared *The New European* in 1989 when the momentous changes were actually taking place. There is a continuing need for reconciliation and pardon on both sides of the old East/West divide. Forgiveness is, as William Blake never tired of saying, the essence of Christianity. It puts a new human face on the severe God of the Old Testament; and wherever Christians themselves have lost sight of it and gained worldly power, they have behaved with no less barbarity than any other group of human beings who believe themselves inspired by great ideals, whether religious or humanitarian. The French Revolution is a case in point and Blake, living at that period, saw clearly the dangers of the Enlightenment: "Mock on, mock on Voltaire, Rousseau." Blake also realised the central significance of Imagination (he always used a capital I). For him it was not just an artistic or aesthetic extra, but the working of the Spirit which gives meaning to political as well as artistic decisions. No doubt he would have seen Barney Milligan's enthusiasm for distributing Gorbachev's speech on the Council of Europe as the result of Imagination! Furthermore he would have comprehended the significance of the less active theological insights of Eastern tradition. The words of another poet, Francis Thompson, come to mind in this connection:

> "From stones and poets you may
> Know nothing so active is
> As that which least seems so."

The second group of contributors are those who express their views about Europe from outside the Council and some even outside Europe. Václav Havel has provided an account of the development of his views on the structure of Europe. He believes, for instance, that it is too much like a cleverly constructed and well-oiled machine (quoted in the chapter sent to contributors – referring to the Maastricht Treaty). This view evoked a strong response and became one of the underlying themes of this book. Indeed it underlies my own view that the European Union's leaders cannot change the relationship with their peoples simply by Public Relations work. Something is wrong at the heart of it. George Bull, the great Renaissance scholar, contributes a short chapter. I said to contributors I was happy for their chapters to be at their natural length. No need to pad Václav Havel. George Carey's insight into the New Europe expresses a clear Christian message and one on which the whole tradition of Christian civilisation, notwithstanding the shallow materialism of the modern world, is supposed to rest.

Colin Tudge, writing from the standpoint of a scientist, paints a black picture of humanity's distant history, one that would surely have satisfied the prophet Jeremiah. There is much to be said for challenging Rousseau's *Noble Savage* and the shallow humanism which has sprung from it. Noriko Hama and Ziauddin Sardar look at Europe with the dispassionate eyes of outsiders and their views may help us to understand what is wrong. To find the guiding principles we need to avoid using religious labels to magnify human conflicts. Diana Schumacher looks at our failure to save the very world our physical existence depends upon. She provides ten environmental commandments to supplement the ancient commandments of Moses.

The ancient commandments needed the New Testament to reveal how the laws might be kept. The modern ones may also need the understanding that will enable humanity to respond effectively to modern man's destruction of the Creation. In his book *Sickness unto Death*, Søren Kierkegaard puts the human paradox in simple terms: "Man's sickness is that he cannot obey." The cure is to obey, that is, to obey the dictates that come from within and which in Christian terms alone give him 'perfect freedom'; just as the member of an orchestra does not achieve his aim by being able to make any old noise, but being able to make exactly the right sound at exactly the right moment.

My hope is that this book will be read with reflection. Readers may care to pause at the end of the first section, and reflect on how they themselves respond to Chapter 2 on a vision of Europe – and especially to Peter Webber's description of Sienna as a city actually constructed on Christian principles – before going on to read the contributions in the second section.

Again, readers may care to pause and reflect before reading the epilogue. They may have better ideas than mine and more to add, and perhaps if a second edition appears, an additional section with readers' responses may be added.

Two final explanations are necessary. Beyond asking authors to respond to the chapter which was sent to them, no guidelines or requests were made. They all approached their task therefore from entirely their own angles. The result may be a touch haphazard or, as today's fashion in philosophy has it, 'chaotic.' The result may be that parts of the jigsaw will be missing but that will hopefully not prevent readers from discerning the overall picture. Indeed too much attention to the details of the nature of the parts can sometimes give an impression of logical coherence without giving much idea of the overall picture – not seeing the wood for the trees. The other explanation is more in the nature of an apology for some of the autobiographical details in this next chapter. It seemed to me that if thought is to be real it must touch on our personal experience and sometimes spring from it. Academic thought will never of itself save the world although it doubtless has its place in reinforcing the directions in which we are going. It behoves us nonetheless always to bear in mind Socrates' estimate of humanity's knowledge. It must also be mentioned that chronological details are repeated in a number of chapters. It seemed to me better that these should be left as they were, since authors included them in the contexts of their own thinking.

Two related points must be added. The first is that Cosmo Russell's contribution – the very first response – was written in 1994. The question arose whether or not it should be updated? It seemed to me appropriate that it should remain as it was since it serves to remind readers of one of the important stages in the evolution of the Council when the countries of Central and Eastern Europe were asking to be reinstated into the European family. It was just after the moment when destiny had presented the British Government with a second opportunity to build a Europe based on values. That second chance was grasped only by the Council of Europe.

The second point is to welcome – and it seems almost like a personal welcome on a living stage – the short chapter by Karekin I, Catholicos of All Armenians, who after promising to write it was struck down by a particularly horrible form of cancer. In his letter to me he simply mentions, "Actually, I wrote it while going through the hardest time of my health condition". I had lost hope of receiving it altogether. Armenia has a special significance for Europe apart from the longer term spiritual and cultural influence. The three terrible genocides of the twentieth century – the 1915 massacre of a quarter of the Armenian people by the Turks; the Jewish Holocaust and the Rwandan slaughter in Africa – are bloody signposts which humanity must not follow in future centuries.

2. A VISION OF EUROPE

John Coleman

Europe has always fascinated me. When I was a child I heard about the way people lived in the Alps in Switzerland and took their cows up and down the mountains according to the season. As a boy I crossed the Channel for the first time at 9 years old in 1937 with my mother to visit an old childhood friend of hers who had married a Dutchman. It was the year of the great scout jamboree in Holland with boys and girls from all the nations of the world present. The Dutch, of course, were great internationalists and keen enthusiasts for the League of Nations on which all our hopes were pinned at that time. Even then, however, I knew the world had a dark side. In the same year I saw the Pathé news films of the bombing of Guernica and wondered how people could bear the violence. It seemed to me unimaginable in spite of the fact that signs of the First World War were all around: men selling matches from wheel chairs by the roadside or mending shoes when they themselves had lost their feet. I had seen them from my earliest childhood and visited the Imperial War Museum with the Wolf Cubs. The Great War, as we called it then, was fresh in the minds of grown ups. I don't think they could quite realise that we children had not experienced it. Only a few years later, however, the dark side dominated our lives once again and we were sitting in an air raid shelter in London experiencing the unimaginable.

Terrible as the Second World War was, it nevertheless brought out some exceptional qualities in people. Everybody began to know everybody else in the part of London where we lived. To my childish perception people seemed to come to life. They all appeared ready to sacrifice everything in a war effort they all believed to be totally justified. Europe seemed to be the cause we were all fighting for. There was a hazy kind of confusion in my mind between Europe and the British Empire. All I knew was that we wanted a world where the terrible crimes of Nazi Germany would never happen again. As we had some very kind German neighbours who were interned at the outbreak of war I was sure that all Germans couldn't be bad.

The post-war period, despite a great flowering of idealism in its immediate aftermath – the army wasn't going to be fobbed off with a promise of 'a land fit for heroes to live in', it wanted the reality this time – gradually became a disappointment to me. People seemed to need a cause and the only cause they appeared to discover was to fill their empty lives with more and more new goods which they had got along quite happily without previously. I also saw a dramatic decline in the quality of goods people were buying with just a few notable exceptions such as motor oil and Bakelite which had turned into the much more robust modern plastic. For some years Britain had maintained its emphasis on keeping the prices of the necessities of life down by means of a pretty hefty tax on luxuries, so that whenever we went on holiday to the Continent we began to feel envious of their much cheaper new cars and new cameras. "Had they," we wondered, "got it right and we got it wrong?" That all began to change, however, and as advertising got into its stride, with television especially, a new materialistic obsession seemed to grip the British people and it was almost a sin not to keep up with your neighbours. It reached its zenith for that era when Harold Macmillan told us that "we'd never had it so good", and the Labour Party began to promise we'd have it even better under them as the white hot revolution of technology forged ahead. Incidentally the former Labour minister, Eric Deakins, in his book *What Future for Labour?* pinpoints this as the moment in post-war history when his party began to jettison its principles.

While all this was happening in Britain the Council of Europe was almost forgotten by the average person and the memory of war was beginning to recede. We heard a lot about economic miracles from Germany and on the Continent the Six formed the Common Market and started to build a commercial Europe which was later called the European Economic Community. NATO, we were told, was the organisation that mattered most and there was much talk of "reds under the bed". One lot of people thought that the Russians were the most treacherous lot of subversives imaginable and were on the verge of taking over the world. Another lot thought that they were really quite friendly. The public were deeply confused and sceptical but feared that the Russians might really be devils – the more so as some of the details of Stalin's atrocities emerged – and therefore it was best to play safe and keep our own devilish deterrents. The logic of the Cold War became entrenched.

It was not, perhaps, until the end of the Cold War that most of us became fully aware of the materialistic foundation of our Western society. So long as the Soviet threat remained it was possible to maintain the façade of a righteous cause. Some of us asked the question: "Is our present way of life what we fought Hitler for?" Surely there was a level at which our basic material necessities should have been satisfied and our minds and spirits should then, in theory at least, have been free to enjoy those other forms of wealth which according to the great philosopher Spinoza are "the things which all can possess alike and where one man's wealth promotes his neighbours".

Everywhere now there is an uneasiness. We are drugged by the need to have ever more and more material goods and yet we sense that if other continents should follow our example, Asia for instance, the result would be catastrophic for the whole globe. Even for us the successful gamblers are the 'fat cats' and the rest have to satisfy their fantasies with the national lottery, with only the remotest chance of becoming a 'fat cat' themselves.

Europe, we are told, has grown out of the civilising influences of Greece and Rome and Palestine and Christianity. The contribution of the Arabs usually gets overlooked but nevertheless should rank in importance with the others. The institutions of Europe have evolved over the centuries from the influences of those sources. There is not much doubt about the Greek, the Roman and the Jewish influences but the precise nature of the Christian influence is not so clear. Anything good or decent gets put down as Christian. If one stands back and looks at the picture of Europe in the latter part of the twentieth century it is hard to gain the impression that it looks particularly Christian. Everybody, or almost everybody, appears to me to be looking not just for their necessities on earth but also for their treasures on earth. Jacques Delors and others have been saying that the European Union must have spiritual and social dimensions but these seem in practice to be little more than extras added on to a commercial empire. The Church, as in most of modern life, seems better at creating an air of respectability over humanity's activities than challenging the assumptions and motives behind them.

In a speech at the European Parliament in 1994 Václav Havel summed up his views of the European Union up to the time of the Maastricht Treaty:

> "I confess that when I studied the Maastricht Treaty and the other documents on which the European Union is based, I had a somewhat ambiguous response. On the one hand, it is undoubtedly a respectable piece of work. It is scarcely possible to believe that a common framework could be given to such a complex and diverse legal and economic order, involving so many different European countries. It is amazing that common rules of the game have been created, that all the legislative, administrative and institutional mechanisms that enable the smooth running of this great body have been invented and that, in so colourful a political environment, agreement on an enormous number of concrete matters was reached and many different interests were harmonised in such a way that everyone will benefit. It is, I repeat, a remarkable labour of the human spirit and its rational capacities.
>
> However, into my admiration, which initially verged on enthusiasm, there began to intrude a disturbing, less exuberant feeling. I felt I was looking into the inner workings of an absolutely perfect and immensely modern machine. To study such a machine must be a great joy to an admirer of technical inventions, but for me, a human whose interest in the world is not satisfied by admiration for well-oiled machines, something was seriously missing. Perhaps it could be called, in a rather

simplified way, a spiritual or moral or emotional dimension. My reason had been spoken to, but not my heart."

It seemed to me that there was only one European institution which could be seen as designed to capture the hearts and minds of Europeans and that was the Council of Europe – Churchill knew all about capturing people's hearts. Cosmo Russell once described it as the parent institution of the European organisations. Today, however, it has degenerated into an antechamber for the Central and Eastern European countries to hang around in whilst they bolster up their economies to the economic level which will permit them to join the economic Union. For God's sake, they are European states and we are all the European family! Do members of a family ask if their brothers or sisters are up to a viable enough economic level to be regarded as members of the family? It takes the blackest of crimes to drive a family positively to disown one of its members. They may fight and argue but the idea of family restrains them and usually keeps them within reasonable bounds. The Council of Europe does not ask economic questions. It can appeal to the heart through the idea of the European family and it certainly has strong moral and human rights expectations. It arose out of the war with Hitler and naturally it is concerned that no one should ever ride roughshod over Europe again. Its task is not to exclude members over any but the most blatant violations of basic human rights and it must always be encouraging better behaviour once the basic abuses have been eliminated. Of course there may be, and there are, disagreements about where the line should be drawn and who should be accepted and who not. So I believe that it is to the Council of Europe alone we must turn to find the soul of Europe, or rather the institution in which the soul of the new Europe should be expressed. Other contributors to this book are all people who have dreams about Europe. Some years ago I heard Lord Dahrendorf speak at the Royal Society of Arts. As he spoke I noticed that he expressed exactly what I thought but had never heard expressed so lucidly before:

"The present space of the European Community is wrong; it is absurd if not shameful to make such a song and dance about our close partners and allies who seek to leave the European Free Trade Association (EFTA) and become members. The present range of what Brussels likes to call competencies, is wrong; Europe cannot be built on an agricultural policy or even the levelling of semi-relevant non-tariff barriers. The present prevailing stance of the Community is wrong; a deeply protectionist Europe is worse than no Europe at all.

The Europe of my dreams is one which is, in the first instance, about the rights of citizens, including those fundamental rights which have a home at the Council of Europe in Strasbourg rather than the European Community in Brussels; it is a Europe which aspires to lifting those who lag behind in terms of economic attainment, social opportunities, environmental standards to the level of the most advanced rather than harmonising everything at the common denominator which is capable of bureaucratic consensus; it is a Europe which sees itself as a stepping-stone on the road to a world order rather than a pretext for drawing a ring-fence round itself to shelter declining industries and anxiously defensive social groups. It is also one which includes, at an early date, the EFTA countries as well as the democracies of East Central Europe. This is a long way from where we are today; but it should not be too much to hope that a Britain which seeks its place at the centre of the European construction – a European Britain – will make a major contribution to turning the European Community from a protectionist bloc into a confident advocate of citizenship rights and international co-operation."

Here there is both a hint of the real importance of the Council of Europe and more than a suggestion that the spirit of Europe should be expressed through the Council and not through the European Community.

In our search for the soul or spirit of Europe we surely can do no better than delve into the Christian tradition which has done so much – so we are told at least – to shape modern Europe. A good starting point, in my view, is Bertrand Russell's *History of Western Philosophy* because particularly in his account of the three great doctors of the Church, Augustine, Ambrose and Jerome, the conflict between the liberal humanist tradition which Russell himself represents and the severe Christian doctrine of the three Catholic saints is dramatically reflected. Taking Ambrose first, which of course is chronologically correct, Russell writes:

"His duties brought him constantly into relations with the emperors, to whom he spoke habitually as an equal, sometimes as a superior. His dealings with the imperial court illustrate a general contrast characteristic of the times: while the state was feeble, incompetent, governed by unprincipled self-seekers, and totally without any policy beyond that of momentary expedients, the Church was vigorous, able, guided by men prepared to sacrifice everything personal in its interest, and with a policy so far-sighted that it brought victory for the next thousand years."

Here surely are echoes of today. Russell is slightly surprised to see Ambrose as a staunch supporter of human rights. The state is led by self-seekers but the Church with the backing of the people is able to check the Emperor. This indeed is true democracy. It is not a mob response but an example of an intelligent and just man gaining the hearts of the people. When Ambrose was accused of inciting the people he retorted instantly that he rendered unto God what was His and even Caesar had to accept that. Russell goes on to give an exceptionally interesting description of Ambrose's life.

> "St Ambrose had every opportunity to seek success in the service of the state. His father, also named Ambrose, was a high official-prefect of the Gauls. The Saint was born, probably, at Trèves, a frontier garrison town, where the Roman legions were stationed to keep the Germans at bay. At the age of thirteen he was taken to Rome, where he had a good education, including a thorough grounding in Greek. When he grew up he took to the law, in which he was very successful; and at the age of thirty he was made Governor of Liguria and Æmilia. Nevertheless, four years later he turned his back on secular government, and by popular acclaim became Bishop of Milan, in opposition to an Aryan candidate. He gave all his worldly goods to the poor, and devoted the whole of the rest of his life to the service of the Church, sometimes at great personal risk."

Russell is unable to conceal his admiration for the way Ambrose led the Church. Alas, he seems to say, there is no similar force today to control the political and commercial power of the modern world. Now, as then, people have lost trust in the authorities but today they know of no effective institution they can trust to oppose them. In AD 390 Ambrose had the most dramatic conflict with the Emperor Theodosius.

> "The next conflict between Emperor and Saint was more honourable to the latter. In AD 390, when Theodosius was in Milan, a mob in Thessalonica murdered the captain of the garrison. Theodosius, on receiving the news, was seized with ungovernable fury, and ordered an abominable revenge. When the people were assembled in the circus, the soldiers fell upon them, and massacred at least seven thousand of them in an indiscriminate slaughter. Hereupon Ambrose, who had endeavoured in advance to restrain the Emperor, but in vain, wrote him a letter full of splendid courage, on a purely moral issue, involving, for once, no question of theology or the power of the Church: 'There was that done in the city of Thessalonians of which no similar record exists, which I was not able to prevent happening; which, indeed, I had before said would be most atrocious when I so often petitioned against it.'
>
> David repeatedly sinned, and confessed his sin with penitence. Will Theodosius do likewise? Ambrose decides that 'I dare not offer the sacrifice if you intend to be present. Is that which is not allowed after shedding the blood of one innocent person, allowed after shedding the blood of many? I do not think so.'
>
> The Emperor repented, and, divested of the purple, did public penance in the cathedral of Milan. From that time until his death in 395, he had no friction with Ambrose."

As I have said, no such institution exists today in which men and women have given their earthly goods to the poor and in which people can place their trust knowing it is not made up of self-seekers. Even giving your worldly goods to the poor today is difficult with the institutionalised charity of the modern world. Well-off people are liable to get their hands on it on its way to the poor. This is not because of the rogues and criminal self-seekers but because of the culture of self-seeking in which most individuals only play a modest part. Cynics say that people are fickle but I believe it suits them to say that; I also believe that people in general respond to genuine selfless leaders. Surely this is what President Havel is really pointing out when he says that people need something they can trust with their hearts.

St Augustine is the next doctor of the Church to whom Russell turns his attention. He, too, gave all his worldly goods to the poor but, being bishop at Hippo in Africa, was obviously not so close to the court of the Emperor. His concern was more with doctrine in a living sense as his Confessions illustrates so vividly with instances throughout his own life and, as Russell so rightly points out, his writings affected the Church for a thousand years until the Enlightenment when the concept of the reasonableness of man and nobility of the savage came to substitute the Christian doctrine of Original Sin. Augustine, Jerome and Ambrose all formed their doctrines against a background of violence and the breakdown of the Roman Empire. When the Emperor was strong and people had the security of its institutions it was easy to believe in the essential reasonableness of man; it was certainly a common belief in the Roman Empire and it triumphed again in the Enlightenment. Russell, of course, holding the liberal humanist viewpoint is prone to ridicule Augustine for his obsession with his own sinfulness. He considered Augustine's concentration on one of his boyhood pranks when he and his companion raided a neighbour's pear tree, although they had their own pears, rather too insignificant for the saint to make such a song and dance about. However, I believe a careful reading of *Confessions* shows that Augustine thought that there was only a thin crust of reasonableness in most human beings which was fragile and concealed savage lusts raging beneath it, so that even the most apparently virtuous people should know that it is only by the grace of God that they are saved from becoming thieves and murderers; indeed he saw that as the significance of Christ's crucifixion between the two felons. The puritan who exclaimed when he saw the murderer being led to the gallows, "There but for the Grace of God go I", understood exactly Augustine's doctrine which left no room whatsoever for self-righteousness.

In his book *Far Away and Long Ago* W. H. Hudson describes the way gauchos in South America murdered their victim. It runs as follows:

> "Darwin writing in praise of the gaucho in his *Voyage of a Naturalist*, says that if a gaucho cuts your throat he does it like a gentleman; even as a small boy I knew better – that he did his business rather like a

hellish creature revelling in his cruelty. He would listen to all his captive could say to soften his heart – all his heartrending prayers and pleadings; and would reply: 'Ah, friend,' – or little friend, or brother – 'your words pierce me to the heart and I would gladly spare you for the sake of that poor mother of yours who fed you with her milk, and for your own sake too, since in this short time I have conceived a great friendship towards you; but your beautiful neck is your undoing, for how could I possibly deny myself the pleasure of cutting such a throat – so shapely, so smooth and soft and so white! Think of the sight of warm red blood gushing from that white column!' And so on, with wavings of the steel blade before the captive's eyes, until the end."

Augustine clearly regarded the pear tree incident as significant because it pointed to the kind of evil he knew to exist in himself. He also tells the story of how he and his young companions forced a gentle and liberal-minded young man to come with them to a gladiatorial contest despite his objections. The young man refused to look at the contestants until one of the gladiators let out a scream as he was about to be killed. At that point the young man opened his eyes and from that moment developed a great passion for the games. This story shows plainly that it was not just what was visible that worried Augustine. The pear escapade was the sign of his own potential for evil and like other Christians of his ilk he believed that he was only saved by the grace of God. In Russell's day the structures of a decent society still appeared sufficiently intact for confidence that men and women could work for and achieve a better world to prevail. Now it is not nearly so certain that they can and the times are more analogous to Augustine's era when rape and murder were common and the gothic soldiers within the Roman army were prone to go berserk and plunge into pillage and savagery so that Augustine's advice to women who had been raped was, to quote Russell's translation: "Tush, another's lust cannot pollute thee". His views on sex and women, although highly unfashionable at the moment, would almost certainly appeal to many feminists who also regard sexuality as somehow a violation of their personalities. Liz Hodgkins in an article in *The Times* made the following points:

> "Sex experts try to make us believe that without frequent sex we will become unbearably frustrated and repressed. In fact the reverse may be true.
>
> Many people discover that their physical health improves during a time of voluntary celibacy. This is because sex brings into play a large amount of stress hormones, which can eventually lead to stress-related diseases.
>
> Although a life of celibacy is popularly imagined to be one of misery, deprivation and continual frustration and repression, it can be the very opposite, and provide a wonderful opportunity to get to know

yourself, understand who you are and what is your real purpose in life. It can also allow you to develop hitherto undiscovered talents.

A period of voluntary celibacy can give you space and time to become autonomous and self-sufficient. It can bestow a powerful feeling of liberation and lightness. It means you can truly reclaim yourself, and become free from the sexual demands of your own body and also the sexual desires of other people, which you may not always feel like accommodating.

It seems to me that sex is more like an addiction than a physiological need. The need for it grows the more we feed it. But once we decide to stop indulging, the desire for it starts to diminish, and it begins to lose its hold, its fierce power over our lives.

We can't live without food, water, shelter and sleep but we can, if we choose, live without sex. And nothing bad happens to us as a result.

We're told that sex relieves stress, but it's actually more likely to cause it, especially if, as so often happens, we are not in total sexual harmony with our partners, or having affairs.

One of the great illusions of our times is that, in order to be emotionally happy and healthy, it's essential to have a full and active sex life from adolescence to the grave. If this were the case, we'd all be happy and jolly. Instead, as we all know to our cost, sexual relationships so often cause pain and suffering to all concerned.

The idea that sex increases human happiness started only with Freud, and soon became an orthodoxy. It is now resulting in great unhappiness as people vainly try to live up to the ideal. And when sex doesn't bring joy and pleasure we can start to blame and hate the partner – or ourselves. But when you decide to remove yourself from the sexual arena, all that 'aggro' vanishes.

If you think about it, sex doesn't really achieve anything. It patently hasn't worked to usher in better physical or emotional health or a more harmonious society.

Perhaps the greatest benefit of the celibate life is that there is more time to nurture valuable friendships. Many happy celibate people, from Stephen Fry to the poet Stevie Smith, have spoken of this. And of course, when you concentrate on friendship rather than sex, there's no fear of being found out if you are having sex with the wrong person. Whoever heard of a celibacy scandal?

So is there a downside, a major drawback? Well, you can miss the physical presence of another person, and you can certainly miss the tranquillising and anaesthetising effects of sex. You can miss the passion, the tumultuous emotions. And it is true that sometimes you will feel odd, as if you're not really part of the human race, not fully living.

> There may be times of sexual frustration and loneliness, possibly of acute pain.
>
> But there's no need to don sackcloth and ashes. You can probably enjoy life's other pleasures even more. And the sense of calmness, of taking control over your own life is priceless."

Augustine values this sense of pricelessness in a similar way perhaps. He was certainly most enthusiastic in recommending it to women, and not from lack of experience. He describes in his *Confessions* how his physical desires had harmed his affections for the mistress with whom he had lived for eight years. He did not condemn lust because it was wrong but because it blinds us to what he believed was the true appreciation of love and life.

Russell is rather dismayed by the concentration of the three great doctors of the Church on the details of piety instead of considering thought and acts of statesmanship which might have counteracted to some degree the ruin of the Empire and the viciousness of that terrible era. Yet paradoxically it was their emphasis on these details of doctrine that created the monasteries as a refuge for civilisation during the ensuing centuries of barbarism. The monasteries have frequently been condemned by those who narrow their view to the most corrupt period of their long history before making their judgements. They should be looked at at their best in order to make a fair judgement of their potential. J. A. Froude points to the period when the monasteries were the best and gentlest landlords in English history and when in consequence a flourishing peasantry existed outside their walls.

The Church in the fourth century was facing the breakdown of civilisation. It is vividly described by St Jerome:

> "The world sinks into ruin: yes! but shameful to say our sins still live and flourish. The renowned city is swallowed up in one tremendous fire; and there is no part of the Earth where the Romans are not in exile. Churches once held sacred are now but heaps of dust and ashes; and yet we have our minds set on the desire of gain. We live as though we are going to die tomorrow; yet we build as though we were going to live always in this world. Our walls shine with gold, our ceilings also and the capitals of our pillars; yet Christ dies before our doors naked and hungry in the person of his poor."

Against this harsh background the harsh doctrines of the three saints of the Church were formed. Now also we are facing a world where the security of tradition is breaking down, where terrorism is on the increase and crime is rising and sex and violence appear to be almost inextricably linked. Liberal-minded people have opened up a Pandora's box and they are shocked at what is coming out. They expected the permissiveness of the age to stop at, say, homosexuals but is it really surprising that paedophiles, for instance, say: "If it's all right for everyone else to fulfil their urges and do what they like, why should we also not do the same? The Greeks and the Romans accepted it, why shouldn't we?"

As the world once again plunges into rough seas a tough discipline is going to be needed to steer the ship through them. Perhaps the way in which total chaos threatens us is different today. Perhaps the barbarians are within the borders of civilisation today instead of outside. The main difference surely is the almost infinite increase and sophistication of technology. But how can this save us? If technology is used to establish the power of a world government, where is the guarantee that a Hitler will not find his way to the position of ultimate leadership – the dream of tyrants throughout the ages? However things go, for better or worse, there can be no doubt that technology will magnify the consequences of our actions, good and bad alike, almost infinitely. Ours is a time when a button can be pressed within a missile launcher and, in the twinkling of an eye, hundreds or even thousands can be killed without the person whose finger was responsible being significantly conscious of what has happened. American psychologists involved in training missile crews are becoming deeply concerned that the people they train are becoming unable to distinguish between practice and the real thing on the battlefield. In the days of bayonet practice the soldier, no doubt, knew the difference between the battlefield and the dummy. Humanity, perhaps, remains much the same in each age. In Europe we have seen "savages" dressed up in different guises in each age. Knowing this, how should we view the developments of our own times? Can we expect the conglomerations of commercial and political interest, which make up the nation-states out of which our present European Union has been formed, to throw up a body like the Church in the dying days of the Roman Empire? Where are we going to find the men and women who are ready to give up all their worldly goods and thereby have the authority in the eyes of the people to rebuke the politicians and commercial magnates of today in the way Ambrose and Augustine did in their times?

Maybe this is precisely where we should look to Eastern Europe. Those who have been through the hardships and perils of those regimes may be exactly the kind of people that the Western world lacks but now needs to speak with conviction and authority. Maybe the Council of Europe, with its concern for human rights and the obligations and values of civilisation which sprung from the background of the war with Hitler, is the right and proper forum to give them expression in the battle against the juggernaut of materialism which the Western world has created. One challenge comes through the words of President Václav Havel and shows clearly that he is no ordinary politician:

> "Throughout my life, whenever I thought about public affairs, about civic, political and moral matters, some reasonable person would

inevitably start very reasonably to point out, in the name of reason, that I too should be reasonable, should cast aside my eccentric ideas, and finally accept that nothing can change for the better because the world is divided once and for all into two worlds. Both of these half-worlds are content with this division and neither wants to change anything. It is pointless to behave according to one's conscience because no one can change anything, and anyone who does not want war should just keep quiet. I often had to listen to this 'voice of reason' following Brezhnev's invasion of Czechoslovakia, after which such so-called 'reasonable' people felt much revived because they had been given a new argument for their indifference to public affairs. They could say: 'There you are, that's the way it goes, they've written us off, nobody cares, there is nothing we can do, everything's in vain, you'd better learn your lesson and keep silent! Or do you want to go to jail?"

This is no more than a restatement of the spirit that has characterised the highpoints in European civilisation, and indeed most other civilisations as well. It is proof that the world can change for the better. The fact that the better may not last is no excuse for not trying to achieve it even if only for a brief, glorious moment. One of those shining European examples is powerfully described by Professor Peter Webber in his book on the planning of Sydney, Australia. It is the city of Sienna, and doubtless like many of the other city states of mediaeval Europe reflects the influence of St Augustine's *City of God*:

> "One of the most admired of cities for its urban qualities, its artistic qualities, the consistency yet variety in its public streets and places and its integrity as a total spatial composition, is the medieval city of Sienna. The distinguished scholar Wolfgang Braunfels studied the thirteenth and fourteenth century records of town meetings to discover how that city operated at the height of its wealth and power, and how the design and alteration of its buildings and public spaces were controlled. We tend to suppose that the formal delights of the medieval city were due simply to the exquisite good taste of the ruling class and the exquisite sensibility of the medieval craftsmen.
>
> Evidence of the political structure of thirteenth century Sienna demonstrates otherwise. Sienna was governed by a democratic assembly 'with so many separate committees that the majority of well-born citizens were occupied for the greater part of the year in the process of governing themselves and in changing the forms of their constitution'. Each year in May a great assembly was held devoted to building and public works and from his analysis of one such assembly held in May 1297 Braunfels observed that:
>
> 'The citizens of Sienna considered each project within the framework of the town as a whole. Many of the resolutions make it clear that no

one was free to build at will and that very strict regulations were enforced. But from the wording of the texts, we learn that this sense of order in town planning arose from a general ideal of what a strong, good, beautiful, and pious city should be. For the Siennese, the ordering of the town was directly connected with the order of life which, in its turn, was a mirror of the order of the Celestial City.'

Usually both the developers and the members of the town council were the influential and powerful families in the city, and all lived their lives within a kilometre or two of each other. They were the representatives of a city which was the state, and they had to live daily with the built evidence of the decisions they had made. Such direct involvement could not but breed understanding, sensitivity and heightened responsibility for their environment."

As with the monasteries, it is easy to ridicule or condemn the city states of the Middle Ages after they had descended into corruption, self-seeking and violent conflict with each other and it is necessary to look at them at the height of their achievement. Who would think of judging a flower after its blossom has faded? Sienna was special and showed that in its eternal moments it reflected the City of God. Plato saw, as did both St Augustine and the Emperor Augustus, the ideals which poor humans have to try and build on earth. Sienna was exceptional because it tried deliberately to represent the *whole* range of human emotion. It was not a chocolate box ideal city state, but represented the harsh as well as the sentimental. The *contradas*, or little districts of which it is composed, have their friends and their enemies. Certain *contradas* hate their enemy *contradas* and regard others with great warmth and friendship. However, the cathedral at the centre represents a principle which they all respect with the result that firm limits are placed on the aggression of the *contradas*. This aggression between neighbouring town and states seems to be so universal that it cannot be simply wished away. It has to be countered by a higher principle which all accept. Perhaps it is difficult to reconcile this with Christian love but I once heard a preacher make it much easier. He pointed out that Christ only said that Christians had to love their enemies. He didn't say they had to like them!

As the new century dawns let us hope that we may see new city states arising across Europe, each with a high degree of autonomy but within a broad framework of their nations and their continent and with respect for the power, whatever it may be, which quells the wild hearts of men and keeps their greed, aggression and rivalry within limits and which exacts respect from all.

After the example of Sienna it is hard to avoid the conclusion that size and morality are closely related, not perhaps the specific kind of Christian morality to which the three saints were referring, but natural morality. We see that soldiers when they travel to far countries outside the influence of their uncles and aunts and cousins indulge in behaviour they would not consider at home. We see that country villagers when they move into the big anonymous cities similarly throw off their normal restraints and although they may not be able to behave like plundering armies certainly lose the restraints of their own local communities. The examples that normal society places on men and women, although different from the concept of the motivation of Christian morality, are more or less infinite and certainly would have been approved of by Jerome and the great leaders of the Christian Church. I noticed in one village in Hampshire where the blacksmith's shop had been changed into a car body shop, that the proprietor had one price for the locals and a different rate for his anonymous customers from further away; surely this kind of anonymity of the customer is what makes it possible for the bigger commercial concerns to eliminate any kind of moral restraint on their behaviour.

The importance of size was once most graphically illustrated by the Victorian historian James Anthony Froude in a lecture to the Devonshire Association for the Encouragement of Science and History. These were his words:

> "Yet as one person is never quite the same as another person, as each has peculiarities proper to himself which constitute his individual importance, so I hope the time is far off when the ancient self-administered English counties will subside into provinces – when London will be England in the sense that Paris is France. English character and English freedom depend comparatively little on the form which the Constitution assumes at Westminster. A centralised democracy may be as tyrannical as an absolute monarch; and if the vigour of the nation is to continue unimpaired, each individual, each family, each district, must preserve as far as possible its independence, its self-completeness, its powers and its privilege to manage its own affairs, and think its own thoughts.
>
> Neither Manchester nor Plymouth are yet entirely London, and I hope never will be. And it is for this reason that I welcome societies like the present. They are symptoms that life is not all concentrated at the heart – that if we are carried along in the stream of national progress, we do not mean to float passively where the current leads us, and that in the present as in the past we intend to bear an intelligent and active share in the general movement of the age."

The modern Church with all its divisions and compromises with the ways of the world no longer seems to have the capacity to undertake this role. What is needed at the heart of Europe is not Britain or any other self-seeking nation-state but some equivalent of the Church as it was in the time of Ambrose and Augustine or the Cathedral at Sienna in the Middle Ages or even the Roman Empire in the days of Augustus when the Emperor himself lived in studious simplicity and from whose court all rich adornings were deliberately excluded. Augustus also put himself in a position to rebuke with authority not the Emperor but the rich families of Rome whose greed had destroyed the Republic.

There may indeed be much wrong with the Council of Europe but it appears to be the only institution which has the potential to judge Europe and to rebuke its political and commercial élites and which could become capable of appealing to the hearts of Europeans in the way Ambrose appealed to the Romans against their Emperor. It will need men and women from the Church and from every other walk of life who are prepared to sacrifice their wealth and comfort as proof of their dedication to this great European cause. The Union cannot do it because it is based on commerce and greed – and is itself in need of constant and severe monitoring. Plato understood the problem when in *The Republic* he set the guardians against the merchants. Like the Church, the guardians were to be allowed to own nothing and were responsible for controlling the greed of the merchants. The failure of socialism seems to have been due to the fact that as one class opposed the greed of another class, its representatives themselves became subject to the same greed. The liberals of the last – soon to be one from the last – century hoped that trade would stop men fighting but unfortunately the harm that can be done through trade wars is often even worse than through military wars. Human greed is encouraged as the engine of trade, not opposed. Whole areas of the world can be condemned to famine because of patterns of trade and all too often trade itself has in the end become the cause of war. If the conservative solution means recurring to the best traditions in human society and conserving them, there is perhaps some hope in it. Unfortunately it seldom means that. What can be said, however, is that the best safeguards against the evils towards which humanity is prone are to be found in small communities where people know one another. And the worst safeguards are where institutions, countries and businesses have grown vast and anonymous. Certainly smallness of the constituent parts would seem to be one of the prerequisites of a 'celestial Europe' and at its heart an institution not reliant upon its buildings and its committees but reflecting the City of God in the way Sienna once did, and having a dynamic that exorcises the self-seeking, the bureaucracy, the empire-building that is parasitic in all human institutions. To paraphrase the words of William Blake: we cannot rest until we have created many Jerusalems in Europe's green and pleasant lands.

Part II – Historical emphasis

3. The first European institution – (post-war)

Cosmo Russell

Cosmo Russell was present with Churchill at the founding of the Council of Europe and played a leading role in establishing the Council of Europe in the minds of the public in the early post-war period. His deep enthusiasm for the fundamental moral position of the Council has never ebbed.

"Bliss was it in the dawn to be alive," sang Edmund Burke on the early outbreak of the French Revolution (he changed his mind later). Some of us privileged to be there in Strasbourg in the dawn of an August morning in the *Aula* (Great Hall) of Strasbourg University in the year 1949 recalled these words. The first session of the Assembly of the Council of Europe had just concluded with a passionate speech from the President, Paul Henri Spaak, in which he informed his colleagues that they had created the first European Parliament and then in the words of the French revolutionary, Danton, adapted, proclaimed *"de l'audace, encore de l'audace et l'Europe est sauvé"*. A United Press correspondent was found feverishly looking through the names of the current members of the Assembly to find the name of Danton. He was glad to be put right.

The Assembly had ended with a debate and the adoption of the European Convention on Human Rights. On a full agenda this was and has proved the most important achievement of the Council of Europe. No one would wish to deny that there was good reason for the act in question. Never had Europe lived through an age in which human rights had been so blatantly violated. To change all this and to put human rights at the undisputed centre of a democratic Europe was surely one positive aim of the new Council about to launch forth. Well before the first session of the Assembly and indeed of the Council's instrument of decision the Committee of Ministers, the European Movement had entered the fray. A committee, chaired by Paul Henri Teitgen of France with Sir David Maxwell-Fyfe of Britain as *rapporteur*, had produced a first draft taking the Universal Declaration of the United Nations adopted in 1948 as its model. This was in anticipation of the Council of Europe whose first meeting was to be held in August in Strasbourg. The Statute of the Council was signed at St James' Palace in London on 5 May 1949.

The European Movement could take credit for this event too. The chain of events started in 1948 with the Hague Congress of Europe chaired by Winston Churchill. This demanded from European governments, starting with the five-power Brussels Treaty of 1948 as a nucleus, a Council of

Ministers representing governments and a parliamentary assembly. It will be recalled that Churchill's reputation and influence were at their zenith in 1948-49. He was in opposition and able to speak freely. He was also able to take a leading part in the European Movement aided by his powerful son-in-law Duncan Sandys, temporarily out of Parliament. Sandys soon became Policy Director of the Movement. Within the Ministerial Committee of Western Union – the Brussels Treaty – of five: Bevin, Schuman (alternating occasionally with Georges Bidault), Spaak, Stikker and Bech, the final decision was taken to recruit Ireland, Norway, Sweden, Denmark and Italy with a view to forming a Council of Europe with the intention of inviting the Federal Republic of Germany at an early date. There was no trouble in accepting that a Committee of Ministers should be the organ to decide action to be taken on proposals from the Assembly. Bevin alone favoured a mixed Assembly with members from the trade unions, employers, universities, as well as members of parliament. He gave way in face of support from all others for an Assembly of members drawn from national parliaments. If Churchill unquestionably influenced the creation of the Council of Europe from outside government, Bevin was the motive power of British, and therefore European, policy in the post-war years as witness the Brussels Treaty, the OEEC (Marshall Aid), NATO and the Council of Europe. Bevin did not care for the European Assembly. He is reported as saying with a splendid cocktail of metaphors, "Once you open that Pandora's Box, you'll find it full of Trojan horses". However, he agreed and when looking at its first draft agenda in August 1949 took the draft Human Rights Convention and suggested it be studied with a view to adapting it to current national need and practice. So back it went to the Assembly from the Committee of Ministers with that message as the final act of their first session. Throughout the following twelve months it was debated by government officials before returning to the Assembly. Then the Ministers decided and the European Convention on Human Rights was signed in Rome in December 1950. With its investigating Commission, its Court of final judgement and its right of individual appeal, the Convention has become over the years the distinguishing mark of the Council of Europe. It has achieved within the Council framework a system of human rights protection that exists nowhere else. Anthony McNulty, its first and greatest servant as Secretary of the Commission once said, "It is the tail that wagged the dog."

It will be recalled that an aim of the Council in its Statute of 1949 is the rule of law and the protection of human rights and fundamental freedoms. Every new member in accepting the aim will in due course sign the Convention and have representation on an investigating Commission and the Court. Today [in 1994] the membership of the Council has grown from an original membership of ten countries to thirty. The major increase has come through members from Eastern Europe following the end of the Cold

War. The wish for those members to be included goes back to the first Assembly in 1949.

If the European Convention on Human Rights was an achievement, so was the Assembly. It has been at the centre of the various phases of the European Community and the revised Western European Union (WEU), which brought defence into European negotiation as an adjunct of NATO (an assembly of parliamentary character has featured in every form of European negotiation since coming into being in Strasbourg). One may recall that in 1949 the Assembly sought to build a practical method of progress – the adoption of series of conventions largely proposed by the Assembly and finalised by committees of government experts. These have dealt with social security, law, cultural and scientific relations and, latterly, the prevention of terrorism. Not every member is ready to adopt every convention right away. It is open to each to adopt at a later date. The method differs from that of the Community but has proved its value over the years with close on two hundred conventions agreed.

Membership of the Council of Europe is now agreed to be the first step in seeking membership of the closer system of European Union. The European elections to a European Parliament take place every five years. But the Council of Europe provided the first European Assembly to consist of existing members of national parliaments. The intention is to ensure that choice of members reflects the strength of political parties present in the national parliament. Where a country is also a member of the Western European Union, members of the Council Assembly also sit in the WEU Assembly.

As new countries join and, in the case of Eastern Europe, newly elected parliaments are formed, the contact between new members and members of old established national parliaments through the Council of Europe develops and ties of friendship and collaboration and a pattern of unity not previously encountered can be established. In 1949, the first Assembly adopted a resolution proposing the creation of empty seats for those European members not yet able to join. Now of course they can. Yet clearly a Council structure made for ten and fifteen can with difficulty do for thirty. That is going to be a pressing problem in particular for the Secretary General of the Council, at present a distinguished French lady. An important factor in the early days was the role of the secretariat of France, Britain, Italy and the smaller countries of Western Europe. For some years past the principal tasks performed by officials drawn from those countries have had to be shared with latter-day members. There was a certain informality in the early days difficult to maintain with a wider membership. Here lies a major task of friendship and understanding for the whole Council membership.

To return to the first session of August 1949. The Assembly met in the specially prepared Aula of the University, suitably installed with interpretation facilities, microphones on the delegates' chairs and additional seating was provided for the press and public. Gobelin tapestries on loan screened the galleries. Upstairs were committee rooms for the main committees on procedure, general (political) affairs, social, economic and legal affairs and, finally, cultural affairs. There was amusement that Churchill chose to be a member of the Cultural Committee but as its Italian Chairman said, "It is natural because he is a great man of letters." At the back of the Assembly there was a very large space converted into a delegates' bar, which in fact was soon invaded by a number of leading Press representatives. They included Randolph Churchill and it soon became known as 'Randolph's Bar'. The Press had a bar of their own. A Hansard had been hired to produce the record and flimsy pages were provided and posted up in the Press Room to keep the Press informed. Arrangements were very make-do at this first and enthusiastic attempt to keep the Press informed.

Such was one practical aspect of the first Assembly, the longest on record. A longer period has never been the case since. A whole fortnight was allowed for committee meetings. Reference has been made to the human rights debate. This was unique and featured outside what turned out to be the main debate in adapting or changing the Council of Europe to become an act of European union. Here, debate turned on what was known as the issue between functionalists and federalists. The former maintained that advance lay in practical adaptation of certain branches of activity, mainly economic, to common control. So the resolution that "the aim of the Council of Europe is a European political authority with limited functions but real powers" was accepted. Hence, of course, the rapid proposal by France and Germany to create the European Community of Coal and Steel. This occurred in the autumn predating the second session of the Assembly by several weeks. Britain made it clear that with home debate on coal and steel nationalisation it was in no case ready to think of merger in 1950. Yet the fusion, between age-old enemies, of the very means of war – and without which war itself was unthinkable – was a matter of importance. In 1973, economically there was no problem when Britain joined the European Community. Throughout that period the calm and good humour of Robert Schuman was an antidote to sore feeling. In fact there was complete misunderstanding of the real difference in Europe. The two strands were for limited delegation of sovereignty to a European authority and intergovernmentalism – the British view. The European Coal and Steel Community succeeded without Britain – with Italy and Benelux joining France and Germany. The next step which occurred in the second session of the Assembly in August 1950 was due to Winston Churchill. He proposed the creation of a European Army. The 'Six', as they came to be called, took Churchill at their own valuation and proposed a European Defence Community. When Churchill returned to power in 1951 it was clear that he had meant an alliance, not a delegation of military power to a political authority. When the French National Assembly refused the Treaty for a

European Defence Community in 1954, the British Government through the instrumentality of Anthony Eden had to find a solution to bring German troops into a Western framework required to bring them thereafter into NATO. The Eden solution was to adapt the Brussels Treaty into a Treaty of Western European Union to include Germany and Italy. So it was and so it has remained. There is a Western European Assembly of national parliamentarians drawn from national members to the Council of Europe Assembly. It is perhaps unfortunate that WEU having played a useful role in European defence in close alliance with NATO should have been used as the political instrument for legalising the break up of Yugoslavia. Seeing that this led to the Bosnian crisis it was no less than a disaster, but this must be attributed to governments, not the institution itself.

With the arrival of 1954 the first chapter in the life of the Council ended. From thenceforward it was to devise its own working methods of a different order to those of the emerging Community. Its task was to draw up European conventions through the agency of the Assembly and committees of government experts to which some member countries would adhere forthwith and others defer joining until a later date. One of the most important has been the European Social Charter of 1960, intended as a pendant to the European Convention on Human Rights by instancing the social rights also included in the 1948 Declaration of the United Nations. This Charter lays down a series of social rights to which each member country can adhere gradually when economically able to do so. In this way the Charter is the only real Charter of Social Rights. It has a review mechanism which meets periodically to hear problems. Its system therefore differs from the Social Chapter of the Maastricht Treaty and would seem to provide a system that some countries would find easier to introduce than the binding proposal of the Chapter.

Over the years it has become recognised that membership of the Council of Europe is a first step for countries wishing to join the Community. Of latter-day members who have joined the Council with intent to join the Community Spain and Portugal are good examples. This means of course that Community countries, through membership of the Council of Europe, are also involved in the decisions of both organisations. It was always the intention of the Council of Europe to aim for a wider unity of the European peoples. By 1994, forty-five years after its creation in 1949, this target could be considered, by and large, to have been achieved.

4. BRITAIN AND EUROPE IN THE POST-WAR PERIOD

Peter Smithers

Peter Smithers embodied the spirit of post-war enthusiasm that wanted Britain to be at the heart of the Europe she had played such a crucial role in rescuing from tyranny. He was Secretary General of the Council of Europe from 1964-69.

The European Movement, and with it the Council of Europe, had its origins in the immediate aftermath of the Second World War. Today it is difficult to imagine the situation in Europe as it existed at that time, so I shall attempt to describe it. In so doing I shall show the reasons for British reluctance to become deeply involved with continental Europe and the lack of political vision which caused Britain to miss the chance to have a Europe more compatible with her own interests and political institutions. Some of this may now seem unfair. It did not do so then.

France

France, for centuries the political pivot of Europe, had been utterly humiliated. Invalided from the Royal Navy in the winter of 1939-40, I was sent to Paris as a naval member of MI6. Arriving in April, I lived through the collapse of that once great country. The very large French army simply disintegrated in front of the German armoured attack. It was no match for the Germans in equipment, strategy or in tactics. On the table in the entrance hall of our office in Paris there was a picture of Marshals Gamelin and Gort saluting smartly at attention. One morning the head of the office, also a Royal Naval Officer, on entering turned the picture with its face to the wall, and without a word stepped into his office and closed the door. Next day I was on my way South in a French Army lorry with an armed escort and all our archives, charged with getting them to a secure place and with arranging accommodation for our staff, all of whom would have faced an unhappy future if caught by the Germans. The first base was at Salbris in the Sologne, not far from Orleans.

As the Germans advanced I was instructed to proceed to Bordeaux to make evacuation arrangements. A British warship would, it was hoped, be available. The roads were already crowded with refugees fleeing South and it was necessary to use maps and to take the country lanes to make the journey. The arrangements were duly made for our staff who were shipped off to England in merchantmen. I slept on board HMS *Arethusa* expecting to sail in her next day: the Germans had bombarded us at anchor during the bright moonlight night. Instead I was instructed to remain behind in

Bordeaux to act as Flag Lieutenant to the first Lord of the Admiralty, A. V. Alexander, who had now taken over from Winston Churchill on his appointment as Prime Minister. He had arrived in Bordeaux in a heavily armed Sunderland Flying Boat to negotiate with Admiral Darlan for the French Fleet. Marshal Pétain was by now installed in the Presidency of France.

The negotiations took place in great secrecy in a Bordeaux hotel. Darlan was absolutely adamant that his duty lay towards the new President and not towards helping Britain to resist the Germans. Excepting for a handful of officers and the great submarine *Surcouf*, which joined General de Gaulle, the French Fleet slunk off to an inglorious inactivity for the rest of the war. One thought with distress of the great French naval commanders of past centuries.

The shame and disgrace of those events and of the years that followed can hardly be overestimated and their effect lives on today. The vast majority of brave and loyal French people had been betrayed into the hands of a German enemy by incompetence and corruption at all levels of government. A trivial example of the latter will suffice. Lt. Cdr. Ian Fleming RNVR arrived in Bordeaux on his way to Lisbon on a mission for the Director of Naval Intelligence. After *Arethusa* sailed we had a day to spare before I joined the First Lord. We spent it getting the refugees who crowded the dockside at Le Verdon into ships bound for England. For this purpose we needed the Harbour Master's barge, but he replied that he could not let the British have it, and we were subjected to a speech about *l'honneur* and *la patrie* and the *vieux maréchal*. Fortunately on leaving Paris, Ian had visited the Rolls-Royce Company which held the MI6 funds in its safe and he was bulging with big French currency bills. He took a large one out and rustled it, and, suddenly *l'honneur* and *la patrie* and *le vieux maréchal* were forgotten, and the refugees, many of them French Jews, had the barge and went aboard. They all reached England.

At that time the owner of a Paris newspaper said to me, "I have lost three-quarters of my paper in Paris and have transferred a quarter of it to Bordeaux. The Germans are advancing. France must have peace." It was as simple as that.

In the last hours in Bordeaux a French officer said to me, "Of course you will go home and make peace with the Germans." The Anglo-French relationship was bedevilled after the war by the unspoken feeling that the British had been saved by the Channel and that they would have done no better than the French in like circumstances. Perhaps. We had precious little left with which to resist. After the war if many French were grateful that we had held out, some of them would have felt better about France if we had surrendered.

I cite these distressing facts, only a fraction of what I observed let alone of what took place afterwards, to emphasise how painful they were to most French people and how devastating to a proud nation, and as background to what took place after the end of the war. The present tiresome struggle of France so long after these events to persuade the world that she is still a 'great power' cutting her own swathe through the errors of Anglo-Saxon policies, arises from the events of those days and of the occupation which followed. In terms of human nature it is understandable and at the end of the war great pains were taken by Britain to try to avoid rubbing salt into the wound of the French ego. For this purpose the activities of the 'resistance', of General de Gaulle and of the participation of the French units in the liberation of France, were built up out of all proportion to the reality. In Britain it was perfectly well understood that this was the case and why it was done.

Italy

I stood on a wooden bridge over a stream in Sologne with some French officers when we were brought the news that Italy had entered the war. Any observant person could have predicted that 'The Mussolino', as my grandmother called him, would make this egregious mistake. By the end of the war it was apparent that the Italian war effort had crumbled in ruins. The Italian armies in North Africa had been even less effective than the French in Europe. The Italian battleships, which had been Mussolini's pride because they carried the largest calibre armament then existing, had proved unusable. The decks bent when the guns fired. And at the Battle of Cape Matapan, Italian naval training had been proved inadequate for a night engagement, the Italian units obligingly sinking one another. Everybody loves the Italians but their war record had not been inspiring.

Spain

General Franco, a much cooler and wiser head than Mussolini, had done his country good service by keeping it out of the war. But he was a military dictator, his sympathies did not lie with the Allies and Spain was not in those circumstances material for a united Europe.

Germany

For the second time in my lifetime the Germans had gratuitously invaded Europe provoking millions of deaths and even more millions of casualties and inflicting indescribable hardship and misery on the peoples of the Continent. In the outcome they too had been utterly defeated and humiliated. I well remember the feeling of disgust with which I crossed the Rhine for the first time after the war. In the interests of a united Europe an effort had been made to portray the Germans as unwilling victims of Hitler. But one cannot divorce a people from their actions as a nation, and this was perfectly realised in Britain. Before Hitler there had been the Kaiser.

Britain

Back in England, immediately after the fall of France and just before the armistice, I was at the Admiralty and working with MI5 on the security aspects of the German invasion. The mood in Britain is difficult to re-create in writing. From the public there was not a word of surrender, or even of negotiation, and yet after what I had seen taking place on the Continent common sense told me that we would be lucky to get away with it. In the Operations Room of the Admiralty there was a notice posted which read 'CROMWELL'. This code word indicated 'invasion imminent'. Every morning there were aerial reconnaissance photographs of the barges lined up ready to bring the German Army. And then, one morning when I went in for the latest information, 'CROMWELL' had been taken down. With hindsight Hitler had lost his only chance of winning the war: knock out Britain before the Americans woke up to what was going on. Britain would and did hold on.

At the end of the war the British Empire was intact, the United States with British support had utterly defeated the Germans, and the whole of Europe, except for Spain, Portugal and Switzerland, was in ruins and in some cases in disgrace. The view from across the English Channel as described in the opening paragraphs of this essay was not inviting. Why give up any British sovereignty to such a repulsive political mess?

The USSR

Britain and the United States did not have a monopoly of glory at the end of the war: there were the Russians. They had indeed put on a stupendous military effort and without them the war would certainly have lasted a very long time and might have ended in stalemate. All eyes in Britain were focused upon this achievement and few paused to consider the political background. Surely the Russians must have the good sense to see that now was the time for co-operation with the capitalist powers in order to ensure that there were no more world wars. In the eyes of the woolly left and indeed of a very large part of the public the Russians could do no wrong. It took several years for this delightful dream to fade away.

The European Movement

It was against this background that in 1948 I was appointed Joint Secretary of the Brussels Conference of the European Movement which took place in 1949. The Conservatives leading the Movement were Duncan Sandys, the driving spirit, Harold Macmillan, Bob Boothby and several other Members of Parliament. The head of the Labour part of the organisation was Victor Gollancz, the publisher, supported by Bob Edwardes MP of the Electrical Trade Union, and one or two others. Senior Labour figures were all in the British Government at that time. The Liberals were led by Lord Layton, also a publisher, and Miss Josephy.

We were confronted by the spectacle of Europe which had been sketched above. Of the three major powers which made up the Europe of 1949 two had been brutal military dictatorships and the third had collapsed. Not much remained. Politically speaking there was nothing in sight but gallant bands in all three countries striving to arrange something better for the future. In these circumstances from a British point of view there was much to be said for creating a single large market, but nothing at all to be said for integrating Britain politically into the remains of Europe when she stood victorious with her Empire and supported by the United States.

At the Brussels Conference it was generally agreed that the single large market should be a first step and this resulted in time in the European Economic Community. Even here, however, an important difference emerged and still exists. The British regarded the single large market as a contribution to freer international trade which was promoted under the General Agreement on Trade and Tariffs, while the French regarded it as a protectionist organisation aimed at rivalling the United States, a difference in perception which persists to this day.

On the political aspects of European union the French, Belgians and some Dutch and Italians favoured a constitutional instrument under which there would be a limited cessions of sovereignty to a central European authority. The British objected to this for two reasons: first, they did not believe that miracles could be worked by signing a piece of paper and second, though this was not said in so many words, there was little attraction to political integration with the ex-dictatorships and the failed French Republic, when there was the Empire and the United States at our side. The division therefore arose between federalists and functionalists. The former were for the piece of paper which we would all sign and subsequently, it was hoped, obey, and the latter believed that much detailed work had to be done in the harmonisation of innumerable details of the society and economy of European states before anything like a federation became workable, let alone desirable. It will be noted that the same division of opinion has persisted down to the time of the Maastricht Treaty and beyond.

There were two events at the Brussels Conference which are worth recalling. Late at night Harold Macmillan rose to speak of the urgent need for a united Europe and for mechanisms to enable us to work towards that end. So carried away was he by his theme that he broke into impromptu and almost, though not quite, faultless French. This was greeted with thunderous applause. Of course, the audience did not know that the whole episode had been carefully prepared, and that a couple of grammatical errors had actually been inserted into what Harold would say to add verisimilitude. Harold and Duncan Sandys were the major British figures who favoured the process of European unity from the beginning.

The other event came at the end of the conference. Winston Churchill arrived to deliver a closing speech from the balcony in Place Kléber, packed to capacity. I stood behind him as he delivered it. *"Prenez garde – je vais parler français"* – in heavily English-accented French. Here was the man who had carried Britain through the war when others were failing, and who had recently said in Zurich: "Let Europe arise". Nobody doubted that he meant Britain to arise as part of it. Disillusion was soon to come.

The Council of Europe

At this time the standing of Britain in Europe was so high, and the desire of everybody on the Continent that we should be fully engaged in the rebuilding of Europe so great, that within reason, any model for the future of the Continent which we chose to ask for we could have had. The Council of Europe was the product of this situation. It would work through its Committee of Ministers to negotiate individual treaties and conventions between member states which over a period of years would bring their societies and economies into a mutually harmonious situation. Then, if at all, would be the time to think of constitutional documents so dear to the French, of which that country had had so many and which inspired so many for Latin America, while Britain has never had one at all.

I was not a member of the Consultative Assembly of the Council of Europe until 1952 so that I was not present at its first meeting after the return of the Conservative Government to power, but memories of it were indelibly impressed upon my colleagues. In view of the words of Winston Churchill and the powerful support for European Unity by Duncan Sandys and Harold Macmillan, both now Cabinet Ministers, nobody doubted that Britain would take the leading part for which all had hoped.

Ominously, Anthony Eden, the Foreign Secretary, did not attend. The Attorney General, David Maxwell-Fyfe, was sent to make the British speech. As it progressed, the atmosphere changed from excited expectation to astonishment and finally to anger. It was abundantly clear that Britain did not intend a vigorous use of the institution to forward the cause of unity. This was followed up by the appointment of a junior and hitherto unknown Foreign Office official as Permanent Representative to reside in Strasbourg and to sit on the Committee of Ministers Deputies which would prepare conventions and treaties for governments to execute. It soon became apparent that he had instructions to see to it that nothing of importance emerged from the Council of Europe. He became the most hated man in Strasbourg.

At this time, when I sat next to Anthony Eden in the Smokeroom of the House of Commons, he would say to me, "Now please do not bore me with Europe." After a debate in the Assembly in which Spaak had made an impassioned speech about the role of the Council in the face of the Soviet menace which had now become apparent even to the woolly left – "It is not the Russians that I fear but our own decadence" – I dined with the then Minister at our Paris Embassy. He was one of the stars of the service, later an ambassador, who had been sent down as an observer. I asked him what he made of the Council of Europe. "Frankly, nothing", was the answer, and this no doubt is what he reported to London. As so often in history what is perfectly apparent to an observant politician is not necessarily so to a trained diplomat. It was abundantly clear to me, to Anthony Eden's long term policy adviser, Ursula Branston, and to many others that we were in the presence of very powerful political currents which would not abate because we found them in some respects uncongenial. If we did not work with them and seek to control them we would be in trouble.

This was simply not understood in the House of Commons. In this respect the Council of Europe achieved an important result in Britain for which it never received credit. It educated Members of Parliament. At the time of the founding of the Council few members of the House of Commons knew anything about European politics. Most knew a great deal about the Commonwealth and Foreign Policy in general, but the internal politics of Europe were a closed book. As the delegations returned from Strasbourg after what were very convivial meetings with their colleagues from other European countries, in a delightful part of the Rhine valley, where good food and wine abounded, they came back transformed in outlook. They did not necessarily return 'Europeans', but at least they understood that something important was going on and they knew something about the problems and policies of their colleagues. My recollection is that a delegation at that time would consist of about twenty delegates with twenty substitutes. The delegation was reappointed each year, with a few changes, so that the educative effect in the House of Commons was cumulative over a period of time.

The Treaty of Rome

But the education took some years and came too late. It was therefore predictable that in due course our continental neighbours, becoming impatient at British obstruction, would decide to proceed without us. It was also predictable that if they did so they would proceed along federalist lines and not along the functionalist lines which were the prerogative of the Council of Europe and which corresponded with the views of the British Government. The Treaty of Rome was seen by its authors as a step towards a European federation. Britain was now faced with a disagreeable choice. It was the fruit of her obstruction of the very process which was the preferred method of proceeding of the British Government. She could reject the invitation to join the Treaty of Rome and be isolated with some of the smaller powers of Europe, or she could join something the structure of which did not correspond with the fundamental principles of her policy. She opted for the former, and even set up a rival organisation on functionalist lines, the European Free Trade Association.

Britain climbs down

When Harold Macmillan became Prime Minister, it was concluded, as it should have been from the start, that if the Treaty of Rome was to go forward we should be in it during the early formative years. It was now rather late. I was the Parliamentary Under-Secretary of State at the time when Harold Macmillan met General de Gaulle at Rambouillet. The main lines of the Community had all been laid out. They got on well together, but there came a point in the discussions when Harold said to the General that he doubted that the latter really wished for British entry into the Community. He was, as it turned out, quite right. The General had not yet fixed matters up to his satisfaction. Some years later when I was Secretary General of the Council I received a visit from the French Permanent Representative who, after beating about the bush, said that the French Government felt 'in a trap' over pressure for British entry into the Community. I was sure that the French Government felt no such thing and that what was meant was that the General, having modified the Treaty to his liking, was now ready to admit us. I passed on the obvious hint. It was late in the day, but still better than being outside: our own past folly had left us with no alternative and we did not get very good terms in the negotiations.

A summary

So it was that Britain at the end of the war saw little need of Europe. Furthermore Europe had been a horrible mess. Britain wanted to see a structure set up which might minimise the danger of any further conflicts and increase general prosperity through a single large market but any cessions of sovereignty were out of the question. In no way did the Government or the Foreign Office feel that powerful political forces were at work in Europe which it was in their interest to accommodate. This was a grave error of perception with which some of us disagreed at the time.

The second error was one of policy. Having obtained in the Council of Europe an instrument of inter-European co-operation and construction very much in line with British thinking, the Foreign Office failed to use it for the purposes for which it was intended. As a result our disappointed partners broke away and set up the Treaty of Rome, a process culminating in the Maastricht Treaty and the Single Currency. British policy thus brought about the exact opposite of what was desired, which was then and is now plainly inimical to British interests.

The future

Thus it is that today the issues which we face in Europe are still the same though they have developed in great detail. Can a supranational structure work in Europe and if so do we wish to be a part of it? Should Europe be a protectionist enclave or part of an open system of world trade? Is it seen as a rival or as a partner of the United States? There is still much to be done to perfect the Single Market, and there is also a very great deal to be done in reconciling the societies and economies of Europe. In these two fields Britain should take a leading part.

From a personal viewpoint I reflect that of the present members of the European Union, five during my lifetime have been military dictatorships, and four of those five are the present major powers. These dictatorships resulted largely from economic hardship, when leaders arose to declare "follow me and I will solve your problems". I am not so simple as to believe that as we enter very dangerous times in the world economy, a repetition of hardships would not bring about a repetition of consequences. I do not believe that the Maastricht Treaty would survive any such convulsions.

Even if no such convulsions occur, the Treaty places the Union in a dilemma. It must enlarge to include Eastern Europe, but if it is to work it must proceed to majority voting, otherwise it would face paralysis. But majority voting would impose upon some of its members economic hardships and social consequences which would be absolutely unacceptable.

As for a single currency, this is a financial exercise prompted by political motives. This is always a dangerous thing in finance. The Director General of EFTA, Sir Frank Figgures, a formidable Treasury mandarin, once pointed out to me that there is really no separating political and economic problems. "So long as everybody agrees on an economic problem it remains economic, and as soon as they disagree it becomes political." With modern electronic processes now in development a single currency is not necessary and in the future would not even be an added convenience. At the same time it must inevitably impose hardship and thus political danger in those countries which are not suited to the economic and financial conditions imposed on all by a central authority. A common currency may work for some time, but in the longer term it is a formula for political conflict and for disruption of the treaty structure.

Finally, the world has changed radically since the Council of Europe was set up. Big is no longer beautiful. All of the empires are gone, so are the federations in Yugoslavia and in all likelihood in Nigeria. The composite state does not work. The United States is no exception. It is a unitary state because until recently all immigrants went there to become Americans. The idea that against the current of events one can set up a successful composite state from the Arctic to the Mediterranean and from the Atlantic to the Urals and beyond betrays the same simplistic thinking which inspired so many constitutions in Latin America, most of which failed because they did not correspond with reality.

All our resources of policy should now be directed to eliminating the many anomalies and absurdities which exist in the Common Market we have created and to making it a constructive contributor to the global market rather than a protectionist island. If we achieve that we shall have taken a very long step forward in the political consolidation of Europe.

5. Europe at the collapse of Communism

Barney Milligan

Barney Milligan is a Canon in the Church of England whose precise role in Strasbourg is explained in the chapter which follows.

"Religion and politics don't mix, and they are better kept apart" – that was how many people used to think: and some still do, but of course, like it or not, religion and politics have been and are inevitably mixed up together. The question is not whether or not they can be kept apart but in what ways they are related and whether it is a creative or destructive relationship. For the ways in which Churches and other religious bodies have related to political structures is a very long and complicated story. There have been times both of persecution and of partnership. At times there has been a struggle for power in which the political side has often, but certainly not always, been the victor. Although in the twentieth century there are an increasing number of countries where the forces of religion count for very little, there have been and indeed there still are many examples of the religious forces being the most powerful in the land: while equally there are countries where the Church can hardly make any decisions without permission from the state; and there are a number of countries, of which the United States and France are the chief examples, where there is a reciprocal agreement that Church and state are structurally totally separate. So it is a strange and paradoxical scene, and full of surprises.

The birth of new international bodies half way through the present century created a completely new scene for which most of the Churches were unprepared. Throughout modern history it was and is the nation-state with which the Churches or other religious bodies had to deal. Indeed it was because of an alliance between the monarch and the Church, be it Protestant or Catholic, that the Church was either recognised or outlawed in some lands, especially at the heart of Europe in post-Reformation times. According to the various official or informal 'concordats' (to use the rather later Napoleonic word) they crowned (or did not crown) their kings; serviced (or did not service) their prisons; armed forces and hospitals with chaplains; and supported or criticised their policies. What, if anything, was the appropriate response now to this new kind of political animal?

It may be surprising or even shocking that most of the Churches were slow to respond; after all the new constructs were set up to safeguard human values, stability and peace – purposes presumably dear to all religions; but none of them have any formal religious structure in the way in which, for example, there are chaplains or prayers or chapels in certain national governments or parliaments. There are several reasons why this is so. First of course the self-evident fact that there was no single Church – or indeed at the United Nations, no single religion – which could properly be asked to provide such a service. Secondly, in the mid-twentieth century when all these organisations were born, the place of religion was less dominant than it had been in the past. But this only serves to heighten the paradox that, while religion itself may have taken a back seat when the post-war international bodies came to birth, it was people of more than usually strong idealism and in some cases, religious faith who were its midwives. As regards the Churches, the fact that the Vatican still retained its universalist attitudes and moreover had a form of foreign service in position with representatives in many parts of the world, made it possible for the Holy See to respond first to the new international bodies which appeared after the Second World War. At the Council of Europe in Strasbourg as in Brussels and at the UN, a diplomatic representative was appointed. But it took longer for the other Churches – and indeed for other organs of the Roman Catholic Church – to come on board the international ship in a formal way.

As for the other Churches and religious bodies, they took time to decide. Among the first – both in the UN and in Europe – were the Quakers and Jesuits – both groups with a strong built-in international sense. At the United Nations, a group from a different religion, the Bahai, also set up their stall. Later, in 1998, the Anglican communion arrived at the UN in New York and appointed to the post Paul Reeves, who, in New Zealand, had the double distinction of being a former Governor-General and a former Primate of the Anglican Church. In the meantime, at the European level, the Roman Catholic Bishops' conferences, now greatly strengthened by the Second Vatican Council, found a new role – and of course a new acronym, COMECE – in their collegial witness alongside the new Community in Brussels. As for the Orthodox, albeit with an ecclesiology markedly different from that of the Western Churches, their response to the European developments was that the Greeks associated themselves with the Churches' centre in Brussels – an association not without incident; and a few years later the Ecumenical Patriarchate in Constantinople set up their own Brussels office. The Ecumenical Patriarch Bartholomew himself paid visits to Brussels and Strasbourg (he made a great impression at the European Parliament especially in the way he applied his sacramental theology of creation to the burning issues of environmental policy and work and employment). I wished he had included the Council of Europe on his itinerary.

But probably the most important development was the least publicised – the initiatives of those lay people from many different countries who were more aware of the ethical and spiritual questions facing them at work than bothered about to which religious organisation they or their colleagues belonged. We may note the early growth of prayer and meditation rooms (the Chagall windows at the UN in New York are a remarkable Jewish contribution). Similar spaces have, over the years, been set up in nearly all the international meeting places. The commitment of the UN Deputy Secretary General, George Muller, and the emergence there, and indeed at the United States Congress, of the Thanksgiving Movement, echoing that remarkable example of 'civil religion' which remains a key date in the US national calendar, have all contributed to a fashion of public spiritual and religious awareness in this wider field of international life.

In all these last cases this was not so much a response by the religious structures themselves, but more of 'in-house' initiatives by religious individuals. Nowhere was this more evident than at the European institutions as they developed in Brussels, where it was the civil servants who made the running. They arranged meetings for prayer and study among themselves, opened an Ecumenical Centre, and later appointed a pastor of the Dutch Reformed Church (Marc Lenders, who has played a key role in this story) to serve there, in the first instance part-time. It was on this base that the Lutheran Reformed and Anglican Churches built their own initiative: they formed an organisation which came to be known as the European Ecumenical Commission for Church and Society (EECCS) which brought the institutional Churches in the member states into the action, informing and involving their members and directing and funding the work. At the same time the 'in-house' programmes continued alongside the new office.

In 1986 the EECCS, which up to that time had concentrated its work in Brussels, had decided to open an office in Strasbourg. It was not only because the European Parliament, by now directly elected, held its public sessions there: it was because the Churches had come to recognise that the Council of Europe had an increasingly important role to play in the evolving European scene. Moreover its competences included many matters with a theological, ethical or spiritual import. The Council of the Churches of the Rhine had had a Lutheran pastor serving there for some time: now, with their blessing, the wider Church body built on what had been already achieved.

The budget, however, was limited and so the office would have to continue to be, at least for the time being, only part-time and this was where I came in. For the end of 1986 was not only a time when I was available to move, but when the Anglican chaplaincy in Strasbourg was looking for a new chaplain who would also be part-time. Thus by a happy chance, the two halves formed a natural double responsibility where the pastoral duties in a small expatriate parish fed and were fed by the wider work in the European field. (For example, to follow the deliberations of a political committee on a subject such as immigration policy and then to be visiting a family seeking asylum in France later the same day certainly kept one's feet on the ground.) The way in which my bishop, with the local Anglican congregation and those responsible in the ecumenical commission, took trouble to set out the terms of the reciprocal agreement avoided the grumbling and bickering which can sometimes accompany these double jobs.

Later, I was to be responsible especially to the Church of England, but did not cease to hold the double appointment as parish priest as well as European representative; nor was it in any way the end of my active involvement with ecumenical partners. There had, to be sure, been some frictions at the time of the change-over and for a while ecumenical relations were very sensitive. But because of the common sense and skill of those who put it together again, notably the new President of the Ecumenical Commission, Klaus Kremkau, and the new (full-time) representative of the Ecumenical Commission, Gerard Merminod (who sadly died very soon after he had retired in the same year as I did), the wounds were rapidly healed and I was able to continue to work closely both with my Protestant friends and also of course with the Catholics. Such collaboration was a crucial component of their job; it made the work much more credible if we were seen to be not necessarily in agreement on every point, but working in close collaboration.

How then did one set out on this task? How was one to understand one's role? I was, after all, not appointed by the European bodies but by the Churches. With my colleagues and partners from the other Churches, I had the obvious task of keeping the home base informed about what went forward in the European corridors, and equally of making sure that the right pieces of paper got onto the right desks in Strasbourg.

This demanded setting priorities, for the agenda was vast and one could not keep up with all of it, still less understand all its intricacies. (I remember that when I was interviewed for the job in Brussels in 1986, I pointed out that if they thought they were appointing an 'expert' they were grievously mistaken and should look elsewhere! What I could undertake to do was to collect a list of those to whom I might go to get the 'expert' view on any subject when I needed to). The priorities which I worked out with my advisory group included human rights, asylum seekers, East/West relations and bioethics. Here was, as is obvious, a need for a substantial squad of 'experts' for these items alone!

The list of priorities does in fact cast an interesting light on what sort of questions my advisors and I judged were the kind of things on which the Churches should have something to say. It was, I recall, confirmed in regard to one of these matters from the point of view on the other side of the counter. When the Council of Europe held a major colloquium on bioethics, Mme la Lumière the then Secretary General, who was in the chair, was insistent that Church representatives be involved and indeed I was always impressed at the way in which our presence and our contributions were welcomed.

There was another perspective here: I believe that all of us in the informal ecumenical group at Strasbourg saw that, beyond that communication and 'ambassadorial' role, we also could provide a space for thinking about the longer-term purposes as to why we were all there. In the various meetings – most of them perforce extremely brief – this was one of the objects we always had in mind. It also had to do with how one saw the role of the Council of Europe *vis-à-vis* the EEC.

For, at an early stage, I concluded that of the two Strasbourg bodies I had to monitor, the Council of Europe had a potential significance as great as that of her more famous and richer daughter, the EEC, and also far greater than was generally recognised. Even in those now distant days before the walls and the statues came down in 1989 and when it seemed that the EEC had far fewer problems than is the case now, there was an oft-repeated cry for time for reflection, for study, for a kind of 'think tank'; as many people felt we needed to think with more definition about where we were going. Events since that time have served only to underline the truth of this.

This is partly, of course, an endemic condition of all political power especially in democratic countries where the short term, influenced as it inevitably is by calculations concerning the next election, has so great a priority over the longer term. With an international body comprising many countries with a variety of dates for many next elections, the claims of the immediate are even stronger and thus the chance is often lost for reflection about international questions in an international setting in a world growing inevitably closer. A diplomat, who has served for many years in the field of international institutions, recently underlined this state of affairs by indicating not only the election questions but also the constant crises which force governments to take a hurried stand under the heat of the moment and thus, once more, "the urgent is more likely to win against the important". In the same address, Sir Peter Marshall spoke of international bodies having special opportunities for shared reflection bringing together politicians and others from diverse backgrounds and countries. The sad thing is that it does not often happen.

In the European scene, attempts have, of course, been made to provide this space especially within the office of the President of the Commission in Brussels. Indeed the small think tank set up by Jacques Delors and continued by Jacques Santer has the title of 'Forward Planning Unit'. Although the work of this group has been and is fulfilling a unique and important role, (and is naturally a point of contact for the Churches) there could be an even greater value in setting the Council of Europe to this task. It seemed to me that the Council of Europe was built for such a purpose and that if it did not exist, it might indeed have been necessary to invent it.

Throughout my eight or more years in Strasbourg I used to produce a bulletin of news and comment. In one of the earlier numbers, which was dated June 1987, I referred to the two major differences between the EEC and the Council of Europe, which led to the first receiving much more publicity than the other. First, the fact that the Community had power, as a supranational body, not only to have its 'own resources' financially, but also to make laws and to ensure their observance; while the Council as an intergovernmental body had no such power (setting aside the more particular legal questions covered by the findings of its European Court of Human Rights) and secondly, that there was a list of 'hard' items on the agenda – economics, trade, agriculture – all potentially full of conflict of interest and therefore newsworthy, which tend to be the concern of the EEC, and the 'softer' items, human rights, education, public health, culture and so on, with which the Council of Europe is concerned.

But it seemed to me then and still does today, that it is the 'softer' subjects which are actually what makes people tick. In my bulletin of June 1987, I tried to express this sense of the priority of 'Strasbourg' questions over 'Brussels' ones. I see with interest, and slight amusement, that, to support this thesis, I quoted two people as diverse as Richard Von Weizsäcker, then President of the Federal West German Republic: "History teaches us that it is usually not disarmament that leads to peace but peaceful co-operation that leads to disarmament...The greatest friend of mutual understanding is culture"; and Clifford Longley, then religious affairs correspondent of *The Times*, who, referring to the 1987 British general election, reckoned that politics was cracked up to be more significant than it is; all the debate was "essentially a trivial pursuit". Thus I argued that the competences of the Council of Europe were less trivial than those of the Community.

In a further bulletin I referred to the exchange of letters which took place in 1989 between the President of the European Commission and the Secretary General of the Council of Europe. It was the first formal correspondence between the two since 1959! Assuming that this might mean business, I asked what relations there might now be between them. "Can mother and daughter", I asked, "find the way to a creative partnership... (as) ... set out in the letter? Some may fear that the Council could become somewhat eclipsed by her more famous and affluent daughter but I have the sense that the Brussels hurly-burly needs the opportunity for reflection which Strasbourg may be able to supply." I went on to say that the Churches certainly need to be present at the points of power-broking and the market place (EEC) but also at the point of study and reflection out of which the bigger decisions may emerge. Could this be a future for the Council of Europe?

When I arrived at my post in 1986, I remember that I found a very different atmosphere in the two bodies which I was to monitor. For the European parliamentarians, life was very busy and full of purpose. After the doldrums of the seventies (of which Christopher Tugendhat writes graphically in his book *Making Sense of Europe*) the Single Act had pumped new life into the arteries of the whole community. Now MEPs were rushing around dealing with legislation which had to go through before the end of 1992 if the Single Act project was to be implemented. There was a deadline, 1 January 1993, by which time the enlarged market of 320 million and the open frontiers had to be realised and this did a great deal to concentrate the mind. My friends in the Parliament were very busy and purposeful at the time. I remember they seemed to have at least three engagements scheduled in their diaries for every hour of the day. Jacques Delors came down regularly to report on the state of the legislative scorecard. Lobbying was intense, morale was high.

But I found a very different mood in the Council of Europe. Here there was a slightly jaded air. The first generation had largely retired and the early sense of purpose was dispersed. The Council seemed uncertain of its purpose and feared that many of its competences might be taken away from it as the Community took an increasing interest in the 'softer' subjects, partly in order to demonstrate that it was not simply a soulless economic technical machine, (this was when they were trying desperately to drop the middle 'E' of 'EEC'). So it started educational and cultural programmes, and some at the Council of Europe wondered which of their clothes would be stolen next.

But soon this would all change. Already there were the signs of what was to come during the next two years. Even in the early months of my posting there were some signals. I will not list them in detail; but from the moment I arrived and began to amble around the corridors of the Council of Europe trying to meet the *fonctionnaires* (civil servants) I constantly found that the person I wanted to meet was "on a mission". "Where?", I asked; to receive the answer not one of the member states but Budapest or Prague or Riga or Leningrad. These early contacts were probably not only harbingers of change, but useful points of contact for the future.

There were signs of a thaw in other circles too. The Helsinki Conference of 1975-76 had brought together countries of both Eastern and Western blocs, including of course, what we then called the two super-powers, to try to establish ways of building confidence where there seemed to be only a recipe for conflict. Their agenda was wide and stretched from arms control to humanitarian matters. Across these 'baskets' (as they were called), when they were able to publish the Helsinki Accords, they wisely set up a process of monitoring which was intended to ensure that promises were kept. A series of follow-up meetings were put into the calendar, each a year or two apart and held in different cities. Thus was born the Council for

Security and Co-operation in Europe (CSCE now, since 1995, OSCE – 'Organisation' having replaced 'Council').

It was these meetings which were monitored by my colleagues in the Conference of European Churches (CEC) – a pan-European organisation which had been set up deliberately so that, despite all the restraints, political, psychological, cultural – the Churches from all parts of the divided continent might not loose touch with one another. Conversation across the iron curtain might thus be difficult, and at times artificial, but it happened. Working with the councils of Churches of USA and Canada whose countries were also involved, the CEC set up a monitoring operation alongside each of the follow-up events of the Helsinki process. The usual plan was to send two Church members – one from the East and one from the West – to spend a week or longer getting to know members of the delegations and making clear by their presence that the Churches from all the countries were truly committed to the search for peace and supported and prayed for those taking part in the Helsinki process; and moreover that they did not allow the political divisions of Europe to stop them working in the partnership across that divide (even though it was sometimes not without problems).

When I came on the scene, these meetings had been under way for ten years. It was the CSCE Vienna Conference which I went to as a member of the Church team in January 1988. It had been going on much longer than scheduled and nobody could be quite sure whether its longevity was good or bad news: did it imply that solid agreements were on the way or was it a sign of impending failure? No one was sure. My opposite number was a young Russian Orthodox priest with whom I got on very well. I enjoyed his company and heard about his wife and family, but he remained somewhat inscrutable and carefully avoided all the convivial sessions that I persistently proposed.

What I remember most vividly about the Vienna meeting however, was the role played by some of the Central European countries which were still of course under Communist control. In some of the smaller consultations to seek agreements and draft and redraft papers – what in their arcane way they called 'non papers' – the chair was often taken by one of those countries known as 'neutrals' – Sweden or Switzerland or Austria – who belonged neither to NATO nor to the Warsaw Pact. We in the Church groups used to get to know the neutrals well and received much help from their advice. The surprise came when some of the members of the Warsaw Pact started to talk as if they were one of the neutrals. They also were clearly acting as mediators on some tough questions where hardliners from East to West were deeply divided. It all sounds so normal now – but it didn't then. Not in January 1988.

It was in 1989 that the real changes came. They were of dramatic importance for the Council of Europe. It was the year of its fortieth birthday. On that day in May the first event was the ceremony to mark the accession of Finland – a country which had never been a 'client' state of the USSR but had not been happy to make any move which would have upset its giant neighbour just a few miles across the sea from Helsinki. Now here they were joining a European body which the Kremlin had often taught was the cultural arm of NATO. As we stood on the terrace in the morning sunshine while the Finnish flag was unfurled, it was clear that the pace of change was quickening.

That afternoon, at the formal proceedings at the University of Strasbourg, they played recordings of speeches made at the inaugural Assembly session in that very room, forty years before. Winston Churchill had declared that this new construction, based as it was on human rights pluralist democracy and the rule of law, was open to any European country which was prepared to espouse its basic ideas and convictions –"even mighty Russia herself; for then indeed all would be well". While there are bound to be differing views on this quotation today with Russia now a member and the consequences of that fact still being digested, in 1989 they were moving and impressive and made all the more so because, at the moment when we heard those words, we knew that Hungary and Poland were signing the first Council of Europe convention preceding their full membership.

It was in July of that same year that Mr Gorbachev came to Strasbourg to address the Parliamentary Assembly of the Council of Europe. His speech was a visionary description not of the details still less the furnishings of the 'Common European Home' of which he loved to speak, but of seven of its foundations. It was clear that the site for Mr Gorbachev's first speech in the setting of a European institution was quite deliberately chosen not in the more powerful and perhaps prestigious arena of the EEC but at the Council of Europe which especially represented the human rights and the rule of law which he now declared were among the foundations of the European Common Home. It was a historic moment of rare hope.

There was at that time a seminar taking place in Strasbourg organised by the Lutheran Centre for Ecumenical Research. It brought together Lutherans from many parts of the world, including the USA. I told them about Gorbachev's speech and distributed copies. The sense of new hope it released was almost tangible, especially among the Americans. It is tempting to be cynical now, but the sense of disappointment, of opportunities lost, of hopes dashed and of political bungling is inescapable.

If the Western nations had indeed grasped the new opportunities open to them at this time half as vigorously as they did after the fall of Nazism, history might tell a different story. If anyone thought of a new style Marshall Plan or similar programmes (and some did) the proposals were not taken up. The way was left open instead for carpet-baggers and strident fundamentalist evangelists. What was lacking was precisely described later by Václav Havel as "generosity and imagination".

But the Council of Europe did react more vigorously to the revolutions, which now transformed the whole European scene. It was not many months after the Gorbachev visit that the Communist regimes to the East of us began to collapse one after another, but before those events broke upon us – indeed only a few days after the Gorbachev visit – another happening grasped our imagination. It was the bicentenary of the French Revolution. Mitterrand's France, and particularly Paris, celebrated the anniversary with enormous gusto. Another triumphal arch on the 'axis' of the Champs Elysées and a pyramid newly opened just outside the Louvre, to house further treasures – all this to the accompaniment of parties and fireworks all over France. It was quite a summer and the theme of Liberty, Equality and Fraternity joined the constellation of slogans which rolled round Europe in the revolutionary year. As the walls and the statues fell, the Council of Europe found itself more popular than ever before. A queue was forming of applicants for membership. Now a new role presented itself as the Council sought to establish itself as an anchor, encourager and above all tutor, of democratic structures and civil society for countries which had been under Communism for many years.

The new Europe, born so suddenly with such amazingly little bloodshed, bringing the remarkable mixture of joy and danger, presented everyone and especially every European body with new mind-blowing questions and the new possibilities. Governments, Churches, political scientists, industrialists, journalists, universities – and the European institutions – struggled to adjust their instruments to the changed landscape. The Council of Europe was not slow to react: its new Secretary General, Catherine La Lumière, had taken up her duties a few days before the visit of Mr Gorbachev and brought a great deal of energy and vision to the task. Soon every part of the Council was addressing new questions in a new Europe.

One of the features of the Council, which qualified it well for addressing the tasks which it now faced, was the fact that it comprised several different but complementary parts. Its two major pillars are of course the political intergovernmental work guided by the Committee of Ministers who represent the member states, and the Parliamentary Assembly, made up of parliamentarians from the national parliaments in numbers which reflect both the size of the country and the party dispositions on the domestic front. There are in addition, the juridical system of the European Court of Human Rights and gatherings of representatives of the local and regional authorities and of the non-governmental organisations. Furthermore, there is the Youth Centre which is closely associated with the Council itself. This amalgamation of the intergovernmental, parliamentary, regional and local, non-governmental, youth, plus the connected but independent juridical system, is unique. All of them were profoundly affected by the openings to the East.

The most eminent and the best-known of the sections of the Council, the juridical process of the European Commission and the Court of Human Rights had begun to address its biggest problem – the delay of its processes (a problem caused, it may be said, by its own success) long before even the first rumblings of the revolutions. The first serious proposals to amend its modus operandi dates from the mid-eighties. But such mills grind slowly. When it began to feel the full force of the wind of change and new members joined up, signed the Convention which they were required to do and allowed the right of individual petition, then the need to streamline the processes became yet more urgent. So they were amended to make it more speedy and efficient. It was at the 1993 summit in Vienna when the member states were eventually able to agree on the new arrangements. Thus the European Court of Human Rights came to adjust to the new problems of scale as membership doubled over five years, but all this took quite a lot more time than had been hoped. As I write, the process is still not fully completed. Yet despite its logistic problems, with co-operation from the member states this should all soon be resolved. This unique legal system is a very valuable contribution to the new arrivals on the European scene. It does not just talk about the rule of law. It does it.

As for the Parliamentary Assembly, it was able to act much more quickly. Before any of the newly democratised countries became members, the Assembly made a dramatic decision: they would accept into 'special invited status' parliamentarians of applicant countries. They might speak, work in the committees and do everything but vote. This created a network of members of parliaments from across the whole of formerly divided Europe, who got to know each other and began to learn to work together. It was of great importance in building confidence in the new Europe.

My ecumenical friends and I used to hold lunch-time meetings for these parliamentarians as for those of the European Parliament when they met. It was particularly interesting to welcome to our home not only Western politicians but some of the Poles, Czechs, Romanians and others, and later, when the USSR had ceased to be, some from the Baltic states. We arranged one meeting early on during these years and invited a Polish MP to speak about how he, a newcomer, felt alongside others who had been in that club for many years. We invited a Frenchman to say how he felt as his familiar assembly point became transformed by the 'new boys' (and girls!). We were fascinated when the conversation turned, without any guiding by our ourselves, to the subject of 'pardon' – that is, as I recall it, a sense that the years of separation required a kind of blessing on a new start and without having any idea of who needed to give or to receive forgiveness, a kind of facing and dealing with the past. It was a memorable and impressive moment. When the Duma started to send a delegation, we found ourselves welcoming a group of half a dozen Russians: one from Vladivostock and another who had flown in from Siberia that morning. In those early days it was only the Council of Europe which provided such a meeting place. It made Brussels seem very provincial.

There were, of course, also some bizarre moments. On one occasion we found ourselves worried but also rather excited that Mr Zhirinovsky might turn up. He was the weird, racist, exhibitionist MP who had not endeared himself to the Jews by his blatantly anti-Semitic remarks. When some of our Jewish neighbours had demonstrated outside the Russian Embassy he had spent a happy evening throwing plant pots at them. Our meeting was the following day. We were ready to telephone the police while keeping a wary eye on the window boxes.

The word 'pillar' tends to be used in Strasbourg Euro-language to describe only the intergovernmental and the parliamentary parts of the Council; but there is some justice in claiming the title for the last two sections. Also, they are certainly important factors in any attempt to build a satisfactory civil society.

Very soon after its founding, the Council took the role of local and regional government very seriously. Indeed, it may be said that more than thirty years before the doctrine of 'subsidiarity' appeared in the formal documents of the European Union in its Treaty of Maastricht, the Council of Europe had grasped its importance and acted on it. For its European Charter of Local Self-Government dates from as long ago as 1958. And for many years the Standing Conference of Local and Regional Authorities (now the Congress) has assembled representatives of the local authorities of the member states every year. Here they have shared common concerns and planned common programmes and also arranged for various committees to meet more frequently and keep the work moving. Here again there was an important job to do in the early nineties to open up to the new democracies.

Before the opening to the East, it had become clear that the Standing Conference would have to change. For within it there was such a variety of levels of authority that such regions as Bavaria and Wales were in the same bag as some market towns or very small local councils. So a process of dividing and separating was started – which of course had to be done with immense tact. The end of this was a new double body – a congress with two chambers – regional and local. This was in fact already up and running by the time that the new Europe was born. It was therefore ready for the task which it set itself of strengthening the regional and local against the national, and helping the countries which had been used to contending with centralised and dictatorial national powers, to make local government work. The conflicts inherited from the former regimes and the new ones which emerged under the new pressures have been sharp and bitter, nor are they in any way solved. It can be claimed that the Strasbourg meeting place has played its part in at least easing the problems and rebuilding on good foundations.

But if the East had to learn to make local government work, the West also had lessons to learn of encouraging decentralisation where governments had for a long time held on tenaciously to their very centralised power, and in certain cases actually extended it. The importance of such a process needs no underlining; local government is a key component of building or rebuilding democratic and healthy societies. For example, it has been said that if Russia is to be brought to political health it will be from her villages. I was delighted to see something of this work.

The 'pillar' with which I personally was mostly involved was the world of 'non-governmental organisations', or NGOs – the voluntary associations which are a key element in the life of any healthy society. Most international bodies make some space for the NGO world. At the UN it is more sophisticated than elsewhere with an effective structure which has spawned some attractive new acronyms 'Kango' or 'Congo' for instance. I compared notes with their office when I was in New York. I found that our Anglican representative put most emphasis on the opportunities of work in the NGO committees. He found that the NGO voice is listened to on such subjects as the rights of the native peoples and environmental questions.

It has been the policy of all the Churches to seek to strengthen the NGO presence in all international bodies. This has been not only because it is the natural slot into which Church and ecumenical bodies may fit and within which they have a place to belong. It is also because the Churches believe in the sort of society represented by the voluntary sector.

The fact is, however, that at every point – whether at the UN or at a regional level, such as the European – NGOs present national politicians and indeed international civil servants, with a conundrum, an extra level of consultation or even negotiation, with which many of them frankly would sooner not be bothered. Those who are wiser, however, recognise that for all their diversity, often surprising, sometimes bizarre – they are an essential part of what democracy is all about. Moreover, there are times when NGOs – especially some of the stronger ones – can get things done which national or even international agencies cannot. This has even been proved in such situations as the Balkan conflict.

At the Council of Europe there is a structure within the Statute which provides for NGOs to be accorded 'consultative status'. This does not mean that they have the right to attend the meetings of expert or standing committees, but they have their own liaison committee and annual assembly and are formally linked with the external department of the Council. This was the formal point of contact between the European Ecumenical Commission (EECCS) and the Council, and it was in fact only a few weeks before I arrived to open the EECCS office that this status had been agreed for us. So I plunged in and was initiated into the NGO act.

NGOs may be a worldwide phenomenon, but at the Council of Europe they were very, very French. Indeed there was no part of it which demonstrated so unambiguously that the Council had spent all its life in France. There were two reasons for this – the first and least important was the fact that the most of the organisations represented were not well off. They therefore could not afford to send people on long and expensive journeys to attend meetings and, accordingly, arranged for someone who lived in or near Alsace to represent them. So the regular work of the NGOs was usually dealt with by the 'locals'. The second reason was that *la vie associative* is an integral part of the structure of French civic society. This was chiefly because of the history of France, and it was due not only to the French Revolution but to the Napoleonic system. For that slippery word *laïcité* is one of the ingredients of *la vie associative*. Although many agencies of the Roman Catholic Church such as Caritas and many educational groups (some of which involved priests) were active among the NGOs, there was still the scent of anti-clericalism.

Personally I did not find this whiff of gallicanism in the least daunting; on the contrary it was stimulating and, I must say, a most agreeable challenge to try, however clumsily, to bring a little Anglo-Saxon pragmatism to the work. The fact that I was usually the only person whose mother tongue was not French, and that their English was either non-existent or not to be paraded publicly, was a complication but not a hindrance. On the contrary, my friends from France decided – apparently enthusiastically – to elect me, a cleric and a newcomer to French culture, to the Liaison Committee and later as a vice-president.

The 'family' of NGOs in consultative status at the Council was very varied and I was surprised at the wide range of associations in this network of over three hundred – from the big players like Amnesty and the International Society of Jurists to groups which, although European – as they were required to be by our Statute – had a very small and focused role. The Commission which I represented was one of the very few non-Roman Catholic Church groups among the active members. There were those who felt that we, representing as we did a large Christian constituency, should have more powerful and prestigious *entrée* to the Council with the possibility of attending and contributing to the standing and expert committees, such as was open to the Roman Catholics through the office of the Vatican Representative. During my time there were indeed suggestions that this might become possible and it would surely be good if it were to come about. I can only say, firstly, that the Vatican delegates (there were three during my time) were extremely helpful to my EECCS colleagues and myself and shared many of their concerns with us as we did in return; secondly, I do not think that it did us – or, I guess, any of our successors – any harm, to have to earn a place from which to speak on matters which were important to us, while at the same time to share in the crucial network of voluntary bodies with all its variety.

Certainly, I was very aware of the privilege of being a vice-president and delighted to hold that office at the time when the openings to the East happened. So I was able to join in the reaching-out to find new contacts which had been impossible before. Many NGOs – which had been illegal or under the thumb of the regime – came out into public view at that time; many found their way to seminars which we and the Council ran in Strasbourg and elsewhere in central European towns. These sessions continue to be an important part of the Council's work and provide a strategic point for co-operation between it and the voluntary sector.

There were also opportunities to go and meet NGOs on their own home territory. In particular I went myself as Vice-President of the Liaison Committee to several countries to tell them about the Council of Europe and especially its work with the voluntary sector and also to encourage them to apply for consultative status. I met with representatives of many associations in Prague, Warsaw, Vilnius, Riga and the following year (1993) in Bratislava and Bucharest. I met many brave men and women who had held to their democratic beliefs throughout the Communist period and some who had suffered deportation. I found also that in some of the work they undertook there were more – or certainly different – problems under a free market system than under state Socialism. In particular, the financial problems for some organisations whose work had been smiled on by the former regime were much more acute. It was a fascinating exercise and I certainly learned a lot more than I taught.

This brief review of the various parts of the Council of Europe and how they tried to adjust to the revolutions would be incomplete without mentioning the European Youth Centre and the foundations which financed many of its activities. Personally, I saw less of this work than I would have wished but what I saw made it perfectly clear that they had been in the bridge-building business ahead of everyone else. Indeed, during the Cold War period there had been some heated arguments about some of their projects which seemed to draw a little too close to the regimes to the East. In the new scene their concern to build a single Europe continues unabated.

It could sound as if the process I have been describing has been a process of the older democracies teaching their tricks to the newer ones: and there is, of course, truth in this, but it has also been, and still is, a learning operation for all. If countries like my own, who have been in the democracy business for quite a long time, imagine that they have no problems at all in building 'civil societies', then they are living with dangerous illusions. For the new Europe spells changes in West as well as East: if the 'old' democracies imagine that all the problems lie to the East of the former iron curtain, we shall all be heading for trouble. It was Václav Havel who pointed out that the growing and changing which countries like his own have to do is really a kind of mirror image of what must be done in the Western world too. Like it or not, we all have much to learn and are very much in the same boat together.

The years I spent in Strasbourg were probably among the most tumultuous of modern times. There has certainly been nothing to touch those heady days when walls and curtains and statues fell and it is difficult to imagine anything on that scale which may now follow. Nevertheless, the time since I left Strasbourg at Easter-time in 1995 has seen more changes in Europe, further shifts of public opinion and some radical changes in the institutions including the Council of Europe. Much, but not all, of this has been the consequence of the revolution as it continues to work its way through the system. Thunderstorms always echo round the hills long after the lightening has disappeared.

The crucial questions always cluster around the arrival of new members – the question of scale: and the time allowed and the time required (not necessarily the same!) to adjust to the increased size – the question of speed. This is nothing new, nor indeed is it unique to Europe: it is part of the dynamic of human history. As ever, then, it is scale and speed which make the difference, the evolution of the then Common Market of six to become the EEC of ten: to the EC of twelve to the EU of fifteen with more coming soon – this evolution, more than changes of political leadership or economic booms or depression, has been the determining factor in the way things have gone and will go on in the future. This process has been at work in all the other European institutions including NATO and of course the Council of Europe.

One important factor in this process is the way in which it clarifies what one believes about the object of the body to which the potential new member applies. In the setting of the EEC, I remember an interesting and revealing encounter in 1988 which threw light on this. A group of Anglican Bishops who were going to the Lambeth Conference were invited to stop off at Brussels en route. They came from Australia, Africa and North America. A full programme had been arranged for them, including NATO, the African, Caribbean, Pacific offices and, of course, the Commission. It was there that one of the young Bishops from Uganda asked the Secretary General what would happen if the USSR (as it then was) were to apply for membership. The question sounded far away and hypothetical not to say naïve in 1988, but David Williamson took it seriously and said that the USSR could not at that time be considered for membership on account of its economic system. I remember that several of us felt that the ways in which the Soviets were at the time treating certain of their citizens was an even more serious disqualification. But although such matters might well have cropped up later, the entry requirements of the European Community were indeed primarily for an economic entity and the Secretary General's answer made that clear.

Recently there has been a filling-out of these requirements to include a human rights clause and the most recent statement of Mr Santer concerning enlargements, to include six more named states in the next few years, makes that clear. But despite that welcome move, economics is still the bottom line.

At Strasbourg, however, it has always been very different. The bottom line at the Council of Europe is not economics, but an entrance examination with questions on the rule of law, multi-party elections, democratic standards and the like together with the acceptance of the European Convention on Human Rights. Although this is clear enough, the actual decision can be a complex and sometimes a contentious business. The Committee of Ministers representing the member states has the final responsibility but does not admit any country to which the Parliamentary Assembly has given the thumbs down. Understandably, the Assembly investigates the situation in the applicant country with great care and sends groups to spy out the land before passing on its considered opinion to the Committee of Ministers. I remember that in the early days of the newly-liberated countries applying for membership, there were some sharp disagreements that had to be sorted out.

I myself was on the edge of one particular case – that of Romania. I was preparing to visit that country to meet with some of their NGOs in the autumn of that year shortly after the 'summit' meeting in Vienna in 1993. At that time there were many reservations about whether to admit Romania. In making my plans for the visit I very much appreciated the help and advice which I received from the Romanian authorities in Strasbourg. But I could not fail to be aware that although I was clearly someone with very limited influence they wanted me to get the best possible impression in view of the decision which was pending. What I found when I got there was a far from satisfactory situation and I heard many serious stories of the way freedom was curtailed and minorities were treated. I also recall some of those I met who were in government presented me with some reassuring signs about opportunities for certain ethnic groups to be represented in parliament. But I am no expert on these matters and I do not put too much weight on my impressions. Whatever the experts and others did in fact advise, it was later that year that Romania was admitted and the news, as I write, is that progress is being made towards a more democratic society and free elections have been held. Whether this is a direct result of membership of the Council of Europe cannot, of course, be proved, but this is certainly the kind of progress that would have been hoped for by those who opened the door.

But, of course, it was Russia which has been and is the greatest test. The first application for membership came well over a year before I left Strasbourg. One remembered Churchill's recorded words at the fortieth birthday party referred to above: "for then indeed all would be well" and one recalled Gorbachev's visit a few weeks later with his hope for a "common home" and then one remembered the bombing of the White House, and then one recalled Chechnya. One also realised that if and when Russia were to become a member, it would increase by over 50% the total area and the total population of the territory of all the member states, thus making a huge change in the balance of the Council.

In fact, after the process had stalled several times and after Chechnya had caused the whole thing to be put on hold for several months, Russia did at last become a full member in April 1996 and the Council is still trying to adjust to the most profound single event of its history so far. Although there are some extremely worrying questions raised about standards which are the very *raison d'être* of the Council (to which we shall turn) it can also be argued that the arrival of the Russian Federation, despite all the complications which it brings with it, is nevertheless a profoundly significant event on the geopolitical map not just of Europe but of the world. It can be argued persuasively that the hopes of peace may have been made just a little more secure by anchoring this huge and unpredictable giant in such a place.

It was about a year later when this question became an extremely lively one, as one of the Council's most distinguished servants over many years, a former Director of Human Rights and more recently Deputy Secretary General, Peter Leuprecht, resigned his post before he was due to retire and took up another appointment in Canada. It appeared that it was not so much Russia but Croatia which was the straw that had broken the camel's back. Before his departure, surprisingly, Leuprecht gave an interview to the local paper. In this he specifically referred to the human rights record of Croatia. And he declared that the Council had become flabby and had allowed the purpose for which it in fact existed to be watered down. With a harshness that was uncharacteristic, Leuprecht also attacked the whole policy of over-hasty "headlong" acceptance of nearly all the countries which had applied which had formerly been under the hegemony of Soviet Russia.

For the Council of Europe there have been all along crucial policy choices to be made which will continue to face those who guide its fortunes in the coming years. The departure of Peter Leuprecht underlines and sharpens those choices.

First there are those who see the Council as a major world player in the defence and safeguarding of human rights and the rule of law. The doctrine is, as it were, put to work juridically in the European Court of Human Rights. There is no part or section of the intergovernmental work programme which does not stand four-square on that foundation. It is therefore of paramount importance that the present member states observe the democratic values of the Council with great strictness. And it is also essential that new members should only be admitted when their human rights record is satisfactory.

In his interview, Peter Leuprecht was not only concerned with the new accessions but with policy to those who were or are already members. He referred to the earlier case of Greece when power was seized by 'the colonels'. At the time the Council of Europe so isolated the Greek regime that international opinion virtually forced them to withdraw. The Council of Europe was not flabby then, he said.

The other point of view is equally clear about the major role of the Council in world affairs but is less absolutist and more pragmatic. Without diluting their title deeds, this view tends to believe that the best chance of getting improvement in the democratic systems and human rights policies of countries who are present members or applicants is by having them in rather than out. It is this practical question which should be paramount.

Presented thus, it would appear that there can be no doubt as to where the Churches would stand. If they do not stand for principle, who does? Surely they cannot condone any fudging? Yet the Churches are also in the business of what may or may not maintain or bring peace and justice. In the period not at the end but at the beginning of the Cold War, such questions were keenly debated. It was Reinhold Niebuhr in the United States who came to represent a school of Christian realism which has had great influence on ethical thinking in many countries and in all the Churches, not only in Protestant tradition to which he belonged. Perhaps his prayer sums it up: give us the courage to change what can be changed: the patience to accept what cannot be changed: and the wisdom to tell the difference. It is an intriguing question to guess what comment he would have made about the most effective way for the Council of Europe to safeguard and extend the principles for which it stands. Certainly, the arguments that human rights and political principles are for use and not to be put in a glass case would have weighed with him, but how much he would have allowed that they may get frayed in their usage is clearly a very nice point, and he, and we too, must admit that at the end of the day, it is a question of degree.

This question – we may call it the Leuprecht question – is not going to go away. The equation is simple. The countries that were formerly under Communism want to join the rest of Europe from which they have been excluded and that means first and foremost that they want to join the European Union; but that size of enlargement cannot happen quickly or the whole edifice would collapse. So the bigger countries of the EU, all of whom are members of the Council of Europe say, "Let them join the Council", adding under their breath, that this will keep them quiet for a little while. But the Council is more than a waiting room. Both clubs may offer advantages to their members. The benefits of the Council of Europe, freedom under the law and so on, are as great as the membership of the market offered by the Union. However, until the big players who have most of the clout in both bodies make it clear that this is how they themselves see it, the Council will not receive the support in the public arena that it ought to have and the importance of maintaining standards of liberal order and civil and minority rights may become undervalued.

I have had plenty of experience of defending the citizens of my own country against the – often understandable – charge of being reluctant, or frightened Europeans. Many is the time when I have pointed out that we were not the only naughty boys and that all countries often drag their feet: sceptics grow in every climate. Nevertheless I do recall being lost for words when the Council of Europe held its first gatherings of heads of state and government – its first 'summit' – in Vienna in 1993 and there were only three countries which failed to send their president or their prime minister: Hungary's Prime Minister was having a heart attack; Turkey was having a general election and had no government; and Great Britain found that the party conference was too important for the Prime Minister to miss even one day. So the Lord Chancellor came and although, as we have seen, the proposed changes in the working of the European Court of Human Rights was high on the agenda and therefore he was a highly appropriate substitute, the absence of the head of the British Government was a shame which I was not alone in feeling keenly.

We must look for something better than this from the United Kingdom and all the members if we can now look forward to a new start. As the Council of Europe approaches its half century, it is to be hoped that there will be a renewed mandate and a new expression of confidence, backed by all the member states. There are three ways in which this can be strengthened. First, by unambiguous public statements delivered in such a way that they may get through to the people. All governments have the equivalent of British spin doctors; we can all get our messages across when we want to. The future of decent standards of public life across the continent – and nothing less than this is what the Council of Europe is about – is too important to be hidden away in a bureaucratic cupboard. Secondly, having agreed what jobs need to be done in the Council's new mandate, it will be necessary to provide the resources to do them.

The third sign that the governments mean business is a little more complex. They call it the 'architecture' of Europe – the ways in which the institutions at the European level relate to one another: the ways in which there may be a common sense division of labour between one another. When the walls and curtains fell many people called loudly for such a clarification. It has not happened yet, but it is not unreasonable even now to hope that ways may be found whereby the EU, the Council of Europe, the OSCE, the OECD and the reborn NATO might agree a sharing of tasks which would both make sense to them and make the policies of their member states more effective. In his "summer meditations", Václav Havel sets out a precise way in which this might happen. As one might expect from such a writer, Havel sees this as a way in which countries would not only commit themselves more vigorously to their common tasks, but also catch the imagination of the people. In addition it would avoid duplication and ambiguity which leads to a waste of time and resources.

The fact that the USA is a member – a very prominent member – of two of these organisations and not of the others is an important factor. The good news is that to have the USA in the equation adds weight to the operation. The bad news is that it greatly complicates the matter. I have myself seen – and wondered at – the ways in which the superpowers dominated the OSCE conference at Vienna: the USA and Russian delegations seemed to call the shots on nearly everything; but as they were themselves often at odds, the lesser delegations were able to make their mark. Four years later when the USSR was no more and there was only one superpower, the USA had an even more dominant position, as I recall from sitting in on a meeting of the G24 group in Strasbourg in 1992, when it seemed as though all the delegations had a kind of deference for the large, articulate and well-briefed American delegations.

If they are stand-offish, therefore, it is not only because they are separated by the Atlantic from the European mainland but also because they are very aware of their status. Who can imagine the USA signing the European Convention of Human Rights? or allowing the right of individual petition? and yet there is an ambiguity in USA/Europe relations, an ambiguity that was never more clearly expressed than at the Paris 'Summit' in 1990. In the process of adapting to the bewildering new Europe which came into existence in 1989, the Parliamentary Assembly of the Council of Europe had suggested that members of Congress and of the Canadian Parliament should be invited to attend as invited guests (as applicant countries did). Everyone – including President Bush – thought it was an excellent idea. I can remember well how, at the next session, the cards USA and Canada duly appeared on the desks they were to occupy, alongside those of the other countries. When the day came, the Canadians were there, sitting in their places, but the members of Congress stayed away.

The fact remains, however, that the United States is already a part of the international European structures, by virtue of her membership of NATO and OSCE and it is worth remembering that when Mikhail Gorbachev spoke of the "European common house", he always reckoned that North America was part of it. Even if the architecture, therefore, has to have a transatlantic wing, which may make the design of the house a little unbalanced or untidy, it is important to remember that we are not after tidiness but effectiveness and coherence. If the powers that run the Council want to demonstrate their commitment, they will design architecture which meets their requirements, even if it looks a little clumsy. Such a purpose is obviously something for which the Churches would want to press.

But that serves to underline the fact that what the Churches may say to the politicians they also need to say to themselves. In 1942, at his enthronement sermon in Canterbury Cathedral, William Temple described the ecumenical movement as "the great new fact of our time". More than half a century later it is hard not to express disappointment tinged even with a little cynicism. And yet much has indeed been achieved. It seems likely that Temple was speaking only of the Churches of Reformation who six years later were to form the World Council of Churches: now since Vatican II the Roman Catholic Church has, despite real disappointments – some of them of recent origin – come very much closer. Temple was also probably not thinking of the Orthodox; yet during the last fifty years they have been actively involved in ecumenism, providing leading contributions and important figures to the World Council of Churches and to the Conference of European Churches and engaging in inter-Church dialogues. By a cruel irony they have become more closed-in from the scene since the time of what is often called 'the opening' to the East. Among the Churches of the Anglican family and of the Reformation, however, there have been further encouragements, some of the most notable being in the European scene. Despite the dark clouds on the ecumenical horizon, there would be much here to gladden Temple's heart, but he would also surely see that we still have a long way to go to heal our differences, some of which have been positively exacerbated by the revolutions of 1989.

The 'great new fact' is however a reality caused as much by the increasing ease and decreasing cost of travel as by theological agreements. International ecumenism is here to stay and the people who did not know one another now do – or certainly if they wish, may do so. In the summer of 1997 thousands of European Christians decided to do just that, and get themselves to Graz in Austria for the second great ecumenical Assembly. Its theme was painfully appropriate – 'Reconciliation: Gift of God and Source of Life' – and it was a moment of tragic irony as well as explosive joy.

The tragedy was that the brave and imaginative attempt to use Graz and its theme as an opportunity for bringing together Church leaders, who had been seriously at odds, failed. The Orthodox Ecumenical Patriarch was to have been in Graz before the assembly. The Russian Patriarch was to attend the assembly. Was it not then the ideal occasion for an East/West meeting? Why should not the Pope come to Graz, so that a signal of reconciled Churches could be sent out from that highly appropriate setting? What exactly went wrong is not clear to this day, and perhaps that is just as well, but the preparations were deemed inadequate and so the whole thing was called off.

The joy was at the ground floor. No problems – Kosovo, Bosnia, Ireland – were solved. Hard questions were raised and discussed and held up in prayer; it was the speakers from the conflict areas who probably had most to say about the nature of reconciliation. But the joy was in the sessions or groups, and in the experience of being together across such wide differences of age and nation and tribe and language and class and culture – eating and drinking, praying and studying – that was Temple's 'great new fact'. It exploded at the final service which was televised and totally confused the broadcasters and everyone else because they simply would not stop dancing and greeting one another for the Exchange of the Peace.

Back in 1986, I knew it was right that the Churches should be in contact with the international bodies born since the war. I knew we should be setting up good two-way communications, fielding Christian convictions into the European processes. I was proud to give a hand with this. What I had not realised was the uncanny parallel between what was evolving in the international and the ecumenical sphere. The problems faced by the Council of Europe (and in the EU and other organisations) and those faced by the Churches in their search for unity were and indeed still are amazingly similar.

The two movements were born next door to each other and almost share a birthday – 1948. In Amsterdam and the Hague – the first Assembly of the World Council of Churches and the Congress of Europe were held. The graph of enthusiasm has gone up and down over the last fifty years with uncanny similarity. The fears of loss of sovereignty in Church and nation have echoed one another with amazing precision.

And now as we celebrate the half-century of the Council of Europe, we find ourselves confronting the same questions in Church and politics. Although there are many difficult problems on the horizon, I list three fundamental questions:

Firstly, can the longing for peace and unity which is to be found at the ground floor, join hands with the official structures of both Church and nation? Can the dance of Graz catch the imagination of the wider world?

Secondly, can we bridge the gap, the major fault line, which separates East and West?

Thirdly, how will those two basic units – the nation-state and the Church – evolve in the coming years?

The first question is partly a matter of political and Church leadership. When, as at Graz, people are enabled to catch a glimpse of a wide horizon, which in no way contradicts their own loyalty for their own Church or identity, then power can be released to help them and those in leadership to achieve their vision. Political and Church leadership fails when it panders to the jingoistic strident nationalism which is a mockery – and a dangerous mockery – of what true patriotism – or true love of one's own Church – is all about. But it is not necessary to hold rallies. It is also to do with quiet projects involving the implementation of educational policies and exchange programmes, and so on.

The second question – the East/West divide – could become very serious and certainly lead to lost opportunities, if we cannot tackle it. In Church affairs the relations between the Orthodox, (especially in Russia, Bulgaria and some other Eastern European Churches) on the one hand; and on the other the Western Churches (in particular the Vatican and what we may well call the Western ecumenical movement and the evangelism of some other groups) including some from across the Atlantic are now at a critical stage. It is not a simple state of affairs, but to put it in shorthand, we may say that the East finds the West lacking in a spiritual dimension, decadent and minding other people's business, while the West finds the East inscrutable, narrow-minded and in some cases racist. But the absurd thing is that we need each other. The more spiritual and less activist theological insights of the Eastern tradition provide precisely the antidote required by the more busy cerebral approach of the West. The West can bring to the Orthodox what has been described (by an Orthodox) as "learning to live in the realities of a pluralist culture".

In the political field the need to find the best forms of collaboration and independence are if anything still more pressing: and despite the 'opening' to the East the dialogue still has a very long way to go. The Council of Europe is well placed to play a unique role in the process. With its 'pillars' of intergovernmental work, its parliamentary sessions, its work with regional and local authorities and with non-governmental bodies and youth – all this provides the framework within which there can be truly creative encounters between peoples at every level. If the Council of Europe is enabled to follow such a programme, there could be a much stronger hope for a Europe not unified but coherent, and able to discover and show a kind of civil society of which we might be proud. As in the Churches, East and West need each other.

The third question facing both the Churches and the political scene is the future of those two basic units of our respective communities – the meaning of 'Church' and the meaning of 'nation'. What do we mean by the word Church? Since the Reformation all of us in the Western Churches – save for the Roman Catholics – have tended to see a Church as closely identified with a nation, or more precisely, with a nation-state. The Orthodox have, since even earlier usually identified their autocephalous patriarchates with a particular territory. The last fifty years of the ecumenical movement have in fact raised a number of penetrating questions about these assumptions. What we are all looking for is nothing less than a new idea of what it means to be a 'Church' if one takes seriously the ecumenical – and international – vision. And this will not mean losing what we know and love, but seeing it in a new and sharper light. Ecumenism is good for the health.

Similarly the idea of 'nation' in an international, or can we say ecumenical, context is being changed dramatically, whether we know it or not, by the international movements of the last fifty years. Sharing sovereignty is going on all the time, and mostly (not always let it be said) to the benefit of all of us. The idea of the absolute sovereign state was an invention of modern history which depends for its vigour on the contrasts with the 'other'. It has been described by a theologian as an 'aberration' and by a journalist as more dangerous than the atom bomb. There is a big difference between a nation-state and a nation, There are regions – Scotland is the most immediate example – which are seeking self-determination in their 'nationhood' but do not want to aspire to be a state.

So much for the questions which we face together in the next phase. But they are questions, not forecasts. Anything can happen. The danger of catastrophe is a real one. The forces of separation could lead to conflict as they have in the Balkans and on a bigger scale. But there is another danger which is as deadly – of a kind of boredom, apathy and sclerosis. Much will depend on the first question. Can the dreams and visions of the ground floor prevail? Can they penetrate the rest of Europe's people? Can Church and politics alike hear what they have to say?

6. EUROPE? – WHAT EUROPE? – THE FUTURE

Robin Guthrie

Robin Guthrie was head of social and economic affairs in the Council of Europe from 1992–98.

For six years I worked at the Council of Europe in Strasbourg and for six years I asked myself and others a question. I asked ambassadors and ministers, colleagues, parliamentarians, students, Church groups, and passers-by. No-one had an answer. The question? It was simply this: why is it, when the British above all have reservations about the Union and its so-called 'federal' tendencies, do they not come round the corner to Strasbourg and say: "This is the kind of Europe we want to see: a Europe of independent states, working together on the basis of common principles and co-operating together on matters of common interest"?

The answer is all too simple, elusive though I found it during those rich years in Strasbourg. But first, some definitions.

Union: "The fact of being united into one political body, especially formation or incorporation into a single state, kingdom or political entity, usually with one central legislature". "The state of being joined into one". As in matrimony, trades union, Soviet Union – and the European Union?

Unity – a somewhat different concept: "The quality or condition of being one in mind, feeling, opinion, purpose or action; harmonious combination together of the various parties or sections"; "The state of being united, joined or in agreement, etc"; "firmly joined in a state of love, agreement, etc"; "All concerned having the same aim".

In other words a 'union' is a single entity in which differences are subsumed within the whole; while 'unity' implies a definable entity composed of separate parts, or a number of different entities with a common purpose.

What sort of Europe have we got? What sort of Europe do we want?

The Council of Europe is one of Europe's lesser-known but still remarkable institutions. Founded in the aftermath of war in 1949 with ten members (Belgium, Denmark, France, Ireland, Italy, Luxembourg, Netherlands, Norway, Sweden, United Kingdom) its stated aim is:

> "to achieve a greater unity between its members for the purpose of safeguarding and realising the ideals and principles which are their common heritage and facilitating their economic and social progress."

Those 'ideals and principles' are specifically *human rights* (the protection of the individual against any overmighty power, including his or her own government), *pluralist democracy* (the freedom of political action) and the *rule of law* (necessitating the separation of the judiciary from the state).

Having defined the aim of the Council, the first article of the Statute goes on to spell out the methods to achieve it:

> "by *discussion* of questions of common concern and by *agreements* and *common action* in economic, social, cultural, scientific, legal and administrative matters and in the maintenance and further realisation of human rights and fundamental freedoms."

The Council's best known institution is the European Court of Human Rights in Strasbourg. The Court is not strictly speaking an organ of the Council, but was established under the European Convention on Human Rights in 1950. It is the only example of a judicial – and effective – enforcement mechanism for human rights anywhere in the world.

The organs of the Council are the Committee of Ministers and the Parliamentary Assembly. The ministers concerned are the Ministers for Foreign Affairs, who meet twice a year; between these meetings their Deputies, who act as ambassadors for their country or permanent representatives, conduct the Council's business. They receive the judgements of the European Court of Human Rights and monitor the implementation of the Court's decisions by the government concerned; they receive and respond to resolutions of the Parliamentary Assembly; and they run the Intergovernmental Work Programme. The different elements of this Programme are entrusted to steering committees of government officials or nominees expert in the relevant fields, covering different aspects of legal affairs, education, culture, social affairs and so on. In this way issues such as football hooliganism, citizenship law, the administration of prisons, the transmission of AIDS through blood transfusion, a census in the Balkans, the conservation of historic buildings, the Convention on Human Rights and Biomedicine, the European Pharmacopoeia, the freedom of the media and a host of other matters, are treated in a manner which enables each country to draw on the experience of others to its own benefit and which, in appropriate circumstances, provides a legal instrument by which the actions of governments and other parties can be judged and corrected.

Ten member states launched the Council of Europe in 1949. By 1989 there were twenty-three, covering the whole of Western, Northern and Southern Europe. When the Soviet empire collapsed it was open to the countries of Central and Eastern Europe to sign up to the principles on which the Council of Europe is founded. This required processes of profound constitutional change and administrative reorganisation, together with vetting and accreditation by the Parliamentary Assembly. As a result of these processes there were, by 1997, forty states in membership of the Council, stretching from the Atlantic to the Pacific and from the Arctic Circle to the Mediterranean. The effects of membership, and the requirements of the conventions – notably the European Convention on Human Rights – are now felt across the whole continent.

The Council has little money and no power beyond that conferred by its moral authority and its legal instruments; nor is it equipped to solve international crises (although it could be, if the governments so willed). What it offers is the application of expertise, on the basis of principles, over time, to the promotion of well-being and the reduction of the risk of conflict for all Europeans.

The Council of Europe is housed in the Palais de l'Europe in Strasbourg. This is an attractive and effective modern building. Immediately inside the main entrance is the entrance hall. A great trunk of wood sprouts from its centre carrying huge beams which link with the canopy outside the entrance and embrace an arena on several levels. This marvellous space is traversed daily by hundreds of staff and visitors. Around it are a newsagent, a bank, a post office and a bookshop, and off it the information centre and at the upper level the parliamentary chamber itself. It can be used for formal occasions such as the ceremonies of accession of new member states, or the reception of heads of state at a summit; but it can be used equally for informal performances by visiting choirs and dancers or exhibitions of cultural developments in member states. There is no comparable space in Brussels where people can move freely and share a common experience.

The European Parliament also meets in the Palais de l'Europe, at least until the spring of 1999 when its new building on the other side of the river is opened. This huge new palace, due for occupation in the spring of 1999, duplicates the huge Parliament building recently completed in Brussels. The parliamentarians conduct their business and hold their committees for the most part there, while their secretariat is housed in Luxembourg. Each of the early members of the Union has at least one Union institution on its territory: the Parliament is France's institution, while its secretariat falls to Luxembourg. The European Court has confirmed, at France's insistence, that the plenary sessions of the Parliament have to be held in Strasbourg. These sessions take place once a month throughout the year, and have been held until now in the same chamber (or 'hemicycle') as the Parliamentary Assembly of the Council of Europe. This adds greatly to the frustration of MEPs and the confusion of European citizens about what 'Strasbourg' stands for. Every month the secretaries pack trunks with papers and the whole caravan migrates up the Rhine in cohorts of lorries, by car, train and aeroplane, to perch in Strasbourg for their plenary sessions.

The origins of the European Union are different from those of the Council of Europe. For centuries philosophers and visionaries have dwelt on the possibilities of a united Europe. A unique opportunity arose after the Second World War, combined with a sense of urgency and a determination that such wars should never happen again. It was vital both to ensure Germany's recovery and to strengthen its position as a bulwark against the Communist bloc. The Ruhr-Lorraine region is a natural economic unit split by political boundaries. In the late 1940s there was a severe problem of over-production of steel and of the absorption by the burgeoning German economy of all the coke produced in the Ruhr, which would have necessitated a limitation on steel production in France, despite that country's reliance on steel production as a key element in its own economic plan. The possibility of uniting the industrial capacity of the two nations had been mooted even in the 1920s, notably by Konrad Adenauer who was now a key player on the scene along with Jean Monnet, Robert Schuman and Alcide de Gasperi. The creation of a single European Coal and Steel Community not only resolved that problem: it ensured that France and Germany could never go to war again (they would be making each others' tanks) and it provided an axis around which the rest of Europe could unite. Six nations did so, and the Union we know today was in embryo. It was a stroke of political genius and a key moment in the history of Europe. Opportunistic though it was, it was firmly based on longstanding philosophical and political ideals and on a clear vision of the future of a united Europe.

The European Coal and Steel Community of 1951 was followed by the Atomic Energy Community (Euratom) of 1957 and the Treaty of Rome in the same year which created the European Economic Community, moving towards "ever closer union". In 1992 the Maastricht Treaty created the Union as we now know it, although one has also to remember that 49% of the French nation voted against that treaty. (The French have problems with the concept of 'Europe'. On the one hand three wars with its neighbour Germany in seventy years make the Franco-German axis crucial to the stability of the state. On the other hand, national interests remain supreme, and for other nations to be 'European' must mean that they approximate to being French. The Greeks and the Danes show no more sign of being capable of that than the British.)

On the basis of these essentially economic early communities, the European Union has progressed from six to nine to twelve to fifteen members. Ultimately it is governed by the Council of Ministers, which is the governments of the member states. The Parliament has limited powers. The Commission has great authority, but far too small a bureaucracy for the huge funds it dispenses. Altogether the Union is an institution of immense wealth, power and potential. Politicians, and journalists, are fascinated by it; ordinary people are not so sure. And it is true that Napoleon, and Hitler, would have loved it: they would simply have moved into Brussels and taken control of the levers of power which have been established there.

Moreover the buildings of the Union are oppressive. They have destroyed large parts of a once delightful city. Each of the main institutions of the Union has recently built itself a palace; but these palaces speak not of democracy, of sharing, of culture or of transparency: they speak of power, they are daunting and difficult of access. Like the new Parliament building in otherwise friendly Strasbourg, they recall the architecture of Mussolini rather than that of the more domestic architecture of the public buildings of the Council of Europe and most of its member states.

Where, then, do we go from here?

The key problem is that the power and the principles in Europe have become separated. The principles lie in Strasbourg, with the Council of Europe. They are not economic: the costs of incorporating those principles into national structures are not primarily financial. In the Council of Europe in Strasbourg virtually all the states of Europe meet on an equal footing; a unity has been established which at last covers the whole continent, in all its diversity of languages, culture and economic variation. But the power lies in Brussels. Sadly, that power is used not to unite, but to divide. The single most divisive factor in Europe is the European Union, separating East from West. It dominates Eastern Europe like a nineteenth-century imperial power. The most important characteristic of the single currency is not whether this or any other country should join it at some point, but what it will do to the continent as a whole. In effect it will dig a ditch as deep as the Iron Curtain and the Berlin Wall were high, roughly down the same geographical divide. If the Czech Republic joins the Union before Slovakia, a whole new frontier, impermeable to vehicles and pedestrians, will have to be built where nothing now exists and people visit each other and their families across a rural landscape without hindrance.

Within the Union similar tendencies can be seen. Indeed so far as the member states are concerned the Union is not so much a union as an arena for the determination of competing national interests. In that lies the answer to my opening question: no politician can risk letting his own people down by not focusing on the Union in order to seek maximum partisan advantage. There is no political capital to be gained by going round the corner to Strasbourg, however much greater the popular appeal of the Council of Europe and the principles on which it is based might be.

How could all our optimism and our ideals have reached this point? How can we talk of enlargement of the Union and set up a single currency at the same time? Faced by these questions, at a seminar I attended a few years back, a senior and respected member of the staff of the Commission finally shrugged his shoulders in answer to the question "What can happen?" and said, "Some kind of earthquake". I do not want an earthquake in the sense of all the destruction that might entail, but I do want a change in the landscape and I do not see any politician preparing us for it, here or abroad.

Tony Blair gets nearer to it than anyone, but the objectives are not yet clear and the far horizon is obscured by the imperative of protecting national interests.

Apart from the question of competing national interests it is clear that the Union itself is out of control. Its huge financial resources, its meagre bureaucracy, its lack of democratic accountability, its ultimate subjection to the conflicting wills of the governments of the member states and its incapacity to tackle the key issues of foreign policy and defence have led it to become at the same time power-hungry within and beyond the boundaries of the Union itself and inward-looking, concerned more with structures than with objectives.

Europe? What Europe? What answer do we give to that question? First of all it must be the whole of Europe, and not just some privileged part. Secondly it must be based on principles, not on economic criteria. Thirdly it must acknowledge differences. 'Harmonisation' in Eurospeak does not mean harmonisation at all, but 'unisonification': that must not be allowed to happen across the whole field of European lives, cultures and economies. Fourthly it can indeed allow for economic groupings, and for the power they will inevitably exercise, but within a broader vision of a Europe entirely united in its principles and capable of determining major issues of common concern.

Curiously enough, the only example I know of where this has already happened is the European Pharmacopoeia. This was established relatively early in the life of the Council of Europe, on the basis of human rights and with the purpose of protecting the individual human being in the crucial field of medicaments. Substantial laboratories have been set up in Strasbourg, and the Pharmacopoeia, now available on CD-Rom, is the key reference point for governments, manufacturers and customers alike. The European Union has in similar circumstances set up parallel institutions to serve the Union states alone (and thus to dominate the continent). In this case it was clear that the European Pharmacopoeia was too far advanced and too competent for any competition: it ranks alongside the Pharmacopoeia of the United States and of Japan to determine worldwide standards in this field, and countries as diverse as Australia, Syria and China are affiliated to it. The Union accordingly decided not to compete with the European Pharmacopoeia, but to join it. All fifteen members of the Union were already members of the European Pharmacopoeia, but now the Union, with its own place on the Commission, speaks for all fifteen members on administrative and political matters while the individual member states speak their own mind on the technical issues with which the Commission of the Pharmacopoeia is primarily concerned.

In the negotiations leading to this situation, the Council of Europe found itself dealing not with DGV in Brussels, which is responsible for health matters, but with DGXIII, which is responsible for industrial development. The objective of the Union was not the protection of the human individual but the single market in pharmaceuticals; its constituency was not the common citizen but the pharmaceutical industry. That objective, perfectly proper in itself, could be absorbed within the overall function of the European Pharmacopoeia as already established in Strasbourg. It is not difficult to imagine what would have happened had the Pharmacopoeia been established first in Brussels and had the Council of Europe attempted to attach its principles and priorities to it.

There is, nevertheless, no point in simply wishing the Union away. It is with us, and will not disappear. The challenge is rather to shift the power of Brussels on to the principles of Strasbourg. In institutional terms this is a daunting task, which will call for imagination and sacrifice in many quarters. Politically it should be easier, particularly if national leaders can offer their electorates a vision of Europe which is comprehensive, principled and productive – the kind of Europe, in other words, which most ordinary Europeans want. With hindsight it is clear that a huge opportunity was missed in 1989, when the Berlin Wall fell and the political geography of Europe was transformed – virtually the 'earthquake' of which the official so presciently spoke. But instead of abandoning the original project, designed for another age and for imperatives that are no longer dominant, we sought – and still seek – simply to extend the empire of Western Europe by incorporating the new democracies of Central and Eastern Europe into our structures and on our economic terms. That is no recipe for the future of the continent as a whole, and we must find a new vision if the ideals and inspiration of those who sought unity in Europe over so many centuries are to be realised in our generation.

Part III – Europe: aims and ideals

7. DREAMING ALOUD[1]

Václav Havel

Václav Havel was President of Czechoslovakia and then, after the division of the country, of the Czech Republic.

In this chapter I want to reflect on how my views on Europe have developed since the collapse of Communism. I shall look back over three significant speeches I made in Strasbourg; two to the Council of Europe which I described as "perhaps the most suitable environment of all for the kind of reflection I wanted to make?" I started with a personal experience of my own: throughout my life whenever I thought about public affairs, about civil, political and moral matters, some reasonable person would inevitably start very reasonably to point out, in the name of reason, that I too should be reasonable, should cast aside my eccentric ideas, and finally accept that nothing can change for the better because the world is divided once and for all into two worlds. Both of these half-worlds are content with this division and neither wants to change anything. It is pointless to behave according to one's conscience because no one can change anything and anyone who does not want war should just keep quiet. I often had to listen to this 'voice of reason' following Brezhnev's invasion of Czechoslovakia, after which such so-called 'reasonable' people felt much revived because they had been given a new argument for their indifference to public affairs. They could say:

> "There you are, that's the way it goes, they've written us off, nobody cares, there is nothing we can do, everything's in vain, you'd better learn your lesson and keep silent! Or do you want to go to jail?"

I was far from the only one to disregard such wisdom and continue to do what I thought right. There were many of us in my country. We were not afraid of being considered fools. We went on thinking about how to make the world a better place, and we did not hide ideas. Our efforts eventually merged into a single, co-ordinated initiative which we called Charter 77. All of us in the Charter, together and individually, thought about freedom and injustice about human rights, about democracy and political pluralism, about market economy and many other things. We thought and hence we also dreamed. We dreamed, both in and out of prison, of a Europe without

---

1. This chapter is based on speeches made by President Havel to the Council of Europe, May 1990 and the European Parliament, March 1994.

barbed wire, high walls, artificially separated nations and gigantic stockpiles of weapons, of a Europe that had discarded 'blocs', of a European policy based on a respect for man and human rights, of a politics not subordinated to transient and particular interests. Yes, we dreamed of a Europe that would be an amicable community of independent nations and democratic states. When I had the chance to snatch a quarter of an hour's conversation with my friend Jirí Dienstbier (later to become Prime Minister and Minister for Foreign Affairs) as we changed machines at the end of a shift in the Hermanice prison, we sometimes dreamed of these things aloud. Later, when he was working as a stoker, Jirí Dienstbier wrote a book called *Dreaming of Europe*. "What's the point of a stoker writing utopian notions of the future when he can't exert the tiniest influence on this future and can only bring more harassment upon himself?" asked the friends of reason, shaking their heads uncomprehendingly.

And then a strange thing happened. Time suddenly accelerated, and what would otherwise have taken a year suddenly happened in an hour. Everything started to change at a surprising speed, the impossible suddenly became possible, and the dream became reality. The stoker's dream became the daily routine of the Minister for Foreign Affairs. And the advocates of reason have now divided into three groups. The first are quietly waiting for some bad things to happen that will serve them as yet another argument in support of their nihilistic ideology. The second are looking for ways to push the dreamers out of government and replace them again with 'reasonable' pragmatists, and the third are loudly proclaiming that, at last, what they have always known would happen has come to pass.

I emphasised that I was not saying this "to ridicule my allegedly reasonable fellow citizens", but for a very different reason: to show that it is never pointless to think about alternatives that may at the moment seem improbable, impossible, or simply fantastic.

We don't dream, of course, just because our dreams might one day come in handy. We dream, as it were, as a matter of principle. Yet it would now appear that there can be moments in history when having "dreamed on principle" may in fact come in handy,

I went on to describe the situation in my country as I saw it then:

> "Following the attack against the students in November 1989, our nation's patience finally gave out, and we quickly overthrew the totalitarian system that had dominated our country for forty-two years. We have set out on the road to democracy, to political pluralism, and to market economy. The press in our country is free, and in a month's time we shall have our first free elections in forty-two years, with a broad range of political forces taking part. I strongly believe that these elections will stand the test in the eyes of all foreign observers as well.

In our country there is spiritual and intellectual freedom; once again, for the first time since the Second World War, all the Catholic dioceses have bishops, and the religious orders are functioning again.

Our state has no ideology. The only idea it wants to instil in its domestic and foreign policy is a respect for human rights in the broadest sense of the word, and an esteem for the uniqueness of every human being. Among other laws, our Parliament has passed some important economic legislation to enact the transition to a market economy and put meaning back into human labour. We are preparing democratic constitutions for our federation and for both national republics. We want at last to give full legal expression to the identity of our two nations and ensure the collective rights of our national minorities. We are a sovereign state, we want to live in friendship with all nations, but if need be, we are determined to defend that sovereignty."

I believed then that we had the right to the status of observer at the Assembly and I was firmly convinced that the Council would understand and accept our application, as indeed it did. But I pointed out that what I said about my country did not mean that Czechoslovakia was at that time an oasis of harmony. Quite the opposite. We were going through an extremely difficult period because we were awash in a vast array of enormous problems that were latent and were only surfacing following our newly won freedom. From the former regime we had inherited a devastated landscape, a disrupted economy and, above all, a mutilated moral awareness.

The overthrow of totalitarian power was an important first step, but it was just the beginning of our journey and there were many pitfalls ahead.

I explained how I believed that there was almost nothing that we were good at and much that we had to learn. We had to learn to create a political culture; we had to learn independent thinking and responsible civic behaviour.

I said that I was not saying all this to gain an undeserved advantage or elicit compassion, but because I am "accustomed to speaking the truth, even in a situation when it might seem more advantageous to lie, or at least keep silent". It is my opinion that the advantage of a clear conscience cannot be eclipsed by any other.

Having briefly painted that picture of my own country, I could then start thinking aloud about the Europe of the future. I stressed that these thoughts were not simply a recapitulation of some far-off dissident dreams but also reflected what I had learned in office and from many conversations with the foreign statesmen I had had the good fortune to meet.

I said it would be pointless to repeat what everybody then believed they knew, that unprecedented prospects were opening up for the future of Europe: "the possibility of becoming a continent of peaceful and amicable co-operation among all its nations".

I spoke of specific measures in this sphere of structures, institutions and treaties that should be created and implemented. I started by assuming that "the structures born of the old system should either be smoothly transformed or merged into new structures, or simply abolished and left to wither. Entirely new structures should be created in parallel as starting points or seeds of a future order." For the sake of clarity, I divided this sphere into four categories: security measures, and political, economic and civic structures, institutions or mechanisms.

I stressed that NATO could become the seed of a new European security system, but that it must change. Above all it must – in the face of its changing role – change its name as well. This should happen, I said, because of a victory of the West over the East. The present name is so closely linked to the era of the Cold War that it would be a sign of a lack of understanding of present-day developments if Europe were to unite under the NATO flag. If the present structure of the West European security alliance can become a precursor or a seed of a future pan-European alliance, it is certainly not because the West will have won the Third World War but because historical justice has triumphed. A further reason for changing the name is its obvious geographical inappropriateness. In a future security system, only a minority of members would border on the Atlantic Ocean. I even suggested that the new security system could have its new headquarters in one of the beautiful Prague palaces near the Prague Castle.

Allow me to repeat a remark I made then concerning nuclear weapons in Europe:

> "These weapons – produced never to be used – have become in the post-war period part of a security model that, paradoxically, ensured peace through a balance of fear. The nations of Central and Eastern Europe, however, paid a heavy price for the efficiency of this nuclear model by remaining in the grip of a totalitarian strait-jacket.
>
> An excessive quantity of any type of weapons, particularly of the nuclear variety, inevitably disfigures the territory on which it is deployed. This applies particularly to those that can only reach beyond their backyards and which we call 'tactical'."

In those now far-off days we welcomed President Bush's proposal to abandon the planned modernisation of those weapons. We saw no point in the weapons in Central Europe directed against us and our neighbours. I emphasised that, in my opinion, the main disaster of our modern world has been its bipolarity, the fact that the tension between the two main powers and their allies was indirectly transferred in one way or another to the whole world. This situation persists to this day. The world is constantly being torn apart by this tension and stifled by the existing superpowers. The chief victims of this unfortunate state of affairs are the one hundred or so states inaccurately called the Third World, the developing world, or the non-aligned world. The anxiety of this world over the possibility that the emergence of a united 'Helsinki' security zone could only widen the gap between the North and the South is understandable but groundless. The very opposite is true. It would be an important step from bipolarity to multipolarity. In addition to the powerful North American continent and the rapidly changing and liberating community of nations of today's Soviet Union, we would have the emergence of a large European connecting link. These three entities, living in peace and mutual co-operation, would indirectly open up new opportunities for a fully-fledged existence to other countries, other communities of countries. The entire international community would start shifting from an arena of peaceful co-operation among equal partners. The North would cease to threaten the South through the export of its interests and its supremacy. Instead it would radiate toward the South the idea of equal co-operation for all.

It was justified, I thought, to speak on the crucial questions of security at length. My exact words in conclusion on this subject were:

> "You will certainly understand why I have spoken so extensively about these ideas here in this Assembly, before the representatives of the oldest and largest political organisation in Europe, one that has such solid foundations and has already done so much useful work. Yes, the spiritual and moral values on which the Council of Europe is based, and which are the common heritage of all European nations, are the best of all possible foundations for a future integrated Europe. I can see no reason why your Parliamentary Assembly and your executive bodies could not be the core around which a future European confederation would crystallise. Czechoslovakia considers all the criteria for the admission of new states to the Council of Europe as excellent: it accepts them without reservations and rejoices that the Council of Europe is opening up to the emerging democracies of the former Soviet satellites, which are now building their relations with the Soviet Union on the principles of equality and full respect of the sovereignty of individual states. I am firmly convinced that the day will come when all European states will fulfil your criteria and will become full members of the Council. The Council of Europe was, after all, founded as a pan-European institution, and it was only the sad course of history that turned it for so long into a merely West European institution.
>
> Obviously, the states that had been ruled by a totalitarian system and now are overcoming its consequences and want, so to speak, to return to Europe, can most rapidly and efficiently do so not by competing and

contending against one another but by helping one another in solidarity. If these countries want to open up to the new Europe, they must first open to one another. The new democratic government in Czechoslovakia, therefore, wants to do everything in its power to contribute to the co-ordination of efforts by the Central European countries to enter various European institutions. That is why we so often appeal to different institutions that are theoretically European but in fact are so far only Western European, to open more flexibly to those who for long years were segregated and who logically belong in them.

The highest level of integration has no doubt been achieved by the twelve countries of the European Economic Community. The countries of Central and Eastern Europe, working on the transition from a centralised 'non-economy' to a normal market economy and trying to enter the world of normal economic relations and achieve the convertibility of their currencies, now look upon the EC as a distant and almost unattainable horizon they should co-ordinate their journey towards. The EC should create some flexible transitional ground, on which the economies of these countries could more easily recover. This would not only serve the interest of these countries, but it would serve the interest of the EC itself and would further the idea of an integrated, democratic Europe.

The harsh lesson of living under a totalitarian system has taught us to respect human and civil rights, and it is no accident that the emerging democracies in our countries have mostly sprung from independent civic movements like the Czechoslovak Charter 77. We cannot forget the soil out of which we have grown and the principles that have governed our struggle for freedom. We therefore realise how indispensable it is that the efforts to integrate states, governments and parliaments be accompanied, or even inspired, by parallel civic efforts. For this reason, I have recently supported, along with Lech Wałesa, a proposal for a European Civic Assembly. I trust that the West European governments will also demonstrate an understanding for this plea.

Against the massive background of this broad 'Northern' or 'Helsinki' security zone, or simultaneously with its emergence, Europe could, relatively swiftly and without the obstacles that until recently seemed insurmountable, become politically integrated as a democratic community of democratic states. This process would no doubt go through several stages and be mediated by several different mechanisms. It may be that in the first stage, say within five years, a community could be established on European soil that we might call the 'Organisation of European States' and, with the beginning of the third millennium, God willing, we could start to build the 'European Confederation' proposed by President Mitterrand. With the gradual consolidation, stabilisation and growing competence of the future confederation, the whole

'Helsinki' security system would ultimately become capable of ensuring its own security, at which point the last American soldier could leave Europe, because Europe would have lost its reason to fear Soviet military strength and the unpredictability of that powerful country's foreign policy.

Every move leading to this goal should be encouraged. The more varied and parallel the attempts undertaken the better, because the greater the chance will be that one of them will succeed. Hence Czechoslovakia supports very different initiatives such as smaller, working regional committees such as Initiative Four (the Danubian-Adriatic Community), and it is studying projects such as Prime Minister Mazowiecki's idea for setting up a permanent political body of the foreign ministers of all European states.

"The time is not too distant", I said, "when some of the republics of the Soviet Union will become completely independent and others will establish a new type of community, whether a confederative association or a looser type. In my view, there is no reason why, against the background of an extensive 'Helsinki' security system, some or all of the European nations of the present Soviet Union could not at the same time be members of a European confederation and of some eventual 'post-Soviet' confederation."

My final words in 1990, when hopes were high, are best reiterated in their entirety:

"In conclusion, allow me to mention an anxiety we frequently meet with nowadays. The fear of all national, ethnic and social conflicts in the Central European arena, which might be fostered by long unresolved and latently spreading problems. This fear leads to the question as to whether our part of Europe will soon become a powder keg of the Balkan type.

It is our common task to exclude the possibility of such a threat and render such fears immaterial. This is chiefly the responsibility of our countries, which must proceed with speed, co-ordination and complete mutual understanding to solve the problems we have inherited. But it is also the responsibility of West European countries, which could help us a great deal by supporting us in this complicated process.

In 1464 the Czech King George of Podebrady sent a momentous message to the French King Louis XI, proposing that he preside over a league of peace and invite Christian rulers to a convention which, on the basis of binding international law, would prevent war amongst members of the union and ensure their common defence. It seems to me that it was no accident that one of the first serious attempts toward a peaceful unification of Europe emerged from Central Europe. As a traditional crossroads of all European conflicts, this region has a particular interest in European peace and security. I am happy to have been able to speak about these matters here in Strasbourg, in a place that was once the symbol of traditional conflicts and is now a symbol of European unity.

Honoured by this opportunity to speak here at the most important European political forum, I naturally devoted my attention to political structures, systems, institutions and mechanisms, but it doesn't mean I am not aware of the obvious – that no truly new structures can be set up, nor existing structures daringly altered, without radical changes in human thinking and behaviour, and in social consciousness. Without courageous people, courageous structural changes are unthinkable.

With this remark I come back to where I started – that is, to dreams. Everything seems to indicate that we must not be afraid of dreaming the seemingly impossible if we want the seemingly impossible to become a reality. We shall never build a better Europe if we cannot dream of a better Europe.

I understand the twelve stars in your emblem not as the proud conviction that the Council of Europe will build a heaven on this earth. There will never be a heaven on earth. But I perceive these twelve stars as a reminder that the world can become a better place if we sometimes have the courage to look up at the stars."

8. INSTITUTIONS AND INSPIRATIONS: EUROPE'S PRESSING NEEDS

George Bull

George Bull is one of the most eminent Renaissance scholars in the world. He is probably best known for his translation of Machiavelli's The Prince *and for his biography of Michelangelo. He is editor of the journal* International Minds.

As well as giving his name to archetypes of the political schemers, Machiavelli, according to Professor Anthony Grafton,[1] "provided the core of the doctrines of 'reason of state' that became the basic political education of modern Europe". These doctrines were intended to help the ruler ensure the permanence and prosperity of the state. Among them was Machiavelli's insistence that when a new state was founded, the new ruler must confront the necessity of imposing new rules and ways, institutions and laws – *nuovi ordini e modi* – and must realise that "there is nothing more difficult to handle, more doubtful of success, and more dangerous to carry through than initiating changes in a state's constitution".

The makers of a new Europe, in Brussels and in the capitals of the European Union, need these Machiavellian insights. Another political thinker worth their attention is Ernest Renan, best known as the author of a controversial work entitled *Life of Jesus*. His prose was magnificent; his political views, like Machiavelli's, are now startlingly topical.

Qu'est-ce qu'une nation? is the title of a little book, still in print, first published in 1869. The nation, Renan reflected (at a time when for Europe – in England and France at least – the nation had embodied the state for hundreds of years) could not be defined in terms of physical or social realities, geography, race, language, religion. Two elements were essential: the memory of a common past, of shared actions, of memorable deeds and works; the regular reaffirmation of a will to live together. The shared consciousness of past history must endure, Renan believed, but a nation must remember the glories and not the disgraces of the past. It was for the people to decide to what nation they belonged. So a nation's existence was relative and contingent.

After pointing out that ethnographic considerations were worthless for the definition of national unity ("truth to tell, there is no pure race") Renan,

---

1. *The Prince* translated by George Bull with an introduction by Anthony Grafton, Penguin new edition 1998.

almost as an aside, remarked that the nation, though endowed with "a soul, a spiritual principle", was not eternal. Nations started and finished: in Europe, the nations would probably be replaced by *"La confédération européenne"*.

However far they may wish, publicly or privately, to travel along the road to a confederation or federation of Europe, political and other leaders in Europe must realise that changes already well underway in the institutions and laws of Europe's nation-states cry out for serious intellectual engagement and debate about the need, and the ways by which, to retain the consent of the great majority of citizens and ensure the "regular reaffirmation of a will to live together".

"One change always leaves a toothing-stone for the next", Machiavelli wrote. Indeed, nothing in progression can rest on its original plan. To ensure the continuance of the "will to live together", where it still exists, as relationships change in Europe between the nation and the community, so is the need to win acceptance for carefully and prudently prepared new rules and ways, institutions and laws ever more urgent. The United Kingdom is gradually realising its "relative and contingent nature" as a nation. Respect for, and an understanding of the vital role of institutions have been remarkable for their absence in the United Kingdom for many years. The great publicly-owned enterprise, the City of London, the long-established world-renowned manufacturing companies, the trade union movement, the independent universities, the relatively uncorrupted and well-educated civil servants, the army regiments, the Church of England, the House of Lords et al., all have been or are being, not altogether without plausible excuse, wrecked or almost casually refashioned by reformers spread across the party system who often show scant awareness of the vital importance of strong and revered institutions in the fabric of a nation.

The direction in Europe may well be towards the development of a confederation of nations, assuming gradually the attributes of a state. In reaction to the fears this possibility promotes, there will be attempts to find an alternative to discredited nationalism through devolution in one form or another, most dangerously based on race or religion. Either way, as old institutions decline or experience metamorphosis (as through the commercialisation of sport) new institutions will have to be created and nurtured. Those who are desperate to retain the *status quo* – *L'Europe des patries*, for example – will also need, nonetheless, to devise new institutions or breathe new life into the old.

The idea of an unchanging, timeless East, whatever truth it contained, has been made obsolete by the spread of stern commercial values and technology. But there are still powerful psychological currents in the East, notably in Japan, that favour a return to ancient ways and customs. Correspondingly, in the West, despite the loss of faith there still exists a general hope for constant renewal and reconstruction. Whether inspired by Europe's Greco-Roman legacy or Judaeo-Christian origins or a fusion of these, the yearning for a civilisation of perennial renewal still affects our history. It helped account for the Renaissance. It was evident most recently through the movement for European unity which began after 1945. This was fuelled by idealism, historical memory and pragmatic sense. But has it lost its bearings?

The great periods of renewal and creativity in European history were fed by both intellectual and spiritual appetite and achievement, from the rise of the universities and the friars, to the Reformation, the Enlightenment, the Industrial Revolution. They were both earthy and visionary.

What has happened to the idealism of post-war Europe which, largely through the Council of Europe, sought to eradicate ultra-nationalistic prejudices? All the fervour seems with the nationalists, not with many who believe that Europe can create greater unity without losing its remarkable, iridescent diversity.

The lack of active idealism may be traced back to the Messina Conference, in 1955, when the European movement turned to economic rather than the then obstructed political routes to unity and, with the 1957 Treaty of Rome, agreed to the launch of the Economic Community in 1958. When the United Kingdom was admitted to the EC in 1973, the political and military potential of the group was further blocked; moreover, the British brought to the EC certainly the memory of a common past, but a past of bitterly disputed actions and memorable deeds from the Henrician Reformation to the Battle of Britain that helped justify the Gaullist belief that Britain's loyalties, like its twentieth-century cultural attachments, went to the West, the open seas, and the Atlantic and America rather than to the Continent of Europe.

Before evaluating and devising the institutions needed to ensure the permanence and prosperity of the state through processes of severe intellectual enquiry, analysis, reflection and debate in a Europe of equally unsettling centripetal and centrifugal forces, we need to re-invent the state. What sort and what size of state will be needed in Europe if Europe is to exert an influence in the world commensurate with its resources and consonant with its ideals? The challenge grows greater almost by the day, especially because of political fissures and economic failure in Russia and the brutalisation in the Balkans. In his magisterial and entertaining *Europe – a History* after surveying great tracts of the rich diversity of Europe's past, Norman Davies warns us that "The old Europe...has passed away...The present 'Europe', a creature of the Cold War, is inadequate to its task. The moral and political vision of the Community's founding fathers has almost been forgotten."

Jean Monnet, I believe, towards the end of his life said that he wished he had formulated plans for an increasingly united Europe on cultural rather than economic lines. For a tangle of reasons, contemporary Europe seems paradoxically to grow increasingly fragmented in its cultural practices and appreciations as it grows financially and industrially more integrated. When, as happens only too often nowadays, I hear crude disparagement of European identity by some fellow-Britons, I groan inwardly at their apparent indifference – perhaps ignorance of – the gloriously rich culture of Virgil and Dante and Milton and Goethe; of the classical orders, mediaeval foundations, the Renaissance and the Enlightenment, of music and medicine, of architecture, sculpture and painting, of analytical and creative intelligence manifested in unique depth and variety in our shared European home since the fifth century BC.

In a useful if inelegant phrase my friend, the economist and journalist Arthur Shoonfield, used to talk of trying "to grope for the shape of the future". The shape of our future Europe as its nation-states pragmatically hand over to the authorities in Brussels, or to fresh common institutions elsewhere, the co-ordinating roles for functions that are of necessity combined (as in the realms of foreign policy, defence, human rights) – with, be it noted, the approbation of most outsiders, including the Americans and Japanese – would be best appreciated and formed in cultural terms, I think. Young people across Europe, among many of whom there is a yearning for the elaboration and affirmation of a distinctly but not narrowly European culture, are like hungry sheep looking up and around and not, alas, being fed. There is, among many middle-aged and older people, a swelling chorus of partly nostalgic, partly prudent individuals, pleading for more attention to be given to the Chestertonian ideals of smallness and local independencies in politics as in trade and industries. The nature of modern technology greatly encourages this. *Small is beautiful. Passport to Pimlico. Devolution. Decentralisation.* All the more reason to intensify our exploration of protean Europe's prolific culture. You could start with Renan's squib.

9. CHRISTIANITY AND THE NEW EUROPE[1]

George Carey

Dr George Carey is Archbishop of Canterbury.

> Behold, I am doing a new thing; now it springs forth, do you not perceive it? *Isaiah 43:19*.

The prophet Isaiah is speaking here of God working his providence through the events of the secular world. The exploits of Cyrus, the Persian King, herald a new order. The prophet senses the beginning of more than a political reordering. Isaiah believed the return of the people of God through the wilderness was imminent, that God was doing a new thing. We cannot claim Isaiah's prophetic assurance, but we sense that we too are approaching more than a new political order in this continent, that God is doing a new thing in Europe today. That is why we can allow ourselves to have fresh hope.

How should the Church offer guidance as the new Europe emerges? Let me suggest four Christian principles.

First and foremost, Europe needs a body of common values and public doctrine. I know that our Western society today is diverse, with people living alongside one another with different religions or none. We must not, however, fall into the trap of thinking that every belief and religion is of the same value – that would be to ignore the claims of truth. Pluralism without common values is individualism run riot, and carries within itself the seeds of its own decay. Without public doctrine there is nothing to hold a community together. It collapses like the Tower of Babel, which fell because the people simply could not understand one another. But the biblical image of a confused world in that story is matched by the image of a united world on the day of Pentecost. The gift of the Holy Spirit was not the gift of a common language: diversity remained. Yet within the languages, the people heard a common theme, a message which, according to Luke, so "amazed and perplexed" them that some reckoned the disciples had been over-indulging in their equivalent of Beaujolais nouveau.

And yet Christianity copes with complexity. In this alone it may offer Europe a model. There is a terrific diversity in European Christian culture:

---

1. Extracts from Dr George Carey's sermon to the Malvern Conference in 1991. The conference was held to consider the crisis confronting civilisation in the light of the Christian faith.

sometimes little seems to unite us. The icon of the Orthodox and the Thirty-nine Articles of the Anglicans are certainly the products of such different traditions that it might seem to observers that we have created an ecclesiastical Babel. But this simply adds to the storehouse of Christian treasures. And in every tradition there is a single loyalty – to Jesus Christ. In a person rather than in a philosophy Christianity finds its common values. And because Christ was a person, Christianity's values are personal – compassion, peace, long-suffering, self-control: those fruits of the Spirit about which St Paul speaks with such eloquence. From that person has emerged the complex web of Christian culture created over the years – a mixture of theology, faith, moral thinking and worship. It would be a tragic mistake to seek to simplify it, to reduce Christianity's diversity in seeking uniformity. That would be to undo Pentecost.

This leads me to my second theological principle – the unique identity of every human being. Each of us has been made in the image of God. Each of us has a unique identity. In the eyes of God, everyone is literally irreplaceable. This principle and truth is reinforced by the incarnation, because in Jesus Christ we are reminded that we are all the children of God, that God's interest in and care for us is greater than that of even the most loving of human parents.

We believe as Christians that the process of finding ourselves cannot be complete until we are found by God. We need to know who we are in the ground of our being. But to realise ourselves we also need to belong. We would find it hard to feel we belong to a Europe so large that it dwarfs us. If Europe is to strengthen its bonds among its member states, it may reduce a person's national identity and offer only a continent too large for finding a new identity. If this is the case we will need to strengthen people's links with their religion and locality. But if we wish to encourage local, regional and even national loyalties, within these loyalties we must retain a sense of proportion. We have all seen how the demise of totalitarian oppression has also released yet another seven demons. The spirit of nationalism is volatile and in some places its flashpoint is extremely low. It can work against common values, against respecting diversity, against a larger vision of human identity. The tragedy of the Balkan conflicts and the renewal of anti-Semitism in Europe are two stark reminders that Europe is not yet properly welded by common values rooted in human identity. And our European partners look on with some apprehension lest British, or even English, nationalism or jingoism should itself keep frontiers barred.

We are less likely to bring down the shutters against the outside world if we uphold the third of my theological principles – to see ourselves as stewards of God's world. The terrible spoliation of Eastern Germany, Poland and Czechoslovakia, and the menacing legacy of Chernobyl remind us of our own responsibilities. The Jewish tradition out of which Christianity grew knew well that we had been placed on earth as God's stewards, which meant not exhausting or exploiting the land; the seventh part of a field left unplanted was a reminder that the soil was his. So the prophet Isaiah says, "Woe unto those who build house upon house till there be no more place".

Europe is not such a conspicuous consumer as the United States; but we come second. It is because of the conspicuous consumption of the West that the planet is faced with diminishing non-renewable resources and increasing world pollution. Here the European community has already shown that in some respects its standards of conservation and its determination to become pollution-free are greater than in Britain. But there are important areas, such as the drainage of phosphates into the oceans, which still remain to be tackled. Europe needs to show that its increasing production is compatible with decreasing pollution and renewable resources.

The Christian theological tradition has much to contribute to the outworking of those principles, for Christians do not seek only limiting prohibitions. We seek instead to work with the natural creation, that we may stand again to overlook the Eden which has been left far behind. As Edwin Muir says in his poem:

> "One foot in Eden still, I stand
> And look across the other land.
> The world's great day is growing late…"

Looking across to other lands brings me to my fourth and final principle – a plea for open frontiers. The common values with which I began suggest that the divisions within Europe should not be the only barriers to be broken down. Europe's own frontiers should remain healthily open to the rest of the world. Our prosperity, our technology, our cultural riches must be shared with a world desperately craving for fairer shares. This is a reminder of our common humanity and of the gospel imperative to stand with the poor. That is its theological base. Like Jesus, we must identify with the marginalised, the outcast, the alienated. That is a clear Christian duty. Ways forward need to be agreed with Europe so that the rich do not get richer at the expense of the poor, so that help to the needy is not just left to private charity and so that there are means of securing justice for those who are powerless and not in a position to defend their human dignity.

The scriptures are strong on remission of debts. That is why the Church must always sound an uncomfortable reminder to our political and financial leaders not to prevent poor countries from developing their potential through charging excessive interest on loans which they took out in their necessity. Europe must share its bread with the hungry, instead of continuing its present practice of building bigger and bigger barns to house its agricultural surpluses (and because the rate of building is not fast enough, in some cases surplus grain is stored in ships). This does nothing to promote common values, or honour human dignity. It is not good stewardship of God's creation and it closes rather than opens frontiers. Those four principles hang together.

Unity and diversity: on being European[1]

This is a very significant time for Europe. The Maastricht Treaty has provoked passionate public debate about our vision of what the European Community should be. Many countries are queuing up to join the different institutions of Europe, but what are they signing up to? What should it mean, to say, "I am a European"?

In this chapter I would like to explore our sense of identity and how we define ourselves in relation to other people. I hope you will forgive me if I begin by describing myself rather elaborately in order to make a point. I am the Archbishop of Canterbury, which means that I am both Primate of All England and Bishop to the Diocese of Canterbury. I am a member of the Church of England, and of the worldwide Anglican Communion. I am a Christian. I have so far identified myself in six ways. I am lucky enough to be a husband, father and grandfather, with strong extended family links. I am an East Londoner, a Londoner, a Southerner, English, British and a citizen of the United Kingdom. I am a citizen of the Commonwealth and of the world. All these identities matter to me. I could easily add to the list, but I shall restrict myself to saying that I am also a European.

My point is that our definition of ourselves as we relate to other people has many layers. They need to be held in balance with each other, not regarded as mutually exclusive. Indeed to assert one level of identity at the expense of others is unhealthy and can be downright evil. We narrow our sympathies behind barriers, we ruin the solidarity between human beings, and we infringe God's commandment to love our neighbour as ourselves. Structures which encourage us to treat other people as beyond the range of our sympathy and concern violate the sacred principle that every single human being is made in God's image and is infinitely valuable.

For me, therefore, being European is precious because it is something additional and inclusive. I do not want to be European *instead* of any of my other identities, but as an extra dimension which brings extra blessings. A jealous Europeanism which seeks to supplant other levels of identity will fail, and will deserve to fail. Moreover, a Europe which sought to erect barriers against the rest of the world would to me be a betrayal, aping the dangerous habits of exclusive nationalism which Europeanism is supposed to overcome.

---

1. From the Archbishop's address to the European Parliament in 1994.

When President John F. Kennedy stood by the Berlin Wall and said: *"Ich bin ein Berliner"*, he was breaking barriers down, not setting them up. He was not in any way downplaying his identity as an American, or as a world leader. He was saying, in effect: "Yes, I am an American and a world leader, and in addition I *identify with you*! I share your values, your aspirations and sorrows, I feel responsible for what happens to you". It is in that positive, inclusive sense that we can enthusiastically say: "Yes, we are Europeans!"

Let me take another example. The Council of Europe gave birth to the European Convention on Human Rights, and we Europeans are rightly proud of that Convention and associated machinery for its implementation. It is not that European human rights are superior to or different from anyone else's human rights! It is not that we seek to deny or frustrate anyone else's rights: indeed, we offer our Convention as a possible model to the wider world. A European convention represents our attempt in this part of the world to achieve progress together, in a way we could not hope to achieve individually, towards what we believe to be good and right. That is surely what is valuable about being European.

There are many other examples. I count among them the removal of unnecessary restrictions to the flow of trade and enterprise, so long as these are not mirrored by extra barriers against the rest of the world. I include the co-ordination of policies for trade and aid towards less fortunate parts of the world. I include the growth of sturdy European policies to protect and enhance the environment. In this and other areas it is surely right in principle to seek to negotiate an agreed framework of shared standards, the observance of which by one member will not, therefore, involve a competitive disadvantage as against the others. Here again, through the European dimension, we can do more to realise our shared values than we could do as competing nation-states alone.

Let me make a distinction. I believe that *national identity* is for most people an important and proper part of how they understand themselves and their place in the world. It is part of the feeling of belonging which need not supplant other levels of identity and obligations. Its natural corollary is a similar respect for the national identity of others. *Nationalism*, on the other hand, is inherently dangerous, because it links national identity to the belief that the nation is entitled to a territorially defined state through which to express its collective will to the exclusion of others. There are brief periods, for instance in 1848 or in the last few years, where nationalist movements pitted against corrupt empires can appear to be the vehicle for noble democratic aspirations; but the logic of nationalism proves otherwise. The logic leads to the repression or removal of those who do not share the national identity and to wars with rival nationalisms with designs on the same territory. Nationalism offers only endless suffering and conflict in Ireland, Israel and Palestine, the former Yugoslavia and throughout the world. It thrives on blinkered refusal to extend sympathy and understanding to fellow human beings and stirring up hatred against the alien Other – hence the frequent usefulness to nationalists of racist stereotyping. We see examples of this trend all over Europe. Nationalism will not tolerate a multi-layered sense of identity and seeks to take the other layers over or eliminate them.

But the universal character of true religion is always a problem for nationalists and racists. It refuses nationalism's monopolistic demands on our sense of identity and loyalty. One of the most dramatic and moving insights recorded in the Bible is the dawning realisation in the New Testament that the 'people of God' are no longer to be understood as a chosen tribe, but as – everybody! The scales fall from the early Christians' eyes as they realise with wonder and joy that God loves every single person equally, that his perfect goodness and salvation is for all people. The writings of St Paul constitute an irreversible triumph of Christian theology over the boundaries of race and nationhood.

Human institutions can so easily run counter to this sacred insight. A mature Europe will remain self-critical. We have recently witnessed the downfall of the political and ideological centralism based on a subjugated population and inflexible economy. What has replaced it is a European diversity of cultures and interdependent economies which brings both hope and dangers against a background of spiritual confusion. I have already considered the dangers of nationalism and racism. There are also dangers in the triumph of free market capitalism, unless structured so as to serve moral ends. Indeed, the German theologian Jürgen Moltmann asks the question: "Is democracy in capitalism possible?" His answer is hesitant. He is rightly concerned that, while the 'free market' requires and encourages individual initiative and liberty, the market itself does not concern itself with those who are unable to succeed and who bear the cost of failure. Moltmann is right to raise the question and draws our attention to the need for social justice which should be the mark of any civilised society, within nations and internationally.

In much of Europe, the Churches have surely helped to model and nurture the values of the new Europe, drawing on our own understanding of suffering and resurrection, of sin and forgiveness, of universal love which transcends all human boundaries, of humility before God. Murderous enmity and intolerance between Churches have given way to much dialogue, ever-closer understanding, constant practical collaboration and joyful acceptance of our diversity. I pay tribute to the way in which an increasing number of ecumenical Church bodies are systematically making available their theological insights, their pastoral experience and their knowledge of fellowship and harmony in diversity, to the various institutions of Europe. The ability of the Churches to bear common witness on social ethics is already highly developed.

Nevertheless, the Churches have more work to do with each other before they can fully realise their potential contribution to the new Europe. We have not yet done enough to deal with our own historical divisions. There is indeed an urgent obligation laid upon all Churches to seek the unity which is the will of God. Our common mission and service is vitiated by our disunity and our unwillingness to acknowledge one another's Churches as full and equal.

Hence, there are two-way benefits from the relationship between European institutions and the Churches. The diversity of Europe meets and welcomes the diversity of the Churches. Diversity need not be another word for disunity but rather a recognition that we all have something to give and share. The diversity which may well be Europe's gift to us all will encourage us to a new spirit of generosity as Churches. Generosity in the sense of recognising the spirit of God working among us and generosity in a willingness to admit failure, faults and weakness. No Church possesses all the truth about God and a simple admission of this fact may well provide a starting point for fresh ecumenical initiatives. In this way, I believe that the Churches need Europe, as much as Europe needs the spiritual vision and energy that Christians can bring.

We shall not strengthen and develop the new Europe on the basis of a spiritual void. Václav Havel has complained of "the omnipresent dictatorship of consumption, production, advertising, commerce, consumer culture" in the Western world, and of a system which "drives each man into a foxhole and purely material existence", undermining the will and capacity to build a good society together. That kind of civic and spiritual impoverishment is a recruiting ground for the false gods of fundamentalist religion, nationalism and racism. Hence, the appropriate response to the hatreds of the past is not to banish belief to a private domain, leaving no shared values to give direction and purpose to the life we live together as a society. Jacques Delors was right to tell Church representatives that "the game will be up" for the new Europe if it fails to develop a sense of shared values with a spiritual dimension as an aspect of European identity. Here again is a reason for intensifying dialogue between the Churches and other institutions of Europe.

The role of the Council of Europe[1]

At a historical turning-point for Europe, full of possibilities for good or evil, it is surely the task of the Council of Europe to represent and articulate a vision and a conviction that the *whole* of Europe matters, not just a fraction or part of it.

---

1. Address to the Council of Europe, Strasbourg 1993.

Certainly, the hopes and values vested in the Council, its conventions and instruments, are part of the soul of Europe and a significant factor in Europe's intellectual and spiritual development.

Not that pluralist democracy and human rights are irrelevant to economic prosperity, either. Surely one of the fascinating and conclusive lessons learnt in recent years from experience around the globe is that long-term, stable, economic prosperity depends to a very large extent on open, democratic structures, effective and impartial administration of justice and a civic culture nurturing liberty, honesty, morality and respect for human rights. One-eyed preoccupation with economic requirements is not only morally flawed, it doesn't work.

On a recent visit to Strasbourg, Her Majesty Queen Elizabeth called the European Convention on Human Rights the Council's "greatest single achievement". Indeed, it is widely regarded as the world's most successful human rights instrument. I can hardly exaggerate the importance I attach as a religious leader to this achievement, or my admiration for those who work so tirelessly to administer and develop it.

But it matters how human rights are understood. A notice seen in a Parisian hotel, attempting to be user-friendly to English speakers, said: "Please leave your values at the desk!". We do not want human rights to be understood like that. Because they ultimately depend on specific and positive beliefs about what is good, it is not enough to regard them as somehow 'self-evident'. They cannot be sustained by utilitarian calculation of what brings the greatest happiness (however defined) to the greatest number. On that basis, why bother about the individual rights of a prisoner? Seen merely as individual entitlements, moreover, rights could encourage an unhealthy concern with self. We need to bring rights and responsibilities together, because both are part of pursuing what we believe to be good. Indeed, a person's rights cannot be effective unless others accept a parallel duty to respect and enforce them.

There is particular danger, it seems to me, if our approach to human rights – or indeed the law generally – becomes too legalistic. If human rights are perceived as essentially a matter for legal experts, the active sympathy of the mass of citizens is switched off, and human rights can begin to seem like a refined minority interest. Only slightly less worrying is another perception that human rights are essentially about the protection of vulnerable minorities, and hence they are the concern of legal experts and liberal pressure groups. That is still much too narrow a constituency, and the Churches have a responsibility to help represent a much wider cross-section of society. For human rights are not only about the rights of minorities, they are above all an expression of the values of society as a whole, and testify to how we view human nature.

Indeed, in my view human rights will only be secured for all people if they represent the active moral commitment of the broad mass of citizens. They require the passionate apprehension and advocacy of each successive generation. They need constant nourishment from our fundamental beliefs about human nature – its dignity and abiding significance. Therefore, as a European and as a Christian, I wish to point out, without apology, the essential and continuing contribution of Christianity to fertilising our collective commitment to human rights.

First, it is well known that the bedrock of the Judaeo-Christian approach to human nature resides in the value we believe that God gives to human nature, irrespective of class, colour or creed. This starting point leads to a rejection of all opinions that divide people into first-, second- or third-class citizens. Any kind of 'ethnic cleansing' which insists on an ethnically homogeneous nation-state is a terrifying form of disobedience of God's will. Civil rights within a society cannot be independent of universal human rights which are the birthright of every person everywhere. These universal and civil human rights require that national identity – of which we may be proud – is relativised in the light of this prior ethic.

Second, Christianity regards humankind from the perspective of *sub specie aeternitatis*. We reject the notion that we are simply finite beings doomed to die and perish without hope. All of us are made in the image and likeness of God and carry within us a divine spark that is precious and unique. This belief in the dignity and infinite value of human life is a crucial part of the legacy of European Christianity. I think, for example, of the many Protestant religious-social movements which have resisted tyranny and injustice. I think further of the codifying of Christian social theory in the Papal Encyclical *Rerum Novarum* of 1891 and *Laborem exercens* of 1981 and *Centesimus Annus* of 1991. In these three documents the Christian affirmation of human beings is presented with classical clarity.

Hence, I affirm most gladly the alliances between the Council of Europe and many other bodies, but particularly the Churches because of their fundamental commitment to human rights as shaped by what we believe about God. When it comes to human rights and morality, there is a never-ending task of education and mission to complement the work of lawyers and judges. Indeed, we must all admit that human rights machinery severed from moral commitment achieves relatively little.

Take some of the precious achievements of the Human Rights Court in Strasbourg. It is good to force certain improvements in the rights of prisoners, but this does not constitute a positive penal policy. Preventing the beating of boys at school is not the same as providing a good education. And limiting the ability of governments to stifle press enquiry does not, alas, of itself produce good newspapers. I make these points, not in any way to belittle the role of human rights machinery in preventing abuses of power, but to emphasise that human rights are the expression of belief about goodness and justice which, by the same token, must be applied to *all* dimensions of our personal and social behaviour.

This is no merely academic point. As I have pointed out already, in much of Europe we are faced with the privatisation of belief. Pluralism is developed to the point where the aspiration to define shared values is lost. The idea of what is good becomes a matter of individual opinion. Absolute values are abolished, since no authority is accepted beyond the individual conscience. Human rights can be seen by some as an expression of this extreme individualism and privatisation of morality. But, in that case, we have no basis for good prisons, good education, good newspapers or good anything in our social life together. Moreover, if human rights are *not* seen as the embodiment of absolute goodness, but merely a lowest common denominator of individual subjective views with no absolute validity, our collective commitment to human rights will be fatally weakened. This presents a huge challenge to the Christian Churches to represent the values of Christianity in such a way that it may once again become the inspiration of individual and social lifestyles.

However, it is one thing to have a wholesome, positive commitment to human rights as an expression of shared values, it is another to enforce them effectively in practice. I am extremely concerned about the major backlog of cases which has built up at Strasbourg. I understand that an individual petition lodged today may face five or six years' delay before adjudication. Justice delayed may be justice denied. Sensible lawyers will often advise their clients not to bother. Governments and state agencies have much less to respect or fear. Moreover, five to six years is a very long time in the life of a new fledgling democracy. Will not the new members of the Council from Eastern Europe feel bitterly disappointed, even cheated, if the long-awaited catalyst of justifiable human rights is postponed *sine die* by administrative constipation? Precisely because the European Convention on Human Rights is such a precious embodiment of our aspirations and values at a critical time of change, reforms to ease the log jam are to me of the highest priority, and I am delighted to note that the Presidency has committed itself to pursuing this matter with great urgency. For, unless something is done, the arrival of new members to the Council will make matters worse and worse. I know that there are different proposals on the table, and endless scope for prevarication. The political will to find a way forward must, however, be summoned rapidly if one of the most substantial collective achievements of Europe is not to degenerate into frustration and ineffectiveness.

It might well be said that my country is part of the problem. I understand that more cases have been brought to the European Court of Human Rights from the United Kingdom than from most other members. Part of the explanation is that the United Kingdom is one of the few members of the Council which has no written constitution and which has not incorporated the European Convention on Human Rights into our own domestic law. British judges cannot enforce the European Convention in British courts, so many cases have to be taken to Strasbourg where the individual can face up to six years' delay. I wonder if this a tenable position. Where is the famous principle of subsidiarity when it comes to the adjudication of such human rights? I confess to a feeling of unease that we in the UK have to rely on a court in Strasbourg to blow the whistle on certain human rights abuses in our own country. There is arguably an element of irresponsibility in leaving our citizens to seek their rights through the lengthy procedures of a Strasbourg court which is struggling with ever-growing responsibilities after the fall of Communism. I hear an argument about parliamentary sovereignty; but if cases are brought to Strasbourg judges anyway, parliamentary sovereignty has already been limited. If we can put our trust in judges in Strasbourg from all over Europe, I cannot myself see why we should not trust our own as well. I dare say there are weighty constitutional considerations which lie beyond the area of an archbishop's expertise and authority. I respect the dilemmas of the policy-makers. But with more and more countries ready to sign up to the European Convention on Human Rights, putting greater pressure on Strasbourg, the arguments for incorporation of the Convention into British law grow more pressing.

The debate must continue and should not be left to lawyers and parliamentarians alone. For the European Convention on Human Rights, as I have argued, represents the aspirations and values of the majority, not merely the entitlements of individuals and minorities. For European Christians, it represents a significant aspect of obedience to God's commandments and a collective effort to reflect his perfect goodness and love for every human being.

10. THE UNION, THE COMMONWEALTH AND THE COUNCIL OF EUROPE

Emeka Anyaoku

Chief Emeka Anyaoku is the Commonwealth Secretary General.

There are some who might argue that the European Union as it stands at present is, in Václav Havel's words, "too much like a well-oiled machine". That has never been an accusation which it has been easy to level at the Commonwealth, although it is increasingly a rule-based association, with many points of common identity with the European Union. I have also conceived the linkages between the two bodies as being essentially informal although, as Sir John Biggs-Davison points out, Winston Churchill was an advocate of a more formal, overarching union between Europe and the Commonwealth.

The Council of Europe in post-war years was seen by many as the institution capable of achieving the ultimate goal of 'ever-closer union' but somehow lost its sense of purpose and mission, perhaps for reasons referred to in Sir Peter Smithers' chapter. As a result, it stood outside the more formal structures of the European institutions.

In recent years, however, it has not only recovered something of its original purpose in the important field of human rights but has been revived as a kind of European 'antechamber', providing an intermediate resting place for ex-Communist countries of Central and Eastern Europe in their journey back into the European fold.

Moreover, as this book argues, the Council of Europe could play a far more important role in the future at a time when the present institutions of Europe are generally perceived as failing to gain the full-hearted support of their peoples.

It is not enough to build upon the clinical application of national self-interest and the cold print of abstract treaties. The Commonwealth has not only survived but now flourishes because, despite its incongruities and dissimilarities, it lives in the hearts and minds of its peoples, not merely as an intergovernmental organisation but as a great congress of professional and non-governmental associations, bound together by a common set of fundamental values. A keen appreciation of this reality may be one of the contributions that the Commonwealth could offer to the European Union; and this book suggests more specifically that the Council of Europe itself could be the true home of those principles which Europe needs and a notable guiding force in shaping the Union, and the world beyond, into the new millennium.

Europeans have never fully understood the Commonwealth. For some it is and always has been a clever extension of British influence. For others who might think they know better, the Commonwealth is an anachronism, a ceremonial gathering of leaders of former colonies who meet every two years to pronounce on international issues, go to a banquet with Queen Elizabeth and then disperse. Most Europeans have heard of the Commonwealth, but very few comprehend what we stand for, let alone what we do.

We did emerge from an empire. But we are not shackled by any imperial dependency. We are a voluntary association of fifty-three sovereign countries which stands for and supports a set of common values. Small and vulnerable states mix on equal terms with large and powerful ones. This allows for a strong sense of intimacy when their leaders come together from time to time and gives small states especially – and the Commonwealth has over thirty of them – an identity and confidence which they would not find in other larger international organisations. In the Commonwealth, they have an authentic voice.

Our mission statement is implicit in the Harare Commonwealth Declaration, adopted by Commonwealth Heads of Government in 1991, which outlines a set of fundamental principles to which all member governments are expected to conform. These include: the concept of good governance and building and strengthening democratic processes; human rights; the rule of law; sustainable economic development; and gender equality. We link the promotion of our basic political values with sustainable economic development in a balanced and mutually reinforcing way.

These are values which we share with the European Union (EU). Our structure, though, is vastly different. This is best expressed in the negative: we are not a trading bloc; we are not a strategic alliance; we are not a regional organisation; we are not beholden to one dominant member; we have no assembly; we were not set up by treaty; and there is no charter. The only formal intergovernmental structure is the Commonwealth Secretariat, a body of some 360 men and women, diplomats, technical experts and others, which I head and which serves as the main point of contact for our fifty-three members.

Behind the Commonwealth secretariat lies a vast network of people-to-people contacts. The Commonwealth is not just an association of governments. It is as much an association of peoples. The fabric of the Commonwealth is a broad tapestry of personal, professional, educational and even sporting ties. The pattern of this relationship – from the highest level among heads of government to the lowliest contact between schoolchildren – is informality.

The Commonwealth is a remarkable example of international co-operation between very diverse countries. Its breadth is reflected in the geographical spread of its membership. It accounts for roughly a quarter of the world's population; it represents every hemisphere; it touches every ocean; and its members belong to each of the world's main regional and economic groupings. And part of its vitality stems from the fact that it is constantly reaching out to a wider world. This geographic and cultural spread allows it to act from time to time as an instrument for building international consensus on issues which touch on the well-being of our planet.

Like the EU, the Commonwealth has not stood still. Both are expanding organisations with a steadily increasing membership which says a lot for the vitality and attraction of each organisation. When Nelson Mandela was elected president of a democratic South Africa in 1994, one of the first decisions of his government was to take his country back into the Commonwealth after thirty-three years in the apartheid wilderness. In November, 1995, Cameroon took its place at the heads of government meeting in Auckland as the Commonwealth's newest member. By the end of the summit, Mozambique had also been admitted.

The modern Commonwealth has never sought the integration that Europe wants. This was a feature of an earlier imperial time, later abandoned as each member government pursued its own national interest in its part of the world. We hear no more of such things as 'Commonwealth tariff preferences'. Freedom of movement within the Commonwealth ceased decades ago. Countries today negotiate their visa regimes on a bilateral basis. Concepts such as 'the Sterling area' are anachronisms. The Commonwealth is not exclusive. Its members belong to their own regional bodies such as the Association of South-East Asian Nations (ASEAN), the Caribbean Community and Common Market (CARICOM), the North American Free Trade Agreement (NAFTA), the Organization of African Unity (OAU), the South Asian Association for Regional Co-operation (SAARC), the Southern African Development Community (SADC), and the EU, and share their experiences. This regional co-operation is part of a wider internationalism in which many Commonwealth countries are making significant contributions towards the creation of new relationships and partnerships. The Commonwealth connection helps rather than hinders this process because it gives countries an enhanced confidence and ensures that their wider ties remain intact.

It is this vast diversity and its informality which gives the Commonwealth its strength and, curiously, its unity. It does not operate on a system of votes. It operates on the basis of consensus which means everyone's point of view is taken into consideration. A common position is reached that all governments can accept. This consensual approach helps it to build bridges across many divides – ethnic, religious, political and economic. Our mini-realist structure also allows us to respond more speedily than would be possible in other more formal and larger organisations.

The process of consensus is followed at all levels: at the biennial summit of heads of government; at ministerial meetings; among officials and within the Commonwealth secretariat. Because of its broad membership and its mixture of peoples, the Commonwealth's experiences and successes are relevant to the wider community, especially to an organisation such as the EU as it moves away from the certainties of Western Europe to preparing for new members from Eastern Europe.

Europe, East and West, is culturally relatively homogeneous; it is also regionally self-contained and easily defined in a way that the Commonwealth most decidedly is not. After all, the Commonwealth spans oceans and continents; Europe has its margins. Without underestimating the variety of Europe's peoples and governments, it is a fact that the Commonwealth presents a much more diverse world.

Pluralism, or social and ethnic diversity, is today a factor in the life of every country and every organisation. If it is not managed carefully it can slide dangerously into divisive, subversive and ultimately destructive forms, producing tension, instability and civil conflict. It is pluralism which, instead of encouraging a sense of common humanity, generates a feeling of otherness. Apartheid in South Africa thrived on such a feeling.

We have seen pluralism at its most divisive when fuelled by racism, chauvinism and xenophobia, especially in the years since the end of the Cold War. In many cases, conflicts that emerged were the result of deep-seated historical rivalries, often fuelled by the reality or perception of discrimination. In other cases they were the product of more recent immigration which had helped to create cosmopolitan societies that were unable to integrate and thus remained prone to instability. We have seen the territorial integrity of long-established nation-states threatened and the prospect of conflict spreading into neighbouring countries and regions.

It is in our common interest that we find a way of living peacefully in a diverse but increasingly interacting world. The Commonwealth, I believe, does set an example. Our experience in promoting consensus and building bridges is relevant to what President Nelson Mandela described as "making the world safe for diversity". We have access in the Commonwealth to a deep well of experience in organising and monitoring elections as well as building and reinforcing those democratic structures that are necessary to sustain democracy and a civil society. At a time of increasing intra-state conflicts, our mediation efforts over the past two years to end or prevent domestic upheavals have involved Commonwealth envoys in places as far apart as Lesotho, Bangladesh, Sierra Leone and Bougainville.

South Africa is perhaps the best example of the discreet and largely unsung manner in which the Commonwealth sets about helping its members overcome divisive legacies of the past. Our envoys helped bring about the negotiations that led eventually to the country's first non-racial elections in 1994. In 1992, along with the UN, the OAU and the EU, we deployed observers to help arrest the spiral of violence that seemed to threaten the negotiations on the transition from apartheid to democracy. We observed the elections. And today we are involved in providing a range of support at local government level and advising and helping to reform and integrate South Africa's civil service. It is in this field of 'capacity building' – the reform and reshaping of institutions, especially the public service, to meet the needs of new democratic societies – that we have established a particular niche.

For example, in the last five years we have assisted sixteen democratic elections in fourteen member states. Our work in helping countries make the difficult transition from one-party or military rule to a genuine functioning democracy – and consolidating that change-over by providing experts and help in such diverse fields as legal drafting, civil service and constitutional reform, local body elections, debt management, and press reform – has been a template for others to follow.

Our experience has shown that pluralism can only be managed successfully, and its divisive tendency contained, if political progress towards democracy is matched by socio-economic development. Economic stagnation tends to unleash divisive pressures in both historically heterogeneous and progressively cosmopolitan societies as different groups seek to protect their living standards. Sustained development, on the other hand, can bring about a situation where all segments of society have a strong stake in stability. It is for this reason that the Harare Declaration – the statement of our fundamental principles to which every member subscribes – linked the defence of political values to the promotion of sustainable development and the alleviation of poverty.

In Auckland, Commonwealth heads of government reaffirmed this link and went one step further. They adopted an action programme designed to advance the Commonwealth's fundamental political values, to promote sustainable development, and to facilitate consensus building. In essence they gave teeth to the Harare Declaration by drawing up a list of measures to deal with member countries which seriously violate Commonwealth principles. This includes situations where governments are overthrown by such unconstitutional means as a military *coup d'état*. The ultimate sanction is suspension from the association. But this extreme step is balanced with other measures which would help the 'recalcitrant' member country return as speedily as possible to democracy.

Despite the contrasts between Europe and the Commonwealth, and the sometimes very different sets of challenges that are faced by both, the Commonwealth serves as a model of international co-operation that could be of some use to Europe. The Commonwealth's experience in managing diversity without creating divisiveness, building consensus without sacrificing individuality, and harnessing the energies of diverse countries to work in mutually supportive ways is of considerable relevance to a Europe faced with integrating an increasing diversity of national identities and interests.

11. The end of the noble savage

Colin Tudge

Dr Colin Tudge is Research Fellow of the Centre for Philosophy at the London School of Economics and is currently editing the Blackwell Encyclopaedia of Evolution. *His books include:* Last Animals at the Zoo *and* The Day Before Yesterday – Five Million Years of Human History.

All of us hear what we want to hear, we listen to the philosophers and poets who flatter us and ignore those who hold up a harsher mirror. So we have listened to Jean-Jacques Rousseau who showed our ancestors as 'noble savages' – compromised by civilisation. We certainly preferred this encouraging vision to that of St Augustine or St Ambrose who saw the human species as barbarians, and civilisation as a thin veneer. As we seek to frame an ethical code for Europe which could be expressed through the Council of Europe, modern archaeology now suggests that Augustine and Ambrose came nearer to the truth than Rousseau did. To judge at least from the actions of our ancestors, human nature is nothing like so noble as we have allowed ourselves to believe.

We human beings are now perpetrating a mass extinction of our fellow creatures that is more rapid and dramatic than any of the past – and it pleases us to think that this is because we have become too 'civilised': we have locked ourselves in cities and lost touch with nature. Inspired by Jean-Jacques Rousseau in the eighteenth century, we like to believe that our hunting-gathering forebears were 'noble savages' living in harmony with other animals. But more and more, the fossil and archaeological evidence shows that this just is not true. The mass extinction of the last few centuries merely continues a trend that was firmly established by the Upper Palaeolithic – the end of the Old Stone Age. That was a time of human diaspora; and wherever we went, the big animals gave way before us.

The evidence came first from North America. Human beings arrived there about 13 000 years ago, walking into Alaska from Siberia via the land-bridge, known as Beringia, which appeared above the waves as the sea-level fell during the Ice Ages.

But when the first people arrived, America already had a native fauna that was astonishingly rich and quite different from the present day. There were wild camels and tapirs and native horses (not the modern mustangs, which were introduced in recent centuries by Europeans); several species of elephants, including mammoths and mastodons; giant ground sloths that had entered North America from the South; and giant relatives of the armadillo known as glyoptodonts, big as a bread van, with dimpled, round carapaces like golf balls. The corresponding carnivores included a long-legged running bear with a short pugnacious face that was about half as big again as a modern grizzly and must have hunted like a giant Rottweiler; and sabre-toothed cats, of which the biggest and best known was the mighty, lion-sized smilodon.

But just a few centuries after the first North Americans arrived, most of that wonderful native fauna had gone. The sabre-tooths, giant bears, camels, tapirs, horses, giant sloths – most spectacular of all – the mammoths, were extinct. So what killed them? Conservative archaeologists have generally argued that it was a change of climate and vegetation. But it now seems that our forebears were to blame; that the first American people perpetrated what Paul Martin of the University of Arizona has called 'The Pleistocene Overkill' – a prelude to the destruction that is now reaching a climax worldwide.

The idea that climate killed the animals is comfortable to live with, but it simply does not fit the facts. There have been at least ten Ice Ages over the past million years – they have come and gone every 100 000 years or so – and none of the others produced such devastation. Given the chance, the animals simply migrate North and South as the weather changes – which is why in the north of England, for example, you can find the fossil bones of tropical hippos and Arctic reindeer, each just tracking the ice as it ebbed and flowed.

By contrast, more and more research favours Professor Martin's Pleistocene Overkill. If the evidence came only from North America it would not be convincing. But the same pattern is repeated time and time again in continent after continent, island after island. Soon after humans appear, the native animals are obliterated. Furthermore, it is the large animals that go extinct while the smaller ones, the shrews and voles, are mostly unscathed. If climate were the cause, the smaller ones would suffer most.

Specifically, North America had forty-five genera of large mammals before human beings arrived – 'large' meaning more than 44 kg, or 100 lb – and only twelve, mostly non-native, a few centuries later. People worked their way down to South America over a thousand years or so and there they confronted no fewer than fifty-seven genera of large mammals – again including camels, glyptodonts and giant sloths, sabre-tooths and so on, plus various hoofed animals unique to South America known as litopterns – but they too were reduced to a dozen genera within a few hundred years. The first Australians arrived somewhere between 80 000 and 40 000 years ago: and Australia quickly lost thirteen genera of large animals, including giant kangaroos and the rhinoceros-like Diprotoson. Now only one native genus of large mammals survives in Australia – that of the big red and grey kangaroos. So it goes on: Madagascar lost its pygmy hippo, its giant tortoises, giant lemurs, and its giant land bird Aepynomisn with its ten-litre eggs, soon after people arrived around the time of Christ. Hawaii lost, among other creatures, its suite of geese and ducks, many flightless, of which the ne-ne is the sole survivor. New Zealand lost its fifteen or so species of moas after the first Polynesians arrived about one thousand years ago. Indeed, of all the land masses on Earth, only Africa seems to have escaped the Pleistocene and modern wipe-out, while in Eurasia the deaths were more drawn out. But then, human beings evolved in Africa, and first reached Eurasia at least a million years ago. The animals had time to adapt to us.

The Pleistocene Overkill hypothesis leaves just one problem. It is easy to see how people could wipe out geese on Hawaii, but could late Palaeolithic people really have wiped out the mammals, sabre-tooths, and giant bears of the Americas? Is it plausible? Well yes, is the answer: all too plausible. Conventionally, indeed, palaeo-anthropologists are wont to suggest that our forebears wiped out the big animals simply through carelessness: they killed what they wanted with no thought for the morrow until they were all gone. Subfossil evidence reveals their prodigality: early native Americans sometimes drove entire herds of bison over cliffs, just for a few steaks and skins. Now, too, computer simulations by Dr Steve Mithen of Reading University show that slow-breeding animals can be wiped out in a few decades even with modest hunting pressure: if mammoths bred at the same rate as modern elephants then they could not withstand an annual loss even of 2%, no matter how many animals there were initially. Clearly, then, the early North American hunters could have wiped out the elephants and other large animals, just by being slightly too greedy.

Carelessness, then, must be the default hypothesis – and the one that scientists are bound to favour simply because it is the most 'parsimonious'. But the simplest explanations are not always the right ones. We seem more likely to get at the truth if we also allow our imaginations to run. For it also seems at least possible that our ancestors knew very well what they were doing and managed the fauna: encouraging the creatures they preferred; eliminating those that were inconvenient.

For consider, first of all, that hunters of the Late Palaeolithic – from around 40 000 years ago on – were not at all 'primitive' in any physical sense. Their fossil skulls tell us that their brains were as big as ours and the archaeological record shows they were innovative – constantly improving their tools, trading more and more widely, and showing increasing skills as artists and potters. If those very same people were around today they would be builders, airline pilots, company directors, what you will. They happened to live at a time of history at which they were obliged, for the most part, to live as hunters and gatherers. But it seems reasonable to suppose that they were good at what they did just as we, their modern descendants, are good at what we do.

As hunters, the people of the Late Palaeolithic surely were supremely efficient: much more so than any other predator that has ever lived. It has often been suggested that human beings are feeble – lacking the massive jaws of the bear, the speed of the cheetah, or the stamina of the dog. In truth, even when considered as simple naked apes, we are powerful compared to most other animals: a fit adult is a strong creature with extraordinary stamina. More to the point, though, is that we are not just naked apes. We have technology and we have enormous intelligence which enables us to co-operate to a degree matched only by the social insects – although we have infinitely greater flexibility.

Crucial among ancient technologies were fire and spear – both apparently developed around half a million years ago by Homo erectus, a species of human being far more primitive than ourselves. Their impact can hardly be overestimated. With fire we can cook, which both purifies and tenderises, and thus enormously expands the potential range of our diet. But also, and even more significantly, fire enables us to control the landscape: opening or removing forest, and burning off senescent grass to encourage fresh grazing and entice the herbivores. Modern Australian aborigines still demonstrate the principles; they practice what the archaeologist Rhys Jones, of the Australian National University at Canberra, calls 'firestick farming'.

The spear is even more fundamental. Simple mathematics shows that in theory, it is more efficient to hunt large prey than small, but large prey is risky. In practice, then, predators commonly focus on creatures that are roughly the same size as themselves: leopards on impalas, lions on zebras, and so on. Still it is dangerous. Every now and again lions are gored and kicked, and die from their wounds. The sabre-toothed cats that lived a few thousand years ago took even greater risks. They apparently attacked animals much bigger than themselves – such as elephants – by clinging around the neck of their prey and tearing the vessels with their blade-like canines. To do this they had to run the gauntlet of horns and tusks. Any lack of technique or loss of nerve could be fatal for the predator.

But the hunter with a spear can deliver a lethal blow without getting remotely within range of the prey's own weaponry. If the first blow is not immediately fatal – no matter. He can simply duck out of site and as modern hunting people, like the Bushmen of the Kalahari, show (or did so at least until the 1950s) can follow the wounded animal until it finally succumbs to loss of blood. For such a prize, it was worth the effort. The spear, in short, offered risk-free hunting. It tipped the balance critically and absolutely in favour of the hunter.

But technologies are merely tools. What really gives power to our species is our intelligence, which enables us to analyse and hence to anticipate, and also to behave flexibly; and perhaps even more than that, enables us to co-operate. Lions co-operate in hunting, but in truth they follow fairly simple routines. The wolf's technique, though more complex and flexible, is still highly standardised. But modern human beings – 'modern' including those of the Late Palaeolithic – can anticipate where their prey is liable to be or lure it to where they want it; and then ambush the animals and drive them into the waiting spears, which in principle can deliver the *coup de grâce* without risk. Furthermore, they can adjust their technique to match the prey and the terrain.

In short, we need not suppose that our Late Palaeolithic hunting ancestors wiped out their fellow creatures simply because they did not know what they were doing. It is at least possible that they knew exactly what they were up to. We can imagine simply on the basis of what we know about present-day human beings (including those that wear suits and live in cities; not just the few remaining hunters) that they would not have hunted creatures such as mammals simply for food. Anything that big and fearsome, and with such wonderful skins and tusks, would surely have been hunted for the prestige. And here – for the prey – is an ugly twist. For prey animals in general gain some protection as the predators take their toll – for the rarer they become, the less worthwhile it becomes to hunt them. Thus 'ordinary' – non-human – predators do not commonly drive their prey to extinction. But for creatures like us, with our new kind of intelligence, hunting for prestige as much as for food, rarity merely becomes a challenge. We can imagine the pride with which young hunters tracked down the last few mammoth herds, in the remotest quarters. In just the same way, in the late 1960s, Arab hunters eagerly pursued the last few wild Arab oryx. Or there is another possibility. If the Late Palaeolithic hunters knew their environment – and of course they did: they were intelligent professionals – they would have realised that their most threatening predatory rivals, the sabretooths and the huge running bears, depended for survival upon the biggest herbivores, like the mammoths. I do not think it fanciful to suggest that the first Americans targeted the mammoths so as to deprive, and hence eliminate, the other big predators; thus making the world a much safer place for themselves. There are modern parallels. Thus it was government policy in nineteenth-century America to eliminate the bison so as to deprive the 'Indians' of their prey-base: and the Americans in Vietnam shot the elephants to deprive the Vietcong of transport.

In short, it seems to me almost beyond doubt that the Pleistocene Overkill is a fact, just as Professor Martin has argued; and it seems at least plausible that it occurred not because our hunting forebears lacked judgement, but because they were competent game wardens who cleaned up the environment to suit themselves. We could argue that the British gentry, this past

1000 years, has cleanedup Britain in precisely the same way – eliminating the wild cattle, the bear, the wolf, and the boar, and the white-tailed eagle, or indeed anything that seemed remotely inconvenient, almost down to the otter and the peregrine. Our species is innately destructive. It is our task, the proper ethic for our age, to override this native destructiveness.

12. The missing heart of Europe

Noriko Hama

Noriko Hama was chief economist of the Mitsubishi Institute and was based in London for many years.

In Oscar Wilde's mesmerising tale of The Fisherman and His Soul, the young Fisherman sends his Soul away from him so that he can marry the beautiful Mermaid. For the Mermaid, being one of the Sea-folk, has no time for a bridegroom with a human Soul. The Fisherman's Soul begs and pleads that it may not be driven away from its owner. But its entreaties are to no avail and the two part company. Upon taking leave of the Fisherman, his Soul asks that it be at least allowed to take the Fisherman's heart with him, for the world is a cruel place and it would be tough going to survive there with no heart. Even this plea, however, is refused for without a heart with what would the Fisherman love his Sea-folk bride? Thus the fisherman's soul has no choice but to go forth into the world heartless. Every year, the Fisherman's Soul returns to the edge of the sea and tries to entice his master out of the waters with wonderful tales of the strange places that the Soul has visited. When at last it succeeds in luring the Fisherman out of the waters, his Soul tricks him into doing many evil things. Rebuked by the Fisherman for its conduct, his Soul replies, "When thou didst send me forth into the world thou gavest me no heart, so I learned to do all these things and love them…"

Man must have a soul, and he must also have a heart. Body, soul and heart need to be kept together if he is to maintain his rightful integrity. This must surely hold true for nations and peoples as well as for individuals. Is that trinity of body, soul and heart intact today for the peoples of Europe? The European Union may be regarded as a body of sorts. But its limbs and organs seem more often than not to be engaged in disparate pursuits that pull the body in opposing directions, and threaten to tear the whole edifice apart. What of its soul? Hopefully, it is that of a seeker of peace, and of unity. Such was certainly the intention at the time of the signing of the Treaties of Rome. There can be no disputing the legitimacy of such aspirations. Peoples who come together under such a flag must surely be able to create harmony amongst one another.

Yet the European Union appears curiously incapable of generating true harmony from within. Turf wars break out at every opportunity, bickering is persistent. What is probably worse, the most bizarre compromises and creative rhetoric have to be applied to paper over radically opposing positions. Some see such ingenuity for keeping up appearances as proof of the Union's growing internal coherence. There may be something in this, but where is the point in putting on a show of solidarity when no one is really sure what it is all for. If the aim is that everyone's vested interests should be kept intact under the guise of collective responsibility, one might as well dispense with the pretence altogether and allow each to go their separate ways without interference.

In observing the European Union of today, one is tempted to quote from George Orwell and say, "I understand *how*: I do not understand *why*". This is not to draw a parallel between the totalitarian nightmare world of Orwell's *Nineteen Eighty-Four* and that of the European Union. To do so would be the ultimate 'thoughtcrime', most certainly politically incorrect, and indeed not at all appropriate. Nonetheless, it is still true to say that the Union seems more and more to be preoccupied with the *how* of keeping itself in one piece, rather than the *why* of the whole exercise. More to the point, the why and the how seem to have lost their initial integral relationship and become increasingly ill-suited to each other over time. There seems now to be no apparent link between the body European, and its soul. The soul cries out for comradeship. But the body cannot co-ordinate its actions accordingly. Only a heart capable of true compassion can fill the widening chasm that divides the two.

John Coleman is perceptive when he cites a preacher who points out "that Christ only said that Christians had to love their enemies. He didn't say they had to like them!" A heart with which to love the European cause, even if your neighbours do not seem all that likeable, is surely what is needed to bring body and soul together in today's Europe.

Could the Council of Europe play such a role? Could it, in fact, be the missing heart of Europe? The potential, at least, would seem to be there. According to Article I of its Statute, the Council was established in order "to achieve a greater unity between its members for the purpose of safeguarding and realising the ideals and principles which are their heritage and facilitating their economic and social progress". This aim is to be achieved "by discussion of questions of common concern and by agreements and common action in economic, social, cultural, scientific, legal and administrative matters and in the maintenance and further realisation of human rights and fundamental freedoms."

Unlike the European Union, the Council's affairs are conducted along strictly intergovernmental lines. This, of course, cannot of itself be said to constitute a virtue. Existing national governments are by no means the best or the most comprehensive representatives of the many and independent-minded peoples that live side by side within the state boundaries of today. Nonetheless, the structure and institutions of the Council of Europe seem to articulate a willingness to uphold diversity such as is not immediately detectable in the workings of the European Union. The existence of the Congress of Local and Regional Authorities of Europe, albeit in a consultative capacity, as one of the three pillars on which the Council stands, must surely be an expression of its awareness for the need to caution against excess centralisation. The role of the Congress of Local and Regional Authorities of Europe is to strengthen democratic structures at local levels, and in particular to assist the new democracies of Central and Eastern Europe to establish effective local and regional governments. Under such an arrangement the smaller entities of this world look to face less danger of being gobbled up by over-arching central control mechanisms that impose uniformity.

The Council of Europe's focus on human rights is also important. The explicit commitment to the protection of an individual's fundamental rights and freedoms which is enshrined in the European Convention on Human Rights is the single most crucial safeguard against a Europe with no heart. There can be no better assurance that diverse cultures, differing lines of thought, and divergent identities will be strictly respected. Heartless suppression of smaller entities can have no place in an institution of this nature.

Yet if the Council of Europe is to truly function as the missing heart of Europe, there would seem to be two points that require some scrutiny. First, there is the question of contemporary relevance. Founded in 1949, the Council of Europe is a very specifically post-war institution. In this respect, it shares a common problem with the European Union in that its capacity to address coherently the issues of today's post-war world is constrained by its very genealogy. Can the Council update itself without jeopardising its original intentions? Can it hold on to its founding aspirations without making itself obsolete? Can it speak the language of today while retaining the voice of yesterday? It started out with a ten-nation membership. It now has thirty-nine members. Can a heart which once beat for ten function with the same precision and aptitude for such an enlarged body as it is today?

The second question is that of economics. While the point is well taken that the Council of Europe "does not ask economic questions" (Coleman), it nonetheless has to respond to them. Many of today's conflicts, and indeed conflicts in general, have their origins in economic needs and desires. Economic questions are ignored at the beholder's peril. Ideals and aspirations have to be tested against the economics of survival. The Council's perspective on economic issues is a social one. It evaluates economic phenomena in terms of their social impact, of their affect on the social rights of individuals. This is an entirely legitimate viewpoint and one that is in keeping with the Council's core concern.

Nonetheless, there are limits to what one can achieve by viewing economic issues through a non-economic spectrum. The vision is apt to become distorted. How can social justice and the economics of competition be reconciled? This is the key question facing the industrialised economies of today but it is perhaps of even more critical relevance in the case of the Central and Eastern European countries, whose fundamental reforms the

Council of Europe is rightly committed to assisting. Social justice and the survival of the fittest are not mutually exclusive concepts. Indeed, how to make the two work in a complementary fashion is the issue.

Creative solutions to this equation are not attainable through a formalistic application of the notions of fairness and equality. In the Lord's vineyard, those who came first are apt to be last, and the latecomers came out on top. This is as it ought to be in the marketplace, where the invisible hand of God operates. The emerging Asian markets have every right to come out first, even though they may be the last to have entered the vineyard of competition. The Central and Eastern Europeans may well feel the same way. Equal access to the vineyard is what they are seeking. A viable response to their demands requires measured economic reasoning as well as the perspective of the social dimension. Is the Council of Europe able to provide this?

When at last, the Fisherman and his Soul are reunited, it is not without pain. "Surely thou mayest enter", said the young Fisherman, "for in the days when with no heart thou didst go through the world thou must have suffered much." "Alas", cried his Soul, "I can find no place of entrance, so compassed about with love is this heart of thine..."

In the end, it takes the breaking of the Fisherman's heart upon the death of his beloved Mermaid for his Soul to find a point of re-entry. Hopefully, the Council of Europe can breathe new life into Europe's future without itself having to suffer critical damage. For such a calamity to be averted, the Council of Europe will need, of its own accord, to open up new vistas for itself. It is well positioned to do so, free as it is from the need to achieve economically unviable and politically unsustainable goals, such as those to which the European Union has bound itself. It is time that the missing heart of Europe was re-discovered and re-united with the body and Soul of Europe.

13. UNITY OF EUROPE: CONSCIENCE OF EUROPE

Karekin I, Catholicos

His Holiness Karekin I is Supreme Patriarch and Catholicos of All Armenians.

So much has been written on this theme of European union that it seems very difficult to add anything that can be considered new. Yet, I will try to offer a personal testimony and bear witness in the context of the Armenian experience of participation in European life.

Let me from the very beginning say that I was not born in a country that falls within the boundaries of Europe in the largest sense of the definition. I was born in northern Syria, in a modest village (Kessab) where from my early schooldays I felt that Europe was close to me. In my early days of life, Syria was under the French mandate. Part of our primary education consisted of French language and literature, even in that remote village.

Later, the European element acquired a greater degree of influence on my education in Lebanon where I continued my education as a seminarist in the Seminary of the Armenian Cilician Catholicosate. The whole cultural climate of Lebanon was impregnated by factors, norms and values of European culture. The two years I spent in Oxford, England, for research study, led me to deeper dimensions of European ethos of Christian and humanistic culture.

With that kind of personal background, as I read my own Armenian history and its unbroken continuity of 1700 years of Christian witness, I see more and more clearly how Armenian history and culture are interwoven with European history and culture.

I realise that geographically and often politically, Armenians have carried on their life outside the orbit of European boundaries. Their history has evolved through constant contact with immediate neighbour countries: Parthia, Iran, Asia Minor, East Syria, Middle Eastern peoples and countries. Yet, Europe in one way or another, has been dominantly present in all the developments of our historical journey and cultural creativity.

First of all, one must consider the basic fact that there is a determinant element of Indo-European ethnic influence on the formation of the Armenian nation. Fundamentally the Armenians are of Indo-European origin. The Armenian language bears ample witness to that historical truth.

Then, for centuries Armenian history was influenced by the Roman Empire and by the culture it brought with it. It is well known by all historians that Armenia was a crossroads for different political, military and cultural forces, through which, and besides the Persian and East Syrian influences, the Greek European elements often entered into play on the Armenian plateau and, indeed, exerted a decisive role on the destiny of the Armenian people as a whole.

The Byzantine Empire is another time and another world which was in an unbroken relationship with Armenia for more than ten centuries. Often the destinies of the two were merged together. Religiously and culturally speaking, Byzantine made a deep impact on Armenian history (see Sirarpie Der-Nersessian, *Armenia and the Byzantine Empire*, Harvard University Press, 1947). Armenians, for their part contributed immensely towards the consolidation and progress of the Empire. Some of the Byzantine emperors, generals and political figures were of Armenian origin (see P. Charanis, *Armenians in the Byzantine Empire*, Dumbarton Oaks).

The Crusaders Movement made Armenia enter into a new era of intense relationship with Western Europe. The history of the Armenian Kingdom of Cilicia (1080-1375) cannot be fully understood and truly assessed without taking into account the impact of the Crusaders Movement. Some of such influences lasted longer than the succeeding waves of the Crusaders Movement itself.

The presence of the Armenian people in Eastern Europe: in Bulgaria, Romania, Hungary and Russia, is such a well-known page of East European history that there is no need to make any further or additional comment.

The nineteenth-century Armenian literary and cultural renaissance is due mostly to direct and constant relations with countries such as France, Belgium, Italy, Germany, Switzerland, Russia, England and others. A large number of Armenian intellectuals, writers, artists and clergymen received their higher education in the European centres of high learning. Returning to their own country and their own people they devoted themselves to the promotion of the ideas and values that they had acquired during their life and study in Europe.

What do we conclude from this very succinct, indeed, sketchy purview? Firstly, religious, economic and cultural progress owes much to the inter-relations, contacts and interchange between nations. Isolation is not a factor of advancement. In that respect Armenia greatly benefited from such relationships, while at the same time offering its share in the pursuit of civilisation.

Secondly, that all influences were not necessarily in the highest interest of the Armenian people. There were influences which enhanced Armenian self-consciousness and cultural richness; there were others which contributed towards the alienation of the Armenians to their ethos and to their relationships with their neighbours. The major reason was that such relationships were often conceived and conducted in terms of exploitation by one side of the other, by the strong of the weaker.

There was a time in recent history when Europe did not manifest that spirit of human solidarity which I consider to be a distinctive part of the European ethos. At the end of the nineteenth century and in the first two decades of this twentieth century, Europe left Armenia at the hands of the Turks, the Ottoman Empire and the Young Turks regime, which perpetrated horrible massacres and even the genocide of 1915 against the Armenian people. Europe acted in such a way that one asks, where was the conscience of European unity and integrity? Thus, Fridtjof Nansen in his famous book, *Armenia and the Near East*,[1] made this poignant observation worthy of serious consideration:

> "Woe to the Armenians, that they were ever drawn into European politics! It would have been better for them if the name of Armenia had never been uttered by any European diplomat."

> "But the Armenian people have never abandoned hope; they have gone on bravely working and waiting... waiting year after year."

> "They are waiting still."[2]

Yet today, after the Second World War and towards the end of this same twentieth-century, when European unity is gaining firmer ground in the conscience of the European nations, indeed, it is a matter of joy for Armenians to see their motherland having recovered its independence. Today, Armenia is a free and independent state constituted on the basis of democratic principles. Today a new and healthier relationship is developing. The unity of Europe surely will take the Armenian partner more seriously. Former injustices have to be redressed. Only through such sound policy will the conscience of Europe give colour and value to European unity.

Finally, what matters above all is the spiritual and moral nature, the intention and direction of such a relationship. We are often tempted to identify progress with material and technological advantages. Europe is not a laboratory for scientific research and inventions. Europe is a spirit imbued with values that have perennial impact. If Europe looks for the fulfilment of its unity, such unity should be enlivened by values of moral nature and scope and not limit itself to purely or exclusively economic, political, technological conditions of power.

---

1. Nansen, Fridtjof. *Armenia and the Near East*, Allen & Unwin, New York, 1928.
2. Nansen, Fridtjof, op. cit, p. 324

Unity of Europe!
What is it for without the *conscience* of Europe?

Such conscience will transform the unity into a unique service for the world on a global level. That is the challenge we are facing as we are preparing to enter the third millennium.

14. TEN COMMANDMENTS FOR EUROPE'S RENAISSANCE

Diana Schumacher

Diana Schumacher is President of the Schumacher Society, founder member of the New Economics Foundation, founder member of the Environmental Law Foundation.

Fifty years on from the first Congress of Europe, the time has come to consider what the Union of Europe really means in terms of belonging; what it means to be 'European', how deep are the loyalties of the member states towards each other and how much mutual benefit has been experienced? Have the strategic, political and social reasons behind the twentieth-century European experiment been fulfilled, or is a new Renaissance necessary to ensure European sustainability in the twenty-first?

The Council of Europe, formally born in London in May 1949 in the wake of the Second World War, was conceived as a means of preventing future wars by building on those cultural values and economic aspirations which were derived from a common European heritage. The Council's role was to strengthen democracy and the rule of law throughout its member states. By substituting an agreed Charter of Human Rights, social justice and economic interdependence for the oppressive dictatorships and nationalistic political ambitions which had been the *casus belli* of the previous half century, it was hoped this time to build a more lasting peace.

This original Council of Europe, in turn, became parent of the European Community and, post-1991, of the Economic Union, having given birth to other affiliated institutions along the way. It has undergone so many metamorphoses established by different European treaties and conventions that, with the plethora of economic overlay, it is now sometimes difficult to discover and define to what extent it is still fulfilling the purpose of the original institution as envisaged by its founders. The Council of Europe was first and foremost about common values rather than economics – about unity in diversity and not about uniformity; about shared integrity rather than institutional integration. It is this gradual shift in emphasis which most concerns the guardians of democracy and cultural diversity as the dawn of the new millennium breaks over a continent struggling to survive in the global market place, with eleven countries now tied into a common monetary union.

As is well known, the post-war European coalition had as its axis the partnership of France and Germany, age-old rivals. Both nations enjoyed a dubious track-record of destroying the elusive European balance of power whenever opportunity offered and both had been severely damaged by war and economic privation during the three preceding decades. If these hostile neighbours could be united with others in the common social, political and economic cause of reconstructing Western Europe whilst acting as a bulwark against the threat of Communist expansion and an attack from the Eastern bloc countries, the continent might prove a far safer place for future generations. The aim of re-establishing human rights, the security of individuals and the sustainability of local communities and culture lay at the very heart of the concept of a federal Europe. In the words of Winston Churchill in his Zurich speech of September 1946, what was needed was: "A remedy which, as if by miracle, would transform the whole scene and in a few years make all of Europe as free and happy as Switzerland is today. We must build a kind of United States of Europe". In other words (and without analysing too deeply the freedom and happiness of Switzerland) the various European states needed some higher purpose to serve as a bonding mechanism to unite them in rebuilding their ravaged infrastructure in the face of what seemed a very real threat from the USSR.

With this fundamental idea of European unity, many different movements were springing up simultaneously and from these the first Congress of Europe emerged in The Hague in May 1948. The main purpose of the Congress of Europe was to demonstrate the breadth of the movements in favour of Western European unity despite their wide regional and cultural diversity. The Council of Europe was set up as a result of the Congress, and was the first European political institution to have an international parliament. In this respect Churchill's vision had been realised. The drafting and establishment of a European Charter of Human Rights and a European Court of Justice to enforce its decisions were also fundamental to the vision but, at this stage, most supporters of a European Federation (including Great Britain, Ireland and the Scandinavian countries), favoured independent intergovernmental co-operation rather than any form of centralised bureaucracy. European *unity*, rather than *union* was the key aspiration.

Such historic details are now of particular relevance since May 1999 celebrates not only the fiftieth Anniversary of the Council of Europe, born from this Hague Congress of Europe, but also the centenary of the very first International Peace Conference inaugurated by Tsar Nicholas II of Russia and the Queen of the Netherlands in the Hague in 1899. The autocratic Tsar had called for a "Parliament of World Peace" (only attended by 100 delegates representing twenty-six nations) in the hope of containing the highly expensive and increasingly explosive European arms race of the late-nineteenth century. It was, of course, an all-male assembly of diplomats, senior military officers, scholars in international law and jurists. Nevertheless, at this unprecedented event were sketched out plans for the League of Nations which was formed after the First World War and from which eventually developed the United Nations after the Second World

War. Even in this very first international peace conference of 1899 were developed the ideas of a multilateral responsibility for global peace and arms control; a permanent International Court of Justice at the Hague, and a Union of Nations with common principles of peace, justice and conflict resolution through mediation and arbitration.[1] It marked the beginning of the modern international system which calls, not merely for international diplomatic discussions to settle disputes, but for structures to be established to settle issues peacefully by mutual agreement.

The Council of Europe was therefore itself at the time marking a fifty-year old historical tradition seeking European co-operation in the maintenance of peace and international jurisprudence whilst recognising the sovereign right of each nation to be responsible for its own internal economic, judicial and administrative affairs. The aim of The Council was "to accomplish a closer union among its members...through the analysis of questions of common interest, through the conclusion of agreements and the adoption of a common action in the economic, social, cultural, scientific, judicial and administrative areas as well as by safeguarding and developing the human rights and fundamental guarantees" (Article 1 of the Statute of the Council of Europe). The assumptions of democracy and justice lay at the very heart of the new union of 1949. The European Convention of Human Rights, a fundamental pillar of the Council's strategy was signed in Rome on 4 November 1950.

The original ten signatories of the Council of Europe, who met in London in May 1949, were Belgium, France, Luxembourg, The Netherlands, the United Kingdom and Ireland, Italy, Denmark, Norway and Sweden. The first sessions of the Assembly were held in Strasbourg, still the Council's permanent seat, although its membership now numbers forty countries.

Soon after the formation of the Council, the Federal Republic of Germany joined. Robert Schumann then proposed closer co-operation through the European Coal and Steel Community (ECSC) to develop, protect and jointly control those industries which had supplied the basic war machine. In 1951 the ECSC was formally established by the Treaty of Paris. These were indeed historic times! The signatories were Germany, France, Belgium, Italy, Luxembourg and The Netherlands, the six countries most committed to European integration. Five of the original signatories of the Council of Europe including the United Kingdom refused to sign, the UK being particularly keen to preserve its own coal and steel industries from EC imports. It

---

1. Nation, Steve and Janet (1999) "One Hundred Years On. The Hague Peace Conference 1899: A background paper for World Peace – Inner Peace Conference 1999", pp. 4-6. It is worthy of note that in 1898 Germany was spending 51% of her national revenue on arms; Britain 38%; France 27% and Russia 23% but on account of her size and resources this amounted to a great deal more than any other country.

viewed these resources as basic for national security, the value of which had been proven in two world wars. Then, in May 1957, the Treaty of Rome – again without the signature of the UK – set the seal on the European Economic Community, (Denmark, Ireland and the United Kingdom only acceded in 1973).

Whereas the original architects of the European Community had planned for a united Europe based on cultural, practical and economic aspirations, the ECSC and EC were now driven primarily by economic and energy-related motives and hence the simultaneous formation of Euratom, the European Atomic Energy Authority. Nowhere in the original vision was it stipulated that economic progress would be the dominant factor of all decision-making processes, nor that mutually binding decisions of member states could be taken by un-elected unaccountable personnel, thereby threatening the hard-won democracy of member states.

There has followed the gradual establishment of different instruments and institutions of the EEC which, operating from Brussels, have further separated the functions of economic and political policy from the much wider cultural and social purposes which had inspired the Council of Europe. Writing in *Europe 92: Reflections from the Underside*,[1] the Reverend Kenneth David points out that the Single European Act came about as the only way for Europe to survive in economic and technological competition against the United States and Japan. However, this would merely "benefit the prosperity of the rich nations of Europe, to the further detriment of the firmly entrenched regional and social inequalities". He goes on to observe that the capitalist system has three characteristics: economically it is very dynamic and capable of renewing itself; socially it excludes certain groups; and culturally it is an intentionally pernicious way to generate a homogenous society. Its coherence lies in the fact that its objectives are investment, profit and economic growth, and as such the European Union is not in crisis since any system is only in crisis in the light of its objectives! That was in 1992!

In fact ever since the 1970s, many had begun to harbour reservations as to what a Europe united by a common desire for economic development might mean in terms of loss of sovereignty, loss of cultural diversity, loss of national and regional institutions, changes in traditions of production, procurement, categorisation, standards, and changes in the distribution of population and wealth. Both threats and opportunities for the different regions became very real. On the other hand, in terms of the original vision of the Council of Europe the Community's collaboration in most respects

---

1. Davis, Kenneth, *Europe 92: Reflections from the Underside – The Challenge to Community Organising* (1992), World Council of Churches, Urban Rural Mission, Geneva, Switzerland.

was initially most successful. There was no subsequent war among the European allies; there was no invasion by the Communists from Eastern Europe; and the European member states did enjoy a period of economic revival albeit initially bolstered by the Marshall Plan. Also, on the eve of the last decade of the century, quite unexpectedly and dramatically, the Cold War abruptly ended. The Soviet Union was no longer a threat and Mikhail Gorbachev, the Soviet leader, astonishingly spoke of "our common European home" and sought EC membership and a newly-united Germany became caught up with unexpected economic and social problems of its own. The Council of Europe was ideally placed to welcome the new fledgling democracies into the European Community.

On the other hand, the European Union was also being significantly enlarged to accommodate new members. Serious flaws then began to appear in the operational structures. The entire machinery was becoming increasingly unwieldy and cumbersome, unable to respond quickly and flexibly to the dynamics of change. Economic growth was driven on at the expense of certain regions, industries and the poorer countries of the Third World, who unwittingly supported this economic 'club' with cash crops and raw materials – without even enjoying the benefits of membership! At the same time the complexities of the different organisations within the Brussels community have obfuscated any pretensions of financial or administrative transparency. The Europe without internal economic frontiers has also become a Europe without accountability.

Because of its inherent philosophy of economics above ethics, the EU also has inadvertently become the global focus of international crime – ranging from the illegal nuclear and conventional arms trade to the illegal dumping of nuclear and toxic wastes, the drugs trade, money laundering, computer crime, child-snatching for their organs, prostitution and pornography, illegal immigration and unbridled terrorism. Perhaps the smuggling of nuclear fissile materials is the most sinister by-product of the new European order with the gene traders running a close second. In his convincingly documented book, *The Octopus*,[1] Brian Freemantle points out that the Mafia of the world and organised crime groups were far ahead of any multinational industry in calculating the enormous economic potential of the European Union and were the very first to go into business as true Europeans, even if they did not qualify by birth or nationality. Nor is there any federal European legal system which is able to effectively contain such well-orchestrated criminal networks.[2]

---

1. Freemantle, Brian, *The Octopus: Europe in the Grip of Organised Crime* (1995) Orion Press, London.
2. David, Kenneth, op.cit.

The EU infrastructure has inevitably also become prey to the manipulations of transnational corporations, with global market control rather than local policies at heart. It is no coincidence that the lobbyists of all the major transnational corporations constantly patrol the corridors of the European Union whilst their European head offices are all clustered around its Brussels headquarters. This European 'free market' is, in fact, anything but free in operation. It is unable to reconcile the opposing forces within its ever-increasing boundaries; unable consistently to maintain the economic growth propulsion of its proponents whilst catering for its ever soaring numbers of homeless, jobless and rootless; and unable to defend itself against the conflicting claims and forces of external interests.

Moreover, although inter-state warfare has largely been prevented within Western and Central Europe, the dramatic rise in unemployment and poverty, together with the crime and violence, referred to previously, vividly demonstrate that social and ethical disintegration have increased at unprecedented rates during a period dedicated to peace and prosperity. The gulf between rich and poor, urban and rural, the productive and non-productive sectors of the Community, has also continued to increase. Dissatisfaction and disillusionment pervade most sectors of society since people have no vote on most issues which govern their everyday lives, and their elected representatives have increasingly limited responsibility under the mechanisms which govern their functioning at the close of the twentieth century. Many now see the European Union's economic dictatorship of 'free trade' as a doubtful alternative to Communism and Fascism. This may in turn pose a serious threat to the future economic and military security and stability of the Union, as the economies of new member states continue to flounder and their expectations become replaced by cynicism and anger.

The external and internal problems and inherent contradictions are now becoming magnified as the size and scope of the EU's initiatives and influence continue to increase at the expense of the Council of Europe. Apparently the only mechanism for checking these had been to introduce yet more categories of bureaucrats operating from Brussels; and an ever-proliferating body of pan-European legislation and ever-augmented regiments of experts, accountants, inspectorates and watchdogs, who are constantly attempting to ensure that compliance and standards are maintained throughout all the member countries. Clearly this has not worked either, as investigative journalists are at pains to point to the overall lack of accountability. In financial matters alone we are, with increasing frequency, made aware of the vast sums of tax payers' money (estimated at £8-10 billion annually) which cannot be traced, or have been allocated to spurious causes such as non-existent olive groves, vineyards and claims for non-existent 'set-aside' land – this despite the evermore complicated and centralised control systems!

More generally, since the EU was formed, agriculture and farming, two of the most fundamental resource bases of any country, have suffered in many regions because of the imposition of the Common Agricultural Policy. This in turn has put stress on cities, as well as giving rise to crises in the countryside. Together with the urban drift to find jobs there is growing interstate social and cultural dislocation owing to the unrestricted internal labour market. European environmental and habitat quality is deteriorating in all but a few regions owing to the combined pressures of natural resource exploitation, production and transportation methods dependent on fossil fuels, and a market economy geared to ever-increasing patterns of consumption. Europe is now living off her capital rather than her income and, although Brussels is awash with accountants there is no bank manager in charge overall to say when 'enough is enough' and to steer the client towards self-responsibility and sufficiency.

Notwithstanding a much publicised policy of regionalisation and subsidiarity, the European Union is becoming unworkable in its present form which is why a restoration of the wider vision of the Council of Europe is so urgently needed for the twenty-first century. Unless the dominance of the richer elements in society is diminished, the most welcome entry of new but poorer member states from Eastern Europe and elsewhere will inevitably add to more confusion and resentment under the present structures. We need to put our own house in order at the same time as encouraging, supporting and integrating new family members.

Whatever may be written or dreamed of the concept of devolution, it is the actual centralisation of economic power which is putting at risk individual liberty, democracy, security and national sovereignty. The 1997 agreement of the Biotech Patent in the face of enormous public opposition; the pressure on European Union members to subscribe to the infamous Multilateral Agreement on Investments (MAI), which was only narrowly avoided; and the New Transatlantic Market Place involving 'public-private partnerships' at all levels were mainly concerned to transfer economic and political power away from the regions and to rob individuals and communities of their democratic and legal rights. This was not part of the Council's original vision. Despite the claimed advantages of a common currency, it is the democratic deficit which must be urgently addressed now in order for the expanded European membership to have any lasting security. To achieve this, the very institutions of the European Union must themselves be reformed and become more accountable, transparent and responsive to regional needs. In short, they need to be giving a moral and ethical lead which provides an enduring example for the newly emerging democracies.

So how might this change of direction come about and which institution could guide and steer the transition? What are the *principles* upon which sustainable community policy for the regions should be based, since sound principles must always underlie any policy of sustainability?

Let me try to answer the second part of this question first so that we can look at some of the principles which such a switch to a sustainable Europe might entail. As suggested in the title, I have listed as an offering, ten interrelated principles or 'commandments' which all represent part of a cohesive whole. It will be seen that they correlate with or overlay each other and, to avoid repetition, I have therefore not devoted an equal amount of space to each as it is hoped that the inferences will be obvious. Taken together the 'ten commandments' might provide a useful checklist for future European development when the time comes to replace those parts of the European edifice which are not working at the end of the old millennium. The ten principles are historically time-tested. Their implementation may entail new structures for local community initiatives, involvement and accountability, whilst minimising long-term costs and risks to the regions.

- The first commandment, which is an essential component to regional and environmental sustainability, is the *Principle of Conservation*. Every new decision or commitment should be tested against this fundamental principal: it is the principle of good stewardship. Conservation, whether of energy, raw materials or manufactured goods, is more efficient than consumerism and was practised throughout history until the second half of the twentieth century. Most communities in Europe reclaimed, re-cycled and re-used materials and products, as is the case with the majority of Third World countries today.

It is true that the European Union, and its predecessor the European Community, have been responsible for very effective and long-overdue environmental legislation on air, sea, water and land pollution, as they have sought to rationalise and impose common European environmental quality standards throughout. The law, when invoked in defence of the environment and local communities against exploitative developments, has an increasingly creative role to play and also in such areas as mediation and conflict resolution. However, the monitoring and enforcement of standards have in experience proved more difficult, again because of the unbridled pursuit of economic growth, including problems of scale and complexity, together with the non-compliance of united corporate and financial interests for which there have been no precedents. New legal initiatives in defence of community and environmental conservation must now become an essential part of any plan for European reconstruction.

A significant proportion of the wastage we see around us comes from the common acceptance of a very narrow and exclusive idea of 'efficiency'. In the European Union generally it relates only to the material side of things; to time and to profit. The principle of conservation, on the other hand, takes a long-term inclusive overview and asks what goods and services actually need to be provided? for whom? by whom? where? for how long? and so forth. To arrive at sensible answers to such questions not only improves overall efficiency but makes people more aware of, and accountable for, waste. Throughout Europe the transport and disposal of waste – especially toxic and hazardous waste – is becoming increasingly costly and dangerous, and disposal sites increasingly scarce and difficult to monitor. One of the key factors in any efficiency conservation policy is therefore to try as far as possible, to eliminate waste at source.

The conservation of energy is one of the most important aspects of environmental sustainability which can be achieved without too much difficulty, once our thinking shifts from the availability of supply to a more efficient management of the demand side of the equation. As Amory Lovins, the United States' energy expert, has been pointing out for at least two decades, we should plan our communities, industries and activities in terms of Negawatts or energy actually saved and not in terms of Megawatts. This means planning energy conservation into every project and pricing fuels more realistically to reflect their replacement costs, and the effects of their impact on the environment.

Water is another area in which Europe needs to develop more effective conservation strategies, as the growth of certain industries (including tourism in arid Mediterranean countries) is putting a very severe strain on resources, while in most regions the water table continues to fall. In order to conserve their own environment it is necessary therefore for each community and region to adopt a coherent water conservation. Otherwise acute water shortages are likely to become one of the most serious impediments to sustainability in the next decade.

• The second commandment for any European development strategy is *The Principle of Appropriate Scale*. As with 'efficiency' there have been many misconceptions regarding 'economies of scale' – that bigger and more centralised control is cheaper, more efficient, faster, more productive and hence more profitable. This is by no means always the case when one looks at long-term developments. Moreover these quantitatively-based economics totally disregard such essentials as the *quality* of communications, of working life, the qualitative needs of the stakeholders, the end use of products and the health of the environment. The economies of scale, as practised in the European community, have proved to be highly wasteful in terms of human skills, transport systems, raw materials and sometimes are even a hazard to public health and safety.

On the other hand, some opponents of the 'big is best' school have been guilty of over simplification, since in planning for all communities and human activities there is an appropriate size for everything. To give a topical example there is need for local community or cottage hospitals with basic resources to deal with minor injuries and uncomplicated requirements. There is also the simultaneous need to provide regional and national hospitals scaled up to become 'centres of excellence' to deal with the diagnosis and treatment of more serious complaints, and the training of highly specialised medical personnel. There are meaningful decisions which have to be taken at the level of the province or state. In the case of environmental protocols, poverty relief and the response to humanitarian or natural disasters, decisions have to be made at an international level to have any significant effect. In the world of ideas, ethics, and the indivisibility of peace and ecology, we need also to base our actions on recognition of the unity of all humankind. This is the *think globally, act locally* principle. The question of appropriate scale for the various institutions of the European Union is therefore of fundamental importance.

The principle of right scale emphasises that the human being and the natural world should always remain visibly at the centre of all human endeavours and organisations. It rejects enormous structures and the sense of isolation, dependence, frustration and the diminishment of human responsibility which these bring. For more secure community structures to flourish, it follows that developments and markets must exist for people and not the other way round as inevitably happens in expanding economic empires. In sharp contrast to people-centred structures are the one hundred largest economies in the world, forty-seven of which in 1998 were financial corporations with strongholds in the European Union and with more wealth than that of 130 of the world's poorest countries.

- The third commandment for European sustainability is that of *Empowerment*. This recognises the need for some form of autonomy and self-determination in community policy matters, whether regarding employment, housing, energy generation, land rights or environmental matters. The principle seeks to ensure the maximum delegation of power and self-responsibility to the grass roots, or at least to the lowest practical decision-making level. In other words it is the principle which underpins devolution. Decisions which take place locally where the knowledge of real needs and local issues are greatest, cut out unnecessary bureaucracy and often make corruption a little more difficult to operate.

Empowerment automatically creates an atmosphere of involvement and initiative. It follows that each community should, as far as possible, be responsible for conducting its own internal affairs albeit within a given budget, in accordance with the laws of the land and other regulations relating to standards, pollution control and so forth. Such local responsibility may not necessarily be in accordance with the objectives of international commercial and financial institutions but are in keeping with the spirit of Agenda 21, and more specifically with Local Agenda 21, which is perhaps the best post-Rio opportunity which Europe has ever had for putting the principle of empowerment into effect. Aimed at encouraging local sustainability, Local Agenda 21 seeks to enable local communities to enhance and protect their environments, meet social needs in an inclusive way and to promote economic viability. Finding the right balance between social needs, environmental constraints and economic goals, is by no means easy in practice and community empowerment is often dependent on education and on providing successful examples of good practice. Great emphasis is currently being placed on the empowerment of women and young people to take a fuller share of responsibility in the running of regional organisations than has happened in Europe in the past. For community empowerment to thrive, the maximum resources and authority should be invested at the lowest practicable level which could be at the level of the municipality or local council. Even today within the European Union, many cities such as Barcelona, Sienna and Lyons provide colourful examples of the richness of local culture, where traditional independence has been allowed to flourish locally.

- The fourth commandment for sustainability is that of *Evaluation* which follows as a consequence of the third. For any responsible democratic development to thrive, individual members must perceive their actions to be useful and valuable, particularly in the adoption of new policies. This means that citizens should have access to the necessary information, and policies should be explicable and transparent before the Community is called upon to participate and evaluate. Unfortunately not all countries in the EU have a Freedom of Information Act which is a prerequisite for any such policy to be effective. There should also exist the means to measure and assess what is valuable and what has been achieved against agreed targets, standards and decisions. This need not always be the conventional quantitative or monetary assessments but rather a qualitative assessment by the community, municipality or region as to how well it has measured up to its own targets.

Traditionally, economic indicators have been an accepted mechanism for evaluating progress. However, indicators of sustainability are totally different and this is an area in which The New Economics Foundation in the United Kingdom,[1] Herman Daly and John Cobb in

---

1. Anderson, Victor, *New Economic Indicators*, 1991, New Economics Foundation, Cinnamon House, 6-8 Cole Street, London SE11 4YH.

America, and a great many others have made very important contributions. Daly and Cobb in their provocative book, *For the Common Good*, suggested that Gross National Damage (GND) should be substituted for the more usual but less meaningful GNP.[1] It will be appreciated that even very negative events such as oil spillages or the impeachment of a President can add very favourably to a nation's GNP! Work on these indicators still continues and, as citizens, we can draw up our own lists of local indicators to see whether the quality and sustainability of the community is progressing or regressing. This would be a most useful decentralised form of evaluation but only insofar as it conveys meaningful information which allows people to grasp what is happening to their own lives and environment.

With over twenty thousand communities in the UK alone represented by thousands of government institutions, one can estimate the multiplicity and variety of indicators needed to monitor sustainability throughout the regions of Europe. In The New Economic Foundation's very useful handbook on community sustainability indicators, the authors point out that the very exercise of setting and evaluating these indicators focuses attention on what is important locally and creates opportunities of working together, and new learning opportunities and partnerships, which in turn tap hidden potential and liberate essential information within the neighbourhood.[2]

- *The Principle of Diversification* is another element important for the sustainability and vitality of all communities or systems since the natural world in all its myriad forms is so very richly diverse. A strategy for sustainable community development would therefore attempt to promote a multifaceted economic and social infrastructure, making the widest possible use of all its resources and the many latent talents of its members. Standardisation, whether of seeds, crops or cultures is the very antithesis of variety and diversity. Crops and communities which are monocultures rarely thrive long term and both deplete and impoverish their surroundings. In this alone, the two opposed ideologies of Communism and Capitalism through a free market have much in common. Both promote conformity and uniformity: both kill the spirit of local enterprise and individuality. Most countries today have examples of community monocultures, where everyone is employed by the same organisation, works in the same industry or uses the same commuter and dormitory lifestyle patterns. The European Union itself and its predecessor the EC have also played their parts in promoting the

---

1. Daly, Herman and Cobb, John, *For the Common Good*, 1989, Green Print, London.
2. New Economics Foundation, *Communities Count! A step by step guide to community sustainability indicator*, 1998, pp. 7-11; 152-155, NEF, Cinnamon House, 6-8 Cole Street, London SE11 4YH.

monoculture industries. It is true that industrialised communities have usually developed because of the economic advantages offered by their geographical location and natural resources suitable for certain industries. But it is also true that most monoculture communities eventually collapse. Once the market for their single product is undermined or subsumed the entire workforce is made redundant and poverty strikes overnight, as was the case with Ebervale and Consett, two UK mining and steel communities respectively.

Monoculture communities generally are extremely vulnerable whereas those which have diversified tend to be more robust. A self-reliant community will therefore actively seek to vary its skills and business enterprises within the same geographical region, producing as many of its basic necessities and marketable goods as energy and nature allow. It will encourage healthy internal transactions of goods and services between members of the community, which will also help to strengthen the social fabric. Local Enterprise Trading Schemes (LETS) and other such initiatives encourage the development of local diversification and yet, unfortunately, the whole EU trend at the turn of the century is towards common currencies, global markets and away from supporting local enterprises and biodiversity. The result has been increasing monetary and political dependency, with the main growth areas being financial services, insurance, surveillance and information technology none of which are indicators of social well-being. The UK, for example, once a farming nation with thriving supporting industries and workshops, is now a net importer of food, agricultural produce and fossil fuels. In other words, the prevailing market forces have driven the productive regions away from self-reliance and, in turn, out of touch with true economic realities.

On the positive side, as the economics of globalisation is destroying the ecological and economic diversity necessary for sustainability, the current financial system is eventually bound to collapse and with it most probably much unnecessary global trading in goods, other than necessary raw materials. This in turn will make way for more complementary currencies such as LETS and Time Dollars. According to Trend Monitor's findings, complementary currencies will soon be connected via an automated internet clearing house, and we can soon expect exponential growth in this type of complementary economy.[1]

• The sixth commandment, related closely to the concept of diversification, is the *Principle of Co-ordination*, without which community life could rapidly disintegrate into chaos and duplication of effort. Co-

---

1. Wyllie, Jan, "Global Economy Monitor: From Consuming to Servicing" *Trend Monitor*, (1998) Portsmouth, United Kingdom.

ordination of regionally varied community policies within an overall framework requires a coherent strategy and constant vigilance. All healthy systems are made up of complementary parts, each one performing its unique function for what one might call 'enlightened self-interest'; but they also exist for the good of the whole. In a healthy community the various activities which are likely to develop when people are encouraged to take charge of their own affairs can lead almost imperceptibly to inefficiency and duplication unless an elected leader or organisation takes responsibility for co-ordinating the whole. There should nevertheless be some flexibility built into the governing system to accommodate change without disruption.

The principle of co-ordination ensures a powerful degree of cohesiveness of the different parts of the community both in relation to each other and to the wider systems of which they are a part. It would seem that the Council of Europe, by co-operating with NGOs at all levels with its Committee of Ministers as the intergovernmental body, with the Congress of Local and Regional Authorities and with the Parliamentary Assembly, could fulfil just such a co-ordinating role. This clearly is not the case as it functions today, and effective co-ordination is unlikely to be achieved unless the current institutions of the Union are creatively overhauled and revitalised. The principle of co-ordination entails 'enlightened leadership with a long-term commitment to sustainability. There should be focus on and learning from systems and projects which can demonstrate successful integration which simultaneously satisfies the needs of individuals, the community, the local economy and the environment. One of the problems which the European Union faces today is unfortunately a divergence of aims of the different partners now that the 'economic miracle' of the 1980s is now a thing of the past. The need is, therefore, to find a means of co-ordinating the diverse regional interests in as flexible a manner as is practicable. It would seem that the Congress of Local and Regional Authorities might fulfil just such a co-ordinating role in future.

• The seventh commandment for Europe is one of *social and environmental justice*. It recognises that the maintenance of a sustainable habitat and environmental security are also basic human rights. Social Justice, as has been mentioned, is fundamental to the concept of the Council of Europe and to the idea of a European federation. In many respects, however, the newly recognised concepts of the rights of the environment itself and citizens' rights to a safe and clean neighbourhood also constitute very important new aspects of social justice which have never so far been properly accommodated.

Traditionally, justice has been concerned with the equality of rights and opportunities and the fair treatment of persons and groups in relation to one another. Environmental justice is only beginning to be thought of in terms of human rights as perceived by the United Nations and its associated institutions. For example, the right to protect one's habitat from development operations and other forms of exploitation by outside interests, and the right to an unpolluted environmental and safe energy supply systems are as important for security as is the right to food, clean water, shelter, clothing and personal security. Environmental justice, freedom from intimidation, corruption and oppression are prerequisites of community sustainability which are frequently overlooked in the cause of economic development. The divine and non-negotiable rights of Nature herself, irrespective of the relationship to human rights are not outside the scope of the concept of social justice.

The guarantee of norms of social justice such as the social contract as safeguarded by the Council of Europe is by no means to be confused by the somewhat sinister proposals for an integrated legal system for the whole of the EU which would seriously undermine national sovereignty and traditional common law. However, organisations such as the UK-based Environmental Law Foundation (ELF), an association of environmental interests, legal practitioners, academic and scientific experts, were set up to provide access to justice for local communities and to guarantee them freedom from the detrimental developments of large corporations and other vested interests. This helps to guarantee the environmental aspect of social justice at community level. Thus, when the European Union speaks of human rights it needs simultaneously to encourage human responsibilities together with effective mechanisms to ensure compliance. This will also help to check unhealthy trends such as indifference and acquiescence to injustice, the infringement of civil and environmental liberties, the suppression of minority interests and so forth. An effective system of social justice also checks insidious, less obvious developments such as *incrementalism*, where temporary, or 'one-off' actions, activities and responses imperceptibly develop into long term strategies, without citizens ever becoming aware of the active progress from A to B. Europe and most industrialised nations abound in structures where one-time temporary experiments and actions have later become the norm, without any open debate or consultative decision being taken. Gene experimentalisation, cloning, food additives and radiation and employee restrictions are but a few, and all are linked with the seventh principle of social justice.

• The eighth commandment of sustainability is *The Principle of Low Risk*. One aspect of this principle which is of particular interest is the precautionary principle which has at last been widely accepted (but narrowly adopted) in relation to the global warming debate. The precautionary principle itself, little loved by scientists, developers, genetic engineers and economists, emphasises that prevention is better than cure or damage limitation when contemplating uncertainties arising from some new development, or strategy. Policy planners need to make a thorough assessment and evaluation of all foreseeable risks and potential hazards before embarking on a particular form of investment or course of action whether in food additives, chemical fertilisers, energy-generating equipment or genetic experimentation. Risks can be economic, environmental, social or a hazard to wildlife, health or future generations. They might take the form of technical accidents and their side-effects which can take place at any level of human activity.

New risks might emerge where developments and innovations transgress time-honoured cultures and traditions and so incite hostile physical, biological or social reactions. In relation to long-term environmental assessments, risk categorisation is under constant review which, in itself, is sufficient incentive to adopt the precautionary principle. Although one cannot evaluate all possible risks in advance, a sound guideline before embarking on new projects, legislation, or investment is to ask whether the proposal is good for the individual? Is it beneficial for the community? Does it create useful employment? And, finally, does it appear safe for the environment? These criteria will also provide more sound and enduring indicators for decision making than risk assessments based on hazard and operational analyses alone.

• The ninth commandment is that of *Unity*. Unity is a prerequisite of any functional organisation, neighbourhood or society. Unfortunately it is a most difficult and intangible concept to grasp, save that it brings about peace, harmony, creativity, and a willingness to co-operate with others for the good of the whole. People are united by a variety of factors ranging from shared values, beliefs, a common culture or mutual interests. It is therefore more difficult to put this principle into practice in a large organisation than a smaller one. Greed, love of power and hope of personal gain will stand in the way and there needs to be a greater spiritual awareness by an enlightened leadership of those decisions and developments which will unite hearts and wills as opposed to those which divide. Unity is inclusive and respects the interests and cultures of others, whilst maintaining a commitment to justice and integrity at all levels. Unity recognises the need for diversity but aims at an overarching system which can bring the various opposing interests into harmony and into a working relationship.

It was this unity of the different interests and states of the various nations which lay behind the vision of Jean Monnet, Altiero Spinelli and Robert Schuman, when they worked together for a federal Europe. Unfortunately, the European Union in its present form has resulted partly from the all-pervasive commitment to economic growth which now overrides some of the other original ideals. Its structures are also partly due to the trend of incrementalism mentioned earlier. A deeper spirit of unity would doubtless be experienced if the various institutions and implements of the EU which currently cause division, could be reformed in the light of a vision which transcends economics. Within the norms of social justice and safeguarding employee rights, some accommodation of regional social conditions and mores must be sought. As Sir Richard Body, MP, so succinctly observed:

"The acid test of whether a problem needs a European solution rather than a national one is quite simply whether it crosses frontiers. Huge numbers of things that the Union now considers its province would be ruled out by that test. They are done in the name of uniformity and would certainly be returned to the member states or the regions if we recognised what is true in politics is true in ecology – namely, variety means health. Uniformity, when it is imposed artificially, means that something is going wrong."[1]

- This brings me to the tenth and last commandment for European sustainability – the *Principle of Replenishment*. The very concept of sustainability, in whatever sphere, recognises that communities cannot continue to live off their environmental capital and ignore their ever-inventive human resources in favour of increased production and technology alone. We *all* need to live off resource income rather than resource capital and in this the European Union and its global partner, the World Trade Organisation, must undergo a very fundamental change of values and ethics.

The principle of replenishment recognises that no society or development can continue according to linear progressions which lead in the long term to mismatches and dysfunction. One cannot continue with more of the same whether it is mining the earth of resources, filling the air with pollutants or the earth and seas with toxic wastes. People, ideas, institutions and systems also have to be replenished and renewed. Somewhere a balance must be struck to restore the natural equilibrium, which is generally cyclical rather than linear. The loop must be closed. Thus in agriculture the soil needs to be renourished and occasionally allowed to lie fallow in the time-honoured tradition. Exploitative agriculture may result in high yields in the short term but gradually impoverishes the structures and leads to diseases throughout the food chain. Petroleum-based agriculture undermines the health of soil, plant, animals and eventually humans.

Non-renewable fossil fuels, of course, cannot be replenished, so it is a matter of some urgency, for a wide variety of reasons, to replace their use with renewable energy forms which have the added advantage of

---

1. Body, Richard. *The Breakdown of Europe* (1998), New European Publication.

minimising pollution. This principle has the advantage of checking imbalances, correcting exploitation and greed and bringing systems back into harmony. In the human workplace systems replenishment can take the form of further educational and training courses; in communities, life education opportunities and time set aside for the arts and culture; for individuals replenishment may mean encouraging the development of skills for the benefit of the neighbourhood. Replenishment is an active willingness to stand back and evaluate what a particular course of action or development has gained from nature, society or the infrastructure of the community, and then to devise ways or means of giving something back. The principle of replenishment reinvigorates, renews and restores. It is the opposite of the 'something-for-nothing' mentality, as it seeks reciprocity.

Conclusion

If the inheritors of the historically rich European cultures, whether Greco-Roman or Judeo-Christian, are to survive the next millennium, they will need institutions and structures based once more on spiritual values, respect for the individual and timeless principles such as the ten outlined above. Ethics will need to replace market forces and the freeing up of local economies will need to replace free trade which merely benefits the rich at the expense of the poor. With unemployment figures in the European Union well in excess of 20 million at the turn of the century, more just and fair methods of production, distribution and job creation must be found, so that human resources can once again be given true value.

Religious institutions on which our common European heritage has been based, have failed lamentably to take a lead in, or to inspire environmental stewardship. They too have subscribed to the mantra of capitalism and 'homo economicus' as was so eloquently outlined by R. H. Tawney in his *Religion and the Rise of Capitalism*.[1] During the twentieth century the technosphere has now finally triumphed over the biosphere and Mammon has flourished.

If one accepts the fact that a 'United States of Europe' as envisaged by Churchill and the others, has not been achieved by the European Union in its present form, and that because of its size and complexity of interests it is not functioning as a unit, there is need to find new ways to revive the concept. The Council of Europe, which itself was established to strengthen democratic structures at the local level and to safeguard individual and community justice, could be suitably adapted. If the European Union were ever to pursue a coherent policy of regionalisation – encouraging and

---

1. Tawney, R. H., *Religion and the Rise of Capitalism*, (1926) Penguin Books.

enabling, as far as possible, local sustainability in the production of energy, food, goods and services, many of the social and environmental problems which currently face member states would be gradually reduced. At the same time the quality of life could be greatly enhanced since a less complicated infrastructure would be required and there would be more local accountability. This, in turn, would act as a brake on financial, fiscal and environmental misdemeanours.

There is also now need to re-evaluate our economic priorities with regard to the once-estranged members of our family from Middle and Eastern Europe in the hope that they can develop along less perilous and more permanent lines, and to secure the future of our common European home for succeeding generations. These prospective new members are from the same common European heritage and their participation in a united Europe must be a radically new one of sharing and co-operation, whilst respecting the individuality and differences of each. Nor should monetary union and 'harmonisation' be a necessary prerequisite for their membership of a federal Europe. By working with sound principles we can still inspire policies of permanence and re-establish the European values of democracy, culture, peace, social justice and respect for the rights of the individual.

So, to return from the ten commandments or principles of sustainability to our first question: How might this change of direction come about and which European institution could direct such a profound policy shift? The Council of Europe would seem the most suitable body to undertake an opportunity for development. Since its inception the Council has continued to champion basic moral and ethical values such as democracy, human rights and the interests of the regions. It is perhaps the only non-religious institution capable of undertaking this mammoth task. For this reason alone its scope will have to be widened, and that of the European Union checked, in order for a sustainable Europe to survive and give leadership to future generations. Its cultural and material heritage demands no less in a world of diminishing diversification and non-renewable resources. Only those more spiritual non-quantifiable attributes of service, self restraint and communal generosity will survive the limitation of Europe's present economic, social and military institutions which are all on the wane.

The Council of Europe could act as the guiding conscience of Europe as was originally intended. By adopting the ten principles as a development of the foundations already laid, championing the rights of the poor, the oppressed, the environment and the traditional values of local cultures and communities, there could be a new start. The Council could also with generosity and humility guide those new members from the former Eastern bloc into a fuller, more participatory collaboration. It could from experience and practice give ethical counsel on a very wide range of topics which fall within its remit but outside the scope to the market place. The Council, together with its consultative NGOs, must now update its structures, reform its institutions and reassert itself as the voice of European unity and integrity. There will be the inevitable opposition from vested interests. To quote Fritz Schumacher, in his essay "Message from the Universe":

> "Let us hope that wiser counsel will prevail; that we learn to subject the logic of production and productivity to the higher logic of real human needs and aspirations; that we rediscover the proper scale of things, their proper simplicity, their proper place and function in a world which extends infinitely beyond the purely material; that we learn to apply the principles of non-violence not only to the relationships between people but also to those between people and living nature."[1]

What better time to begin this new renaissance and reformation than in a jubilee year at the birth of the new millennium in the year of Our Lord 2000 AD? It is to be hoped that the success of the original visionaries of the Council of Europe will find renewed resonance before it is too late.

---

1. Schumacher, E. F. "Message from the Universe", *This I Believe and other Essays*, Green Books, (1997) Dartington, Devon, UK.

15. EUROPEAN MUSLIMS AND EUROPEAN IDENTITY

Ziauddin Sardar

Ziauddin Sardar is a writer and cultural critic and editor of Futures, *the monthly journal of policy, planning and futures studies.*

Europe came to an awareness of itself in direct relationship to the Muslim world. Today, the Muslim world is testing the conscience of Europe. The greatest test is whether Europe can overcome a millennium of simplistic and constructed ignorance and deal with the diversity of problems afflicting the Muslim world according to Europe's own best conception of itself. Kosovo and Iraq are the two most obvious, and entirely different, even diametrically opposite cases where Europe's ability to reason with the nature of Muslim existence is called into question. The Muslim world comprises one fifth of humanity; around the globe Muslims are embroiled in a series of diverse social, economic, political and human problems that test the quality and practice of European conscience. And Muslims are now the largest single minority within Europe. The operation of European conscience is no remote foreign policy concern, it is a test of whether Europe will be able to live in peaceful, constructive plurality at home every bit as much as abroad.

The trouble is, there is no starting afresh, no clean slate on which to forge a new relationship. History, for both Europe and the Muslim world, is significant, and a significant impediment. Substantively, the idea of Europe is nearly contemporaneous with the inception of Muslim civilisation. The idea of Europe as the physical location of Western Christendom, the heir to the Western unity of the Roman Empire, takes shape in confrontation with the early, rapid expansion of a developing Islamicate civilisation. The Battle of Tours, unfortunately, to which we could add the Crusades, the fall of Constantinople and Granada, the battle of Lepanto and the Siege of Vienna are not dead letters in either European or Muslim purview. The spirit of confrontation has marked all periods of interaction of Europe and the Muslim world up to and including the present. The genuine legacy of confrontation constructs a deformed relationship that obscures far more than it reveals. A millennium is far too long for the legacy of these conflicts to persist. But there is no point in trying to overcome them by pretending they do not exist.

Attaining a new mutual understanding as a basis for coexistence means transcending the realities of history. It is not appeals to history, but the ability to unmake the conventions of history that will determine whether Europe is ready to live in a pluralist world in the next millennium. The fate of the Muslim world, along with many others, depends on such a humane determination. This is not to suggest there is no need for rethinking on the Muslim side of this cohabitation equation, there is. Putting Europe first in the need to overcome the legacy of prejudice is an honest reflection of the dynamics of power in the world forged by European-born ideas of dominance.

In essence what is needed is a shift from the dynamic and ethos of power and dominance to the dynamic of principle, the best principles that inform and educate our conscience on the 'ought' and 'should' of resolving human problems. As a mutual process this requires a new ability to debate matters of principle, both European and Muslim. The prospect this opens is one of dialogue, a dialogue in which many areas of common ground will and can be found. Dialogue, conscientiously and courteously engaged in, will also disclose common problems, similar conundrums that are as resistant to simplistic resolution on both sides. While there can be no dialogue without acknowledging the problems constructed by shared history differently experienced and interpreted, the most necessary condition for the dynamic of principle is acquiring the ability to listen and learn across the divide of difference. Difference has to be seen as a source of constructive possibilities, not an unacceptable, irreducible force that can only breed division that ought to be got out of the system if at all possible. Creating genuinely pluralist societies requires making the leap to the true meaning of tolerance as a basis for free enjoyment of civic rights and responsibilities. True tolerance is accepting the validity and right to full expression, not merely of that with which one disagrees but of that which one finds objectionable even unacceptable. Tolerance is the legacy Europe would like to think has come out of its own horrendous religious wars. The European Muslim community tacitly finds the claim moot – in their experience there is still much work to be done to achieve real tolerance.

Secularisation is the complex historic process by which Europe sought to accommodate virulent religious difference within its own boundaries. But the ambit of those who could be included within this studied secular toleration was always limited. Jews could only apply for admission on the grounds of wholesale assimilation, often including conversion. Assimilated or not the fate of Europe's Jews in this century is known. In recent decades the emergence of secularism as a full blown ideology begs many questions for people in the West and is a serious area of contention. It is no secret that Muslims in Europe, especially in Britain and France, are also embroiled in these issues. Whether it is the Rushdie affair or the issue of *hijab* as it is being fought out in France, the experience of Muslims leads them to the conclusion that Europe is not ready to extend conscientious principles of equal toleration to them. It also leads European Muslims to conclude, along with many of their fellow European citizens, that there is a sharp and unresolved distinction between a process of secularisation and an ideology of secularism. Muslims are not the only ones who feel that the ideology of secularism so ascendant in Europe places real problems in the way of discussing matters of principle. In European terms these principles actually derive from conscientious religious ideas inadequately translated, and incapable of proper debate in secular terms. There are many issues of ethical and moral concern in science and society where only the language and concepts of a religious world-view provide the means to discuss human fears and determine what is acceptable and appropriate. Such issues do not only trouble the sensibilities and conscience of Christians, they are matters of common concern on which debate from different perspectives can be constructive for both Christians, Muslims and representatives of the many other faiths now present in Europe. To engage in dialogue that constructively empowers difference, however, requires a major effort on the part of Europeans. Europe is the seedbed and breeding ground of all of the West's idealised notions of universals. It is deeply attached to the notion that these universals are the only possible universal statements – once found they are binding on all. Alongside this universal determinism is the self-assurance that European scholarship, as objective impartial inquiry, puts them in possession of a clear understanding of what Muslims, and many others, believe, think and know. Both assertions are wrong, to put it baldly; or inadequate and partial ideas, to state the matter politely. Europe desperately needs to acquire the ability to let Muslims define themselves, their beliefs, ideas and aspirations in their own terms, freed from the confines of European interpretation of what is a Muslim definition of belief, ideas and aspirations. Both sides approach the definition of universals in their own distinctive fashion. A willingness to allow those distinctions to emerge as constructive parts of an on-going dialogue, rather than difficulties to be papered over as unfortunate, offers the best prospect of deriving genuine universal acceptance of common principles, rooted in and vigorously supported by distinct and different systems of belief and thought.

Turning away from the vast body of interpretation that convinces Europe it knows what Muslims believe, how they think and what are the essentials of their world view is the hardest task, and is properly placed first. Europe's ideas about Muslims and Islam have been fashioned and filtered through a millennium of opposition, trepidation and false characterisation. It leads Europe, which is so conscious of its own diversity, to consider Muslims and Islam as an ascribed monolith, a mass with no means for differentiation, diversity or dynamic interpretation. In keeping with history, today the Muslim is a stock character whose persona is fixed and given by Europe's misrepresentations of Islam. In our time the Muslim is the terrorist bent on mindless revenge and awful violence and the female held in enforced retreat behind her shrouds of *hijab*. With such characters dialogue seems fruitless. A closer look at the European Muslim community, living and shaping itself within the European Union, nearest at hand offers a swift antidote to this time-honoured body of ideas and interpretation. The European Muslim community is a new community wrestling with the complex problems of nationality and identity, essential problems posed to all Europeans in the debate about the future course of European Union. The European Muslim community is the very essence of heterogeneity. Muslim citizens in any one European country come from many different nations, speak different mother tongues, have significant cultural differences and diverse racial and ethnic origins. They are not one distinctive minority in any country, they are many minorities with one linking bond. The most powerful impulse making them into a community is the existence of general antipathy to Islam, which is often a stronger force for communal unity than their Islamic affiliation.

European involvement in flashpoints around the world, where the ubiquitous Muslim terrorist or Muslim bogey man has become the opponent, puts pressure on these minority communities, draws them together with a common sense there is no genuine acceptance of them as citizens of any European nation.

The heterogeneity of the European Muslim community also extends to their Islamic outlook. Coming from many backgrounds they represent many different schools of Islamic thought and diverse traditions of interpretation of Islam embedded in their mother cultures. Acquaintance with the reality of the European Muslim community is the best antidote to the idea of Islam as a monolith. A more realistic understanding of the authentic, inherent legitimate diversity of thought that is possible within an Islamic perspective has considerable implications for European policy options both at home and abroad. It is important to appreciate that this European-born Muslim community is better educated both in European and Islamic terms than any other Muslim community in the world.

By virtue of living in Europe, they have access to better education in the basics of their religion, better access to materials on Islamic thought, history and contemporary ideas than if their forebears had remained citizens of the Muslim world. Indeed, the Muslim diaspora in the West is often in the forefront of thinking, writing and articulating contemporary interpretation of Islam as a system of ideas for living. The Muslims of the West are influential in many of the great debates within the Muslim world. On the other hand, it is also true that as a defensive strategy many Muslim organisations in Europe seek to foster particular ideas of tradition that are conservative, reactionary and antithetical to Western culture. The entire diversity of Islam as belief, thought and practice is to be found within Europe. Closer acquaintance with European Muslims is perforce a matter of embracing multiplicity and heterogeneity in all its implications, and all on Europe's own doorstep.

Maintaining the conventions of history risks making the European Muslim minorities into a disaffected, dissatisfied community united by a common sense of being unjustly treated and misunderstood. The alternative possibility is for Europe to cease thinking of Muslims as a uniform entity and begin accepting the diversity Muslims understand and recognise about themselves. Acceptance of this heterogeneous community and openness to its internal debates wrestling with very real and valid questions about nationality and identity can be a constructive encounter with plurality, the very plurality Europe itself needs if it is to develop as a genuine union of nations and peoples.

The European Union, for all that it harks back to the original universalist idea of Europe, is perplexed by its own convoluted questions of nationality and identity. What it is to be European is a question that must be asked by citizens of fifteen nations, who must come to a new relationship with their own history. Muslims, grounded in Islamic ideas of supranational identity, each individual being a citizen of a worldwide *ummah*, a community of believers, must also wrestle with the meaning of modern nationalism. Within modern nations in both Europe and the Muslim world there is a variety of affiliations – religious, ethnic, linguistic – that add complexity to the question of identity in the context of the nation-state. It would be instructive for Europeans to explore the historic answers developed in Islamic political thought on the questions of nationality and civic rights. In Islamic thought a strong sense of universalism was combined with very weak and very different concepts of nation as an operative unit of polity. This was blended with a strong universal and undifferentiated sense of civic rights that included from the outset the extension of these rights across a heterogeneous population. The performance of the Islamicate model in history is by no means perfect, but it is a long history of practical experience with plurality generated out of the complex issues of nationality and identity. When it comes to making sense of history and contemporary experience the European Muslim community has much to contribute to the 'European' question. The idea of European union has given new impetus to nationalisms, whether it be Mrs Thatcher's 'Little England' mentality or the politics of Jean-Marie Le Pen in France. Nationalism as a European concept forms a fault line along the meeting of the tectonic plates of the contending ideas, the other plate being the idea of Europe as a pan-national community originating from a shared culture which is grounded in the unity and ideology of Christendom. Both are authentic parts of European history, they pull in contradictory directions and alternate as centripetal and centrifugal forces in the history of ideas and politics in Europe.

It is appropriate that nationalism should be a vexing problem for Europe. It is Europe that defined and bequeathed to the world the concept of the modern nation-state, one of the most brutal, fatal and dehumanising legacies of colonialism for the non-Western world. The concept has been no less fraught with blood for Europe. Contending nationalisms are the history of Europe. The nation as a totalitarian concept, the supreme identity, is the legacy of the French Revolution gone rabid. Romantic nationalism, the idea of a people and their cultural/folk identity as a natural basis for a nation was the reactive antidote to revolutionary thought that turned just as rabid. The roots of Nazi National Socialism and its racism are derived from romantic nationalism, as are the conundrums of the Balkans now and in history.

The nation as one people, one language, one identity with an innate right to exist is a potent idea that is seemingly accepted as a universal principle. It derives from European ideas, yet it is actually and historically untrue of the composition of virtually all European nations as well as virtually all nations around the globe. The nation-state is simply a mess, socially, culturally, and most of all politically. Unpicking this unholy mess is a problem Europe shares with the rest of the world. Incidentally, it is unholy because there is no religious philosophy that specifically warrants the concept of the modern nation-state, centuries of God on our side notwithstanding. The 'One Nation under God' across the Atlantic pond could only resolve this inherited problem of European ideas by strict separation of Church and state, a matter that is still causing them considerable difficulties.

The modern nation-state does not answer important questions of identity, either in Europe or elsewhere in the world for all its citizens. Identity is a more basic ingredient that has been overwritten, displaced and marginalised as well as brutalised into submission by nation-states and their simplistic nationalism. The establishment of the European Union has revitalised older, still extant identities within Europe. Unfortunately, the supremacy of the set of ideas associated with nationalism and the nation-state make the politics of identity a mixed blessing. Marginal identities grasp the ideology of becoming a nation-state in their own right as the only option because the idea of the polyglot, heterogeneous state has no valid place in the repertoire of modernity. It has been the work of centuries in Europe to build up the commonality of a single, singular national identity, backed by imagery, ritual and ceremonial support. Establishing such uniformity on a secular basis that includes different religious persuasions is the origin of all the concepts of civil rights in Europe. But that state operates and delivers these civic rights only on the basis of an undifferentiated nation as a whole, denying autonomy and self determination to minority identities.

The politics of identity has acquired the odium of being aggressive, destructive and fragmentary, the end of civilisation as we know it. This reputation persists, notwithstanding the acceptance that national policy often produces real civil injustice in the treatment of minorities. This argument has been fought out within Europe, among the Basques, in Ireland, as much as it constitutes the crisis of Kosovo and afflicts country after country whose national borders have been created by colonialism around the world.

Looked at more closely, the European Union is its own answer to its own problem. The operation of the Union has empowered and enriched regionalism, and thereby revitalised marginal identities. The strong and well-funded regional policies have enabled Europe to uncover its older complexity. Both Welsh and Scots nationalists, for example, have eagerly embraced European Union. As political parties they have been disproportionately represented in Europe. Access to European regional funds has been constructively and creatively used to give new vibrancy to the cultural life of their erstwhile marginal identity, as well as their battered and impoverished economies. It can be argued that the British politics of devolution could only have happened within the context of Europe.

To develop further according to its own principles of democratic accountability the European Union will have to find answers to the conundrums in the nexus of nationality and identity. The answers all lie in the direction of setting identity free from the single vessel of the nation-state, accepting the celebration of identity that is not a necessary part of nationality nor the sole definition for membership and rights within a nation-state or supranational federation of states. It is here that the emerging European Muslim community, as well as the older marginal identities of European minorities, can play a vital role as constructive participants in defining and refining the possibilities.

The future for a genuine European Union requires the construction of a consensual understanding of heterogeneity, a consensus that respects and accepts multiple identities. If the European Union can embrace plurality at home it will develop a new potential to appreciate the complexity of problems elsewhere. Operating on its own conventions has given European governments an unenviable record in their acts of commission and omission in trouble spots around the world. The former Yugoslavia is an obvious example. Throughout the long agony of Bosnia the lines of contention were seen as competing nationalisms defined along religious lines. Europe proved itself incapable of hearing what the Bosnians repeatedly insisted they were standing up for – a plural, not a Muslim state, that was true to their history in the face of a militant, totalitarian and ethnically dominated Serbian nationalism. The NATO solution was to separate out different identities and deny plurality, a tacit victory for Serbian nationalism. The enforced resolution in Bosnia also ensures that the problems of nationality and identity will be a continual source of problems for generations to come. The imposed singular identities will be active ingredients in political competition for national control and access to limited resources. In Kosovo it is the rights unfailingly ascribed to nations that impede support of what are supposed to be universally accepted human rights. Once again Serbian nationalism is able to manipulate the *problématique* of European ideas while it denies legitimate human rights and self-expression to the diverse community of ethnic Albanians. There is a bankruptcy of ideas in the West when it comes to finding humane resolution to the problems of the Balkans. Western intervention, hidebound by its bankruptcy of ideas, solidifies the problems by forcing everyone to adopt the untenable lines of simplistic nationalism so familiar to Western ideas. Alternative principles, principles that have been part of Balkan existence for centuries and which might offer an indigenous basis for sorting out their own problems find no support among Western power-brokers. Just as elsewhere in the world, the dynamic of power and its repertoire of ideas that derive from the history of Europe and the West end up giving most support to the unconscionable and unprincipled, in spite of the best ideals of Europeans.

In instance after instance around the world European Muslims see European governments support the *real politik* of power and nationalism despite the grievous shortcomings or outright abusiveness of regimes in power. Saddam Hussein is the most notable, but by no means the only, example of this procedure. Popular aspiration for reform in many parts of the world embraces the legitimisation of Islamic ideals of justice and equity. Unfailingly this language of hope among the hopeless is seen as an inherent threat and opposed by the power and dominance of the West. In response, allegiance to spearhead movements of popular discontent comes to embrace more and more hardline, reactionary and obscurantist Islamic ideologies whose militancy is directed towards becoming a mirror image of the power and dominance dynamic of the West. What is ground out of the system by this pincer movement of action and reaction is genuine opportunity for humane answers. So long as power is more important than principle, forging the contemporary meaning and operation of conscientious principle is not an option and gross abuse and neglect of basic human rights and needs remain the lot of millions of people around the world.

How does this unending cycle of backing the wrong options for the wrong reasons come to an end? There is no simple answer but there are many difficult possibilities. As Europe moves to define itself in new terms it has the potential to learn a new openness to alternative options in the sphere of politics and social reform that have traditional and popular support in other parts of the world. If Europe genuinely opens itself to welcome and encourage the development of a distinctive Muslim community within its own boundaries it can find that principled dialogue at home uncovers new possibilities for understanding. What dialogue makes visible and possible within Europe builds the possibility of taking more informed and more principled positions on trouble spots abroad. A distinctive European Muslim community is not only concerned with issues of nationality and identity in the sense of: "Are they Muslims before they are British or French or European?" – whatever that last component may imply. What this new, well-educated community must wrestle with is what it means to have a fully operative Islamic identity in the context of European nationality and identity in the twenty-first century. Openness to the debates within the European Muslim community would reveal a lively and questioning attitude to many issues that have a common resonance for all Europeans. Islam has a rich repertoire of concepts such as *adl* (justice) *istislah* (social interest or welfare) or *khalifah* (stewardship of common resources). This inheritance leads many European Muslims to believe that they can participate in common cause in the context of European politics and social action from the standpoint of their Islamic identity.

There are European Muslims who see this as the humane and principled plural alternative, an alternative that leaps beyond old ideas of assimilation and contemporary virulent secularism. In fact it is a reversal of the old equation: difference of religious identity becomes the spur to finding common ground, common cause and commitment to act in concert with fellow citizens of different backgrounds and persuasions.

It may come as a shock to Europeans to realise that Islam insists on, encourages and validates an open, tolerant plural approach to politics and the creation of community. It may also be something of a revelation that Islam has its own tradition of ideas on human and civic rights, obligations and responsibilities, environmental duties and obligations and just as many vexing ethical dilemmas in the field of science and medicine as concern Europeans in general. It is axiomatic for European Muslims that these Islamic principles have not been seen in action in Muslim nations for centuries, but that does not make them irrelevant. There are European Muslims who see the best expressions of conscientious principle developed in the West as Islamic, that which is good, humane and promotes human welfare has every right to be claimed as Islamic wherever, and by whomsoever, it has been devised. It will be an acid test of openness and plural possibilities if Europeans could come to the conclusion there just might be good, humane ideas within the fabric of Islamic thought that they too could utilise. If both parties can see human welfare and human betterment as a common objective good ideas and sound principles can be adopted wherever they originate. It is not the brand name but the quality, applicability and appropriateness of the solution, its ability to bring about human betterment, that should be our aim. In other words we should not assume we have already discovered the last word on universals leaving only a battle of wills, a bid for dominance to decide whose universals get to be adopted. Europeans can do better than that – Catholic, Protestant, Muslim, Jewish, Hindu, Buddhist and secularist alike.

A European Muslim by definition is a person with multiple affiliations that contribute to their identity. European Muslims are concerned citizens of the European nations of their birth, to whom they owe allegiance. It should be accepted that their concerns begin and revolve around how to contribute to the welfare and betterment of their country and society as a whole, and not merely to define enclaves in which they can exist as Muslims, a breed apart from their fellow countrymen and women. European Muslims can be constructive and positive agents in making a plural society a reality in Europe. In which case European Muslims can help Europe to be a more constructive force in resolving the human problems of poverty, oppression and conflict around the world. Globalisation, the buzz word for the twenty-first century, can only be controlled, ordered and made conducive to uplifting the human condition equitably around the world if we can place pluralism at the centre of our thinking. Globalisation that is not based on universalism through diversity would be the next totalitarian system. Untempered and unbalanced by commitment to pluralism, globalisation would carry many of the most virulent and bloody conflicts of the twentieth-century into the next millennium. As globalisation is now constituted and operated, the European Union is as prone to being swamped and overwritten as any other identity. The dynamics of power and dominance are incapable of creating a humane, plural global order. We have to look to the dialogue of principle to secure our human future, whoever we are, whatever our particular set of multiple affiliations in the Europe of tomorrow.

Part IV – Epilogue and appendices

Epilogue

John Coleman

One clear conclusion emerges from most of the contributors in this book. It is that somehow, at some point in the development of post-war Europe, we lost our way. The high expectations so vividly expressed by Cosmo Russell and summed up in the words of Edmund Burke who spoke at the outset of the French Revolution, evaporated almost as rapidly. The dark clouds of the violence evoked by the former and Cold War of the latter writer left little room for hope.

George Bull traces Europe's problem back to the Messina Conference and feels that the mistake was to create an economic community. He speaks of our shared European home as existing since the fifth-century BC and of the gathering of culture that has happened since then. And yet, he points out, we have turned our backs on all that and tried to create an economic entity based on a very shallow materialism. It might be said that we have looked at the leaves on the tree that wither and die every year instead of considering the roots that persist through the centuries underground.

Sir Peter Smithers traces the lack of 'active idealism' back to the post-war period in which he himself was involved with the Council of Europe and, in particular, to Anthony Eden's lack of interest in European affairs. Churchill, of course, showed a great deal of interest in European affairs immediately after the war but fundamentally he wanted mainland Europe to create a kind of European United States, while he worked to shape the new Commonwealth out of the old British Empire. Sir John Biggs-Davison who worked closely with Churchill at the time believed that each would be creating its own structures and in due course they would be linked rather like the parts of a space station being linked up in space.

There is a consistency in Churchill's view which goes back to the early 1930s. Churchill wanted to bring the Soviet Union in with Britain and France to check the development of Nazi Germany. In Parliament he expressed the hope that Russia would join Britain and France as "a Soviet Socialist state strongly armed to maintain its national independence and absolutely divorced from any idea of spreading its doctrines abroad otherwise than by example". After the war there was a clear divergence between Churchill's view and that of the Americans. The American view was clearly expressed by Noam Chomsky:

> "The general framework of thinking within which American foreign policy has evolved since the Second World War is best described in the

planning documents produced during that war by the State Department planners and the Council for Foreign Relations who met for a six-year period in the War and Peace Studies Programme, 1939-45. They knew, certainly, by 1941-2 that the war was going to end with the United States in a position of enormous global dominance. The question arose: 'How do we organise the world?' They drew up a concept known as Grand Area Planning, where the Grand Area is defined as the area which, in their terms, was 'strategically necessary for world control'."

After the war President Truman brought that thinking to practical fruition in his famous speech of 1947, the core of which has come to be known as the Truman Doctrine. The essence of it is contained in that speech :

"There is one thing that the Americans value more than peace. It is freedom. Freedom of worship, freedom of speech and freedom of enterprise. The pattern of international trade which is most conducive to freedom of enterprise is one in which the major decisions are not made by governments but by private buyers and sellers.... that pattern of trade which is least conducive to freedom of enterprise is one in which decisions are made by governments. That was the pattern of former centuries. Unless we act and act decisively it will be the pattern of the next century."

Truman made it plain that this was America's aim. Europe was rebuilt with Marshall Aid. Commercial economic power became the basis for European integration. Professor Swann, one of the leading authorities on the economic history of the European Economic Community, stresses this point:

"The latter [the US] had in mind that the aid it was to give should be linked with progress towards unification. This is a particularly important point since it indicates that from the very beginning the European Movement has enjoyed the encouragement of the US."[1]

A knowledge of this background makes it much easier to understand why the hope that prevailed at the end of the war faded and why the Council of Europe became the Cinderella of European institutions and why a Europe based on a firm commercial foundation flourished and expanded – and indeed why Harold Wilson once commented that the Treaty of Rome was a Magna Carta for the multinationals of Western Europe.

It is being widely realised that the result of following the Truman Doctrine is a world run by the big corporations. David Korton makes this argument this powerfully in his book *When Corporations Rule the World*.[2] I once

---
1. Swann, Dennis, *Economics of the Common Market*, (1970) Penguin Books.
2. Korton, David, *When Corporations Rule the World*, (1988) Kumarian Press.

heard him challenged by a woman who said, "These corporations are only collections of people", and in response he said, "No, they are collections of legal documents." A recent article by David Rockefeller in *Newsweek* (1 February 1999) "New Rules of the Game: Looking for New Leadership" indicates the point at which we have arrived. In it he wrote:

> "In recent years, there's been a trend towards democracy and market economies. That has lessened the role of government, which is something business people tend to be in favour of. But the other side of the coin is that somebody has to take government's place, and business seems to me to be a logical entity to do it."

It is one thing for governments to put a lot of unnecessary restrictions on trade, which is surely undesirable, but it is something else, and highly questionable, if commercial interests – which if separated from other interests used once to be called 'vested interests' – become so powerful that they can decide what governments are able to do, become in effect the government. This kind of thinking certainly does not represent the outlook of the Founding Fathers of America. Quite the reverse. Lincoln thought government should be of the people, by the people, for the people. Surely if he'd meant of the traders, by the traders, for the traders, he would have said so.

To understand a little more about the European dilemma – and clearly it is the American dilemma also – it is necessary to look a little more deeply into the background of the American situation. In 1869 the Victorian historian, James Anthony Froude, was giving his inaugural lecture as Rector of St Andrew's University in Scotland. It was on education. He said:

> "An eminent American was once talking to me of the school system in the United States. The boast and glory of it, in his mind, was that every citizen born had a fair and equal start in life. Every one of them knew that he had a chance of becoming President of the Republic, and was spurred to energy by this hope. Here too, you see, is a distinct object. Young Americans are all educated alike. The aim put before them is to get on. They are like runners in a race, set to push and shoulder for the best places; never to rest contented, but to struggle forward in never-ending competition. It has answered its purpose in a new and unsettled country, where the centre of gravity has not yet determined its place; but I cannot think that such a system as this can ever be permanent, or that human society, constituted on such a principle, will ultimately be found tolerable."

That is perhaps America's misfortune: that it has global power but it is still constituted on that same principle. It is trying to cope with world power when it perhaps needs to be grappling with its own brilliant adolescence. For all their faults, Britain and the other European nations have a social stability which puts the spirit of competition more into its place. The Truman

Doctrine is surely an example of carrying on with that spirit long after it has served "its purpose in a new and unsettled country".

A personal anecdote may not be out of place here. Thirty years ago I was driving across Argentina and I stopped by the roadside near to a group of lorries. One of the drivers came up to me and asked if I was North American. I said, no, I was British. "Oh," he replied, "We used to hate you but now we hate the North Americans." I thought at the time that that was the penalty for having world power.

It seems to me that on both sides of the Atlantic we need to be looking much more deeply into our own roots and traditions. Americans might be looking at the thoughts and ideals of their country's Founding Fathers. We in Europe should be looking into the culture that has shaped our continent since the fifth century BC. Before doing that, however, one more glance into the future – if the route suggested by David Rockefeller is taken – it is now made possible by Stephen Vines, author of *Hong Kong: China's New Colony*. Writing in *The Independent* (19 January 1998) he poses the question whether businessmen really are the best people to run governments:

> "If only governments were run by successful businessmen, wouldn't that make them work far better? It's an interesting idea but one which could be quickly dispelled by a trip to Hong Kong which nowadays is run by a former shipping tycoon.
>
> Those wishing to make the trip seated in the first-class compartment of an airline had better wait until the end of the week because from today many of the seats will be taken up by a gaggle of tycoons travelling at the Hong Kong taxpayer's expenses to the first meeting of the Chief Executive's council of advisers (note that business-minded Hong Kong calls its head of government the Chief Executive).
>
> Jetting in for the meeting are such luminaries as the media tycoon Rupert Murdoch, Karl-Hermann Baumann, the chairman of the German conglomerate Siemens, Cor Boonstra, the head of Royal Phillips Electronics in the Netherlands, Maurice Greenberg, the boss of the insurance giant the American International Group and Shoichiro Toyoda, the veteran chairman of Japan's Toyota Motor Corp.
>
> Yes, there is no doubt that the Chief Executive, Tung Chee-hwa, who was formerly the head of the Orient Overseas shipping line, has gathered some of the biggest names in the global business community to advise him.
>
> They are arriving a week after Mr Tung completed a round of meetings with groups of legislators. Without exception all those elected by a process of universal suffrage, a minority in Hong Kong's exquisitely rigged system, emerged from their meetings saying that Mr Tung had no intention of listening to them."

Epilogue

The Western world must certainly confuse those with a different frame of mind and different assumptions about life, whom it confronts. Ziauddin Sardar shakes us. He forces us to see that there are others who see things through different eyes. He is gentle, however, in comparison with an account of the situation described in the *Admiralty and Horse Guards Gazette* (the official journal of the British Army and Navy) of 1902 at the time of the Boxer revolt in China. My grandfather was editor and wrote the piece himself:

> "The terrible rumours from Pekin are now only too fearfully confirmed. There is practically no doubt now that every European man, woman, and child has been put to the sword.
>
> Righteous as is the indignation which is universally expressed about this frightful business, it is nevertheless imperatively necessary to keep cool heads. Rabid articles of the type published by the *Globe* and similar absurd papers, crying aloud for Pekin to be given over to massacre and burned with fire, are simply fanning the devouring flame of Chinese national feeling, and are calculated to make the Chinese at large make common cause with the ferocious anti-foreign sentiments of the Boxers and their followers. Many thousand Europeans are yet in China, and it is deplorable that their lives should be put in jeopardy by hole-and-corner scribes, who, writing for a vile wage, only think of cadging to the unreasoning indignation of the mob. The always sane *Westminster Gazette* points out that there is no possibility of collecting a force which will be able to scatter itself over China or pursue the Boxers into the interior, and to attempt any such thing would be to court disaster. All China, I might add, is aflame with revolt against the hated 'foreign devil'. The assertion is a sweeping one, but it is justified by the reports which come from various parts – North, South, and East.
>
> The fearful massacre throws a terrible light upon statements made by a 'Boxer' in London in an interview of which an account appeared in the *Daily Express* so long since as June 13th.
>
> His words, in view of what has since taken place, were really prophetic:
>
> 'You bring us' said this Chinaman in effect, 'inventions which we do not want, a religion which you yourselves are divided upon, and these things, in defiance of protest, you force upon us. You even seize our harbours and towns.
>
> Against all this we protest.
>
> And now, having carefully considered the matter, we, of the so-called Boxers' Society, have decided that the only way to get rid of you is to kill you. We are not naturally bloodthirsty. We certainly are not thieves. But when persuasion and argument and appeals to your sense of justice are of no avail, we find ourselves face to face with the fact that the only resource is to put you out of existence.

Consider your missionaries. They come, as I have said, with a new religion, upon the main principles of which they are literally divided amongst themselves. They tell us that unless we accept their doctrines we shall suffer eternal punishment. They frighten our children and the more weak-minded of our older people, and create all kinds of dissension between families and individuals. No wonder that we will not tolerate them.

If we wanted your railways and machines, we could, of course, buy them; but we do not. We have no use for them; we have learned to do without them. Yet you say you will force us to buy them, whether we will or no. Is that just? I say it is impertinence – an outrage.

We could if we chose overwhelm the rest of mankind. That we do not do so is due to the perfection of our civilisation, our philosophy, and our morals. We number 400 000 000 human beings, and who could withstand us if we chose to assert our power? Do you think we are unconscious of it? On the contrary, we understand it only too well. Let the white races of the earth appreciate the fact that we and not they are its masters.

Let us alone and we will let you alone.' "

This, with Sardar's contribution, reminds us that the two areas in the world which are likely to be stirred up and inflamed are China and the Muslim world unless the greatest understanding is exercised on all sides. It is tempting to judge others by our own standards of human rights. To a Muslim who sees us bombing other Islamic countries it may well appear that we are condemning him for minor crimes. He might well think that we see the mote in his eye but fail to notice the beam in our own. Many Muslims must feel that while Christians call Christ the son of God and Divine in fact they, Christians, seem to their eyes to take very little notice of this teaching. Indeed, they may feel that they themselves pay far more attention to his words although they regard him simply as a prophet.

There must indeed be a list of things that strike Muslims as a bit odd, to say the least. Christ's injunction that his followers should give up their worldly goods in favour of treasures in Heaven must seem more honoured in the breach than in the observance. The Christian saints of the early Church would have appeared convincing. Ambrose and Augustine have already been mentioned. How much greater the understanding between Christian and Muslim might be if when those of other faiths than ours visited our cities they saw them organised as Sienna once was or if they came across societies of people "living lightly" as Walter and Dorothy Swartz describe in their book of that title.

Froude speaks of England's past in contrast to what was then her Victorian present:

"In those past generations, when the English character was moulding itself, there was a virtue specially recognised among us called content. We were a people who lived much by custom. As the father lived, the son lived; he was proud of maintaining the traditions and habits of his family, and he remained in the same position of life without aspiring to rise from it. The same family continued in the same farm, neither adding to its acres or diminishing them. Shop, factory, and warehouse were handed down with the same stationary character, yielding constant but moderate profits, to which the habits of life were adjusted. Satisfied with the share of this world's good which his situation in life assigned to him, the tradesman aspired no higher, endeavouring only in the words of the antiquated catechism, 'to do his duty in that state of life to which it had pleased God to call him'. 'Throughout the country there was an ordered, moderate, and temperate contentedness, energetic – but energetic more in doing well the work that was to be done, than in 'bettering' this or that person's condition in life. Something of this lingers yet among old-fashioned people in holes and corners of England; but it is alien both to the principles and the temper of the new era. To push on, to climb vigorously on the slippery steps of the social ladder, to raise ourselves one step or more out of the rank of life in which we were born, is now converted into a duty. It is the condition under which each of us plays his proper part as a factor in the general progress. The more commercial prosperity increases, the more universal such a habit of mind becomes. It is the first element of success in the course to which the country seems to be committing itself. There must be no rest, no standing still, no pausing to take breath. The stability of such a system depends, like the boy's top, on the rapidity of its speed. To stop is to fall; to slacken speed is to be overtaken by our rivals. We are whirled along in the breathless race of competition. The motion becomes faster and faster, and the man must be unlike anything which the experience of humanity gives us a right to hope for, who can either retain his conscience, or any one of the nobler qualities, in so wild a career."

How different the response of other faiths would be if they met the Christians of those past generations. As it is they meet that which was first whipped up in Victorian England and was carried on even faster in the United States of America. How hard it must be for the naturally slower, more contented people in 'holes and corners' of the world to understand what is happening. It is not surprising that they turn to fundamentalism. My thoughts on this were vastly reinforced as I read David Selbourne's *Our Moral Evasion*.

There is another evil on our side which I believe we pride ourselves on being rather free from, and that is intolerance. People with deep convictions can fall, and all through Christian history have fallen into that trap. St

Augustine was as fundamentalist a Christian as it was possible to be and yet he could pose himself the question of whether Plato was a Christian. He also believed in laying up his treasures in the other world. In Augustine's belief God could work outside time and space. He could choose whom he would save. Augustine was humble enough to recognise this and yet through the centuries Christians – Jews and Muslims as well probably – have passed harsh judgements on other faiths. It is simply a refusal to believe that the essence of truth can only be revealed through the outward form of one particular faith which is not the same as the easy notion that all religions are equal.

At the very heart of Ziauddin Sardar's contribution is the crucial point:

> "Muslims are not the only ones who feel that the ideology of secularism so ascendant in Europe places real problems in the way of discussing matters of principle."

To many, Christian behaviour in history must have seemed like that of wolves in sheep's clothing. Secularism may soften the effect. Rather than discuss it I prefer to give a concrete example from personal experience. In 1993 I joined a parliamentary visit to Armenia led by Lord Shannon, which included a three-day visit to Nagorno Karabakh. There was a shaky cease-fire at the time which fortunately has held. For diplomatic reasons ambassadors could not visit the war zone so they were particularly anxious to talk to our group. I recall rather vividly the Iranian ambassador, who had been rather quiet and unforthcoming, suddenly coming to life when Sir Trevor Skeat, the Conservative MP, who was with us, spoke of some matter of principle to do with relations with Armenia. "Do you put that before your trading interests?" he asked. "Of course," was the reply. Immediately the ambassador spoke with great enthusiasm saying that both religions were religions of peace and if we are true to them we cannot fight each other. Interestingly Armenia was the first country in the world to become Christian and it remains so. There is no secularism there. Their faith is woven into the life of the country. This is especially significant because when Turkey and Azerbaijan imposed a blockade on Armenia it was the Iranians who opened their borders to send in vital supplies. This surely has something to do with the mutual respect that exists between the two religious peoples of the region.

This exemplifies Sardar's point about secularism and gives special poignancy to the contribution from the Head of the Armenian Church. Although not mentioning the Council of Europe it is clear that he intends to describe the ingredients for true European unity.

Muslims would see in Diana Schumacher's remarkable contribution a 'check list' which many of them would understand perfectly and believe by implication they could find in their own religion. The world today does require a new set of environmental commandments not so much to add to, or alter the ancient Commandments but to cope with a global situation of industrialisation and mass production that previous centuries never had to face. The whirl of competition and all those things it has spawned – the arms races, the corruption, the deceptions of advertising which goes far beyond informing – threatens our world in no less deadly a fashion than weapons of mass destruction. There may well be much more to be said on the subject of this book. It is an almost infinite theme. In the 1970s Marion Boyars, the publisher, brought out a series of books called *Ideas in Progress*. The aim was to add the responses of readers of the first editions to succeeding editions. I hope the same may be possible with this book. I would like to think, in Churchill's words that: "This is not the end but possibly the end of the beginning", the beginning of a new era in the construction of Europe in which conscience plays the leading role. "Healthy federations," said Froude, "must grow. The only stable bond of union is mutual goodwill!"

Expediency may have made it necessary to concoct some kind of union to cope with the disastrous effects of the two murderous wars of the twentieth century. Conscience and reflection must rectify that structure and transform it into something infinitely better for the twenty-first century. It will not be enough to be merely democratic. We must revert to those principles which occasionally gave examples of stability in human society in the past. The Council of Europe seems to me to be the one institution in the very complex European structure of today through which people of conscience can work to apply the necessary guiding principles for our 'common European home'. It is one of the illusions of the modern world that peace and prosperity necessarily go together. There can be little doubt that severe deprivation can cause conflict and war. People will fight over the necessities of life. What is not so clear is that they will stop fighting when they get what, from the point of view of deprivation, is considered enough. On the contrary, unless some self-regulating force comes into play expectations know no bounds and consumerism doesn't reach a point at which it stops. Here is where stoic and puritan play a valuable role. There is a danger in looking back to an idealised epoch but the truth is that history is cyclical. Civilisation goes up and down. Trade is a necessity but yet it can lead to our modern consumerism and destruction of the very world in which we exist. At best humanity struggles up a difficult and rocky path and needs the favour of Providence if it is not to slip over to the left or the right.

A. Europe's spiritual guidelines

Cardinal Franz König

Cardinal Franz König was formerly the Archbishop of Vienna.

In 1976 on the occasion of the award of the European Prize, the Belgian statesman Tindemans stated that Europe had for four hundred years spoken for all mankind, but was now silent. Tindemans made his point one year after the close of the Helsinki Conference on Security and Co-operation in Europe. The Helsinki Acts have been signed by European states from both West and East of the Continent.

The silent Europe of today is divided into an Eastern bloc and a Western bloc. The Europe which for centuries spoke to the whole world stretched from the Atlantic to the Urals. Presumably the Russian head of the government had this in mind when he spoke of a "common house of Europe" on the occasion a short time ago, of the visit to Moscow of the West German President.

Without being arrogant, we can even today declare that no single continent or region of the Earth has contributed more to the development of today's world, or has had such influence, as Europe: through its ideas, its systems of philosophical enquiry, its science and technology, inventions and research, its Christian faith but also through its atheism, its idealism and its materialism. The colonial empires were all formed in the European mould.

We should also draw attention to those values which, arising from its Christian heritage, were carried by Europe beyond its frontiers. I am thinking of its love for the family, respect for life, recognition of the value of work, spirit of enterprise, as well as its struggle for tolerance and its efforts to achieve co-operation and peace. This is all the more apparent when we consider the Christian roots of Europe: for neither Christianity itself nor any of the other great world religions have their beginnings in Europe. For those, we have to look at Asia and the Indian subcontinent, for it is there that not only Buddhism, Hinduism, Shintoism, the Jewish and Islamic religions, but also Christianity began. Laotse and Confucius had their homes there. On the other hand, Europe did, through Paulus and the Roman martyrs, accept Christianity under the Roman emperors until the edict of Milan on the basis of the old Roman Empire. In the course of time this Continent became the dynamic missionary centre for the whole world.

For one glance at their common history shows clearly how the spiritual strength of Christianity caused the other Romantic, Germanic, Slavic and

Hellenic peoples to grow together into one spiritual family of states. Christianity combined so successfully with the self-consciousness of the various nations and linguistic groups of Europe. For example, in this wide spiritual area the Roman monastery of St Boniface was a centre of Byzantine learning, where the Latin West could meet the Greek, East Roman and Slavic worlds. From this very monastery came for instance Bishop Adalbert of Prague. French, Greek or Latin bishops were not only appointed but fully accepted in Italy, Germany, Eastern France or the North, just as earlier Irish and English scholars and bishops had been accepted in Western Europe. Still today the cathedrals of Europe, Christian art and the Christian literature held in Europe's monastery libraries bear witness to this spiritual world. However, the ancient inheritance of the Greeks and Romans was itself protected by the monasteries, and in this way historical continuity was maintained that means that it is from the pre-Christian building stones of Roman-Greek and Slavic peoples that an all-embracing European unity was constructed.

These brief examples are intended to show how our Europe of today – divided as it is into two separate spiritual worlds – still holds fast to a common longing for a new Europe of tomorrow. The German ambassador at the Conference for Security and Co-operation in Europe (CSCE) in Vienna, Ekkehard Eickhoff, stated in a press briefing that the Vienna Conference had helped to give expression in a number of ways to the wish European nations had to strengthen the sense of community which all felt fundamentally. So it is, let us say once more, certainly no coincidence that Gorbachev spoke of a 'common house of Europe'. In the knowledge of this common history, the question now arises for us: What does this all signify? What meaning does the Europe of today have? Is there here a task for tomorrow? Does there still exist a European consciousness, a European striving and planning forward into the future?

Along with the CSCE Conference on the political front, the European Catholic Bishops' conferences have been active in pointing time and time again to Europe's common spiritual heritage. The Second Vatican Council re-awakened interest in the spiritual aspect of this common heritage. This new interest in Europe as a spiritual community was summed up by Pope John Paul II in an impressive confession made during his pilgrimage to Santiago in Spain.

In this context another question arises: to what extent is the determining power of Christianity still alive in our Continent? Is not this spiritual power also essential, if a torn Europe is to be woken from its lethargy?

This underlines once again the fact that this Continent – and in its wake the others – is facing the question of how it is possible to reconcile progress in science and technology with the preservation of spiritual values and moral principles. This tension between scientific progress and the maintenance of spiritual values together with personal responsibility has today become plain to see in the contrast between a Christian religious view of mankind and a Marxist view of the world and the human being. This conflict has its roots in nineteenth-century Europe, and so its resolution today is a task for Europe.

The opposition between knowledge and belief, in the sense in which it formed the basis for the Marxist as well as Christian view of the world in the nineteenth century, has today been overcome.

The complementarity of knowledge and belief is recognised in our days and given prominence. The recognition in Europe of this relation between knowledge and belief has set in motion a great dialogue, which is being followed with interest in other continents. However, in recognition of its history and the fact that it has now set itself this task, Europe is expected to play a leading role in it.

The Second Vatican Council emphasised this dialogue and gave it prominence. Three Vatican secretariats were born out of the Vatican Council, and show clearly the direction being taken by the essential spiritual dialogue taking place in Europe. First of all the dialogue to promote Christian unity (Secretariat for Unity); next, the promotion of discussion with other world religions (Secretariat for non-Christian religions). The third dialogue concerns discussion with non-believers (Secretariat for *non credentes*), in other words talking with materialistically oriented humanists and atheists. These three Secretariats in Rome show those three directions which are clearly emerging as tasks for Europe today. Europe, silent until now, should once again be heard and once more take up her role as spiritual leader because of the historical background to these three directions of dialogue.

Ecumenical discussion among Christians is also linked with the dialogue between the great monotheistic religions: Judaism, Christianity and Islam. We have here a difficult and great task for the future, one which touches Europe first and foremost. But through its history Europe is prepared for this theological task. The relaxation of the tension between Christians and Jews has begun, a tension which does exist and which includes a European tradition of anti-Semitism. Further progress now needs to be made. It will be achieved through the introduction of new ways of thinking, a strong boost to which was given by the Vatican document *Nostra Actate* (Catholic Christianity and the non-Christian religions).

Dialogue with the Muslims is touched on in the same document, and is a pressing question because of both Europe's history and the present-day situation. Particular attention needs to be paid to the struggle to divorce religion and politics, in the light of events in the Muslim world. If religion and politics appear as opposites it is of disadvantage for both sides, however the same is true if they are brought too closely together.

The discussion with other world religions began very promisingly last year and at the instigation of Pope John Paul II. This debate has indeed been heard in other continents, especially in Asia; however it received new meaning and new emphasis in Assisi. The discussion with the advocates of materialistic humanism, with the *non credentes*, gives rise to the question of how to resolve the conflict between an atheistic (whether of a Marxist or pragmatic nature) and a religious view of the world and mankind.

In India therefore, one hears arguments such as "India may import scientific and technological knowledge from Europe, but that it is capable of providing superior religious and spiritual values". By this, the Indians are telling us that a technical world without religion will inevitably lead into a cul-de-sac. Our endangered environment, the dangers of nuclear power as well as the question of the meaning of human existence want to make us aware of the same.

The way Europe was going without the spiritual strength of Christianity has led into a cul-de-sac. Such a world would result in the overturning of traditional values, which means technology placed before morality, the scientific world considered more highly than the human being, the victory of materialism over the spiritual world.

Despite bloody conflicts and spiritual crises, which have severely shaken the life of our Continent, one thing is clear after two thousand years of history: Europe has no identity without Christianity. Those common roots out of which the civilisation of the continent has grown are to be found in history. From those same roots come Europe's dynamism, her enterprise, her capacity to spread ideas constructively even into other continents – in short, everything for which she is famed.

So even Christians must use the difficulties with which the old continent is today struggling as a means to strengthen themselves in unity, so as to find once more their origins and to revivify those true values which once formed the spiritual unity of Europe. Christianity is the godparent of Europe, and despite all their diversities this has kept the European nations bound together spiritually. Thus the crisis in European culture is in no small measure also a crisis of Christian culture.

B. Scientific Method Applied to History[1]

J. A. Froude

James Anthony Froude was the eminent but controversial Victorian historian of the Tudor period.

Ladies and Gentlemen, – I cannot but congratulate this country – my own country in which I was born and to which I am proud to belong – on the formation and the success of this association. There was a time when Devonshire was, to use a modern phrase, the most advanced county in England. During the hundred years which followed the Reformation, Lancashire and Yorkshire, Durham and Northumberland, were the strongholds of old-fashioned opinions. They were places where everything that was old was consecrated, and new ideas were intolerable. Somersetshire, Worcestershire, Cornwall, Devonshire, were the chief seats of the staple manufactures of England. They were progressive, energetic, full of intellectual activity, taking the lead in what was then the great liberal movement of the age. The knights and squires of the North were wrapped up in themselves. They rarely left their own houses. They rarely saw the face of a stranger, unless of some border marauder. The merchants of Plymouth and Dartmouth were colonising the New World, and opening a trade with every accessible port in the Old. The Hawkinses, the Drakes, the Davises, the Raleighs, were the founders of the ocean empire of Great Britain; while, on the other hand – for mental energy is always many-sided – Devonshire, in giving birth to Hooker, bestowed the greatest of her theologians on the Church of England.

Times have somewhat changed. The march of intellect has moved northward. The soil up there, after lying fallow so many centuries, disclosed the reservoirs of force which were stored in the coal measures. The productive capacities of the island shifted in the direction where there was most material for them to work with, while Devonshire rested on its laurels. Improved means of communication – roads, canals, railways, the electric telegraph – have diminished the importance of the smaller harbours or towns, and thrown the business of the country into a few enormous centres. The agricultural districts have been drained of their more vigorous minds; while from the same and other causes local peculiarities are tending to disappear. There were once many languages spoken in this island. There are now but

---

1. An address to the Devonshire Association for the Encouragement of Science and Literature, 19 March 1869.

three. Even our own Devonshire dialect, which Raleigh used at the court of Elizabeth, is becoming a thing of the past.

Yet as one person is never quite the same as another person, as each has peculiarities proper to himself which constitute his individual importance, so I hope the time is far off when the ancient self-administered English counties will subside into provinces – when London will be England in the sense that Paris is France. English character and English freedom depend comparatively little on the form which the Constitution assumes at Westminster. A centralised democracy may be as tyrannical as an absolute monarch; and if the vigour of the nation is to continue unimpaired, each individual, each family, each district, must preserve as far as possible its independence, its self-completeness, its powers and its privilege to manage its own affairs, and think its own thoughts. Neither Manchester nor Plymouth are yet entirely London, and I hope never will be. And it is for this reason that I welcome the formation of societies like the present. They are symptoms that the life is not all concentrated at the heart – that if we are carried along in the stream of national progress, we do not mean to float passively where the current leads us, and that in the present as in the past we intend to bear an intelligent and active share in the general movement of the age.

C. THE TWO COMMONWEALTHS: CONTINENTAL AND OCEANIC[1]

Sir John Biggs-Davison

The late Sir John Biggs-Davison was an author and Member of Parliament in Churchill's post-war administration.

There should not have been a Treaty of Rome in 1957. There should have been a Treaty of London in 1947. Britain could then have shaped a united Western Europe as its undisputed moral leader. Had she not fought on alone against the Axis when all her allies had been struck down? In fact, no!

We British were never alone in 1940. The Commonwealth stood with us from the start. Russians and Americans, for their part, waited to be attacked, and emerged the only victors. Roosevelt and *naïveté* clasped hands with Stalinist barbarity. For the 'FDR', Churchill was the imperialist, not Stalin. Europe was vivisected and partitioned between Soviet domination and American protectorate.

Europe's oceanic empires were broken and balkanised. Most of the successor states lacked the sociological basis of political independence. Their primitive millions were delivered from European paramountcy to the freedom of massacre and famine. They became victims of East-West conflict and the intrigues and mischief of anti-colonialist colonialists. Nearly a century ago Disraeli warned his countrymen that if the British Empire were perversely indifferent to "the feelings and fortunes of continental Europe" it would become "the object of general plunder". That it indeed became.

Another, some would say greater, Conservative statesman, Lord Salisbury, said in 1888, that "we are part of the community of Europe and we must do our duty as such".

In 1917, that climacteric year in which the future super-powers Liberal America and Bolshevik Russia stepped out from the opposite wings to the front of the world stage, Milner, man of Empire, and a member of the War Cabinet under Lloyd George (whom he had accompanied to Russia), was talking to Sir Henry Wilson.

---

1. This article is reprinted from the journal *New European*, Vol. 1, No. 3, 1988.

That redoubtable Ulsterman told Milner that the British Empire "was too scattered and too thinly-populated to stand alone in a jealous world. Englishmen must be either 'Americans' or 'Europeans'".

Field Marshal Wilson's prescription for post-war Britain was a strengthened system of alliances with France, Italy and Belgium: support for Turkey; a Middle East policy which did not put the Arab and Muslim world at odds with France and Britain; and a Germany "reconciled with France as an equal member of a Grand Alliance strong enough to hold the balance between America, Japan and Russia".

"The Americans should stay out of Europe." The policy (associated with another Wilson, the President of the United States, with his Fourteen Points – four more commandments than the Almighty!) of "fomenting the militant nationalism which was the chief enemy of peace" was "a game that two could play at".

Many, not all, right-wing Tories agreed with Wilson's thesis: but America seemed so rich and populous and Europe, General Smuts lamented at the Imperial Conference of 1917, "suffers from an exhaustion which is the most appalling fact of history".

The Field Marshal knew that America could never be the friend of the British Empire and that a balkanised Europe would again be explosive to the undoing of both Europe and Empire.

The First World War exhausted Europe, the second left her partitioned and in ruins. On 25 November 1943, when victory in Europe was assured but not achieved, General Smuts shared with the Empire (now the Commonwealth) Parliamentary Association some 'Thoughts on the New World'.

He predicted that after the war three of the Great Powers would have disappeared from the Continent, leaving Great Britain and Russia, "the new Colossus", reinforced by the reduction of Japan. The glory of the British would be unparalleled – and their poverty.

Smuts went on to posit three world powers: "Russia the Colossus of Europe, Great Britain with her feet in all the continents, but crippled materially here in Europe; and the United States of America with enormous assets...and potentialities of power beyond measure." He rejected union between the British Empire and Commonwealth and the United States. Anglo-American collaboration was "one of the greatest hopes of mankind" but, as a "political axis", it would be "one-sided".

What then should be done? Smuts proposed a closer co-operation with "those smaller democracies in Western Europe which are of our way of thinking [...] and which are of the same political and spiritual substance as ourselves". Standing by themselves, they were lost. Their place was with "the next worldwide British system".

The great Afrikaner pointed out that the Commonwealth was a group of sovereign states. As sovereign states, each of the nations could say, with perfect safety: "That is our group: why are we not there? With full retention and maintenance of our sovereign status, we choose that grand company for our future in this dangerous world."

Between the wars (and after) Leo Amery campaigned for Imperial Preference. With Churchill, he interested himself in the Pan-European Movement created and inspired by Coudenhove-Kalergi, who urged Continental integration in close communion with the British Empire, and the Briand plan for a 'European League of Nations' within the wider League, conceived of, in proto-Gaullist terms, of a grouping of sovereign states. These visionary schemes came to naught. It was Hitler's New Order that awaited Europe.

After the second war, Leo Amery strove with Churchill for a United Europe. With Julian Amery, I myself had some part in the Council of Europe's Strasbourg Plan of 1951 to join Commonwealth and other overseas partners of European powers in a vast economic area based for trade on two-tier preference. Backbenchers are sometimes wiser than their governments and the plan was unanimously accepted by the Consultative Assembly of the Council of Europe, where I held the post of Secretary to our Conservative delegation.

Two post-war Labour Governments and the Conservative administration that took office in 1951 failed Europe by denying her leadership and therefore failed the Commonwealth too. France took the initiative from which Britain shrank. She received American backing for the European Coal and Steel Community and Euratom. Their supranational flavour was repugnant to Britain. More disastrous still was the rejection of the Strasbourg Plan, for it could have realised the vision of Henry Wilson, Smuts and indeed Ernest Bevin who wanted to prolong the concerns of the Western Union (now enlarged as the Western European Union) into Africa.

In 1957 the six states of the European Economic Community confronted Britain with a 'continental system'. In 1959 Harold Macmillan's administration responded with a league of seven maritime and peripheral states, the European Free Trade Association which would have formed a single industrial zone but excluded agriculture. Then in 1961 Parliament endorsed negotiations designed to reconcile adherence to the European Communities with Commonwealth responsibilities and EFTA obligations. I stated my own attitude in my General Election address of 1966: "We must take our place in Europe. Our long-term aim should be a European Commonwealth, linked in London with the British Commonwealth, allied with America, and reconciled with Russia." In 1973, after two rebuffs from

Gaullist France, Britain made a successful application to join the Communities.

She was 'Johnny Bull come lately'. The mould had been set. It could not be broken to suit Britain's convenience and 'that of the Commonwealth'. True, reasonable trading arrangements were negotiated for much of the 'new' Commonwealth including those members now comprehended by the Lomé Convention. But preference for the 'old' Commonwealth went into reverse.

Yet, if 'multi-cultural' Britain is European, so is Canada, with her main roots in Old France and the British Isles; and the former Prime Minister, Pierre Trudeau, sought a counterpoise to United States penetration and predominance with a 'contractual link' between Canada and, the Community. 'European' too are Australia and New Zealand. During the negotiations in Brussels for British entry into the Communities, Mr (now Lord) Rippon pleaded with some success – access for New Zealand butter is still a running battle – the case of 'three million Europeans' at the Antipodes. Recently Mrs Thatcher spoke of strengthening Britain's relations with New Zealand.

The impulse of Europe is more than that of a market. Europe is not limited to a Treaty area. The Community has crossed the Pyrenees. Europe is not bound forever by the wire and watch towers of the great partition. Europe is a civilisation and a bond of interest and the 'old' Commonwealth is a prolongation of a Europe that in a sense extends from the North Cape to the Cape of Good Hope.

The empires of East and West are in decline. Nationalist tremors shake the land mass of Soviet Eurasia. United States prospects are obscure. Pacific overtakes Atlantic. So Britain in Europe, still a partial Europe, must needs keep old friendships in repair. In their centenary year the Royal Australian Regiment mount guard at Windsor and Buckingham Palace. At the same time, Australian fellow subjects queue with aliens for immigration at Heathrow – while some of those we and they fought for our own and others' freedom go in through the gate of Community privilege.

The Community should have taken more heed of the comparison made by a celebrated President of the European Commission, Dr Hallstein, of Britain's Commonwealth link to a dowry for European nuptials.

As we build, and extend, a New Europe, let us be mindful of the old Commonwealth. Europe must not become, as Jung feared "a mere hyphen between America and Asia".

D. A FEDERATED EUROPE

Peter Unwin

Peter Unwin is the Director of the David Davies Memorial Trust. He has been the British Ambassador in Budapest and Copenhagen and Deputy Secretary General of the Commonwealth.

Sixty years ago, David Davies sat down to write a book about the future of Europe. He finished it at the height of the Phoney War between Christmas and New Year, 1939. The German and Soviet partition of Poland was complete. The Red Army was attacking Finland. The United States remained staunchly isolationist. All depended on Britain and France, which stood resolutely on the defensive. No one could see how the dictatorships might be defeated. It was a strange time to be planning Europe's destiny.

But people everywhere were eager for hope in a better future, and the book was published early in the following year, 1940, before Hitler's attacks on Denmark, Norway, the Low Countries and France. It appeared in the yellow jacket which adorned all books in Victor Gollancz's famous series on contemporary political and international issues. Its title was *A Federated Europe* and it covered, if in a summary 140 pages, all the issues which such a project raises. Sixty years later it is interesting to compare Lord Davies' approach with the European Union as it is, and as it may become.

Davies' approach was avowedly political. He wanted a system which would give Europe the blessings of peace, freedom and justice when once the democracies had defeated Germany and set the captive European nations free. He believed that federation, or failing that confederation, could guarantee those blessings as the nation-state could not. Old Europe, he believed, could learn from younger, federal societies such as the United States, Canada and Australia. He was not much interested in economics.

Davies envisaged a European federation including almost all European states. Germany, defeated, would embrace democracy. So, by implication, would Italy and Spain. The Balkans would get their act together. Turkey, though marginal to Europe, had earned its membership. He excluded Russia on three grounds: its size, its geographical position, and the improbability of it embracing democracy. Curiously enough, Davies envisaged that the self-governing dominions might be members of the European federation, led into it by Britain, the leading member of the Commonwealth family. He ruled out the United States. It was too large, and if it were to join the federation's centre of gravity would inevitably shift to the other side of the Atlantic. But in any case the United States – which in the winter of 1939

Lord Davies shows clear signs of despising – was selfishly isolationist. It had left the field to the dictators. Above all, it had conceived the League of Nations, then abandoned it; and the League which was left had proved itself inadequate in itself and a frustration to the creation of a federated Europe.

The federal Europe of Davies' dreams was in most respects a minimalist affair. It would settle disputes between its members and conduct the continent's external affairs. It would supervise sanctions against offenders and – a sudden leap to a maximalist position – it would control a federal defence force which would hold a European monopoly of heavy weapons: aircraft, tanks, artillery, battleships. But Davies saw measures of economic integration such as a customs union and a common currency as matters for which individual member states might volunteer or not as they chose. He envisaged federal taxation only to the extent that it was necessary to finance the federation's military and political institutions. The federation's constitution should be amendable only by the free vote of member states. And every member should have the absolute right of secession after a period of notice.

Davies wanted a President of the Federation elected by a college of heads of state for a single four-year term. He envisaged a senate elected by popular vote, with two members per country, irrespective of size. He wanted a directly-elected house of representatives, with a member for every million people. In Davies' time this produced a senate of fifty-four and a house of 406 representatives. And he saw both houses jointly electing the executive of the federation.

The European Community took a very different route from Davies'. It started with a political aim: to build an "ever closer union of the peoples of Europe". But in its early years it used only economic building blocks, and it has carried economic integration far beyond Lord Davies' conception. Slowly, and with infinite difficulty, it has more recently begun to build the political federation which was his starting-point. And it is still wrestling with the difficulties which he identified. Fears for 'sovereignty' and fears of a superstate are both problems with which Davies dealt. As is the problem of 'tolerance' in a continent with a tradition of the opposite; and Lord Davies rather quaintly calls the German rape of Poland an act of 'intolerance'. He deals also with the problem of other, competing loyalties, for example to the Commonwealth or to the global community.

Nevertheless, the structure which A *Federated Europe* describes is not all that far removed from what may be the structure of the European Union in the early twenty-first century. The two great exceptions are, of course, economic integration, which makes up so much of the warp and woof of today's Union; and Lord Davies' military force, his federal monopoly of heavy weapons and of coercion.

There NATO does what he saw a European federation doing. It does it essentially because, ever since 1941, the United States has belied his expectations. It committed itself to the destruction of the dictators, shored up a devastated continent and has remained involved in it ever since. If ever American resolution falters it will be time for the last piece in Lord Davies' jigsaw puzzle, a real, federal European militia capacity. But if it comes, that piece will be fitted into a structure much more complex and, in the achievements of the European Union, much richer than the limited, essentially political federation he envisaged sixty years ago this year.

E. THE OCTOPUS: EUROPE IN THE GRIP OF ORGANISED CRIME[1]

Brian Freemantle

Brian Freemantle gave up his career as foreign editor of the Daily Mail *to write books on the KGB and the CIA as well as to investigate organised crime. The following is an introduction to his book* The Octopus: Europe in the Grip of Organised Crime.[2]

The first true Europeans, men and women who totally embraced the concept of a frontierless, free-market union, were not politicians with a vision of a European Community: they were crooks. After almost four unhampered decades the crooks are still here, working a goldmine, taking hundreds of billions of pounds a year. While the fifteen current nations of the European Union bicker about sovereignty, monetary union, and cohesive military forces, organised crime has set up shop throughout the European continent – and beyond – for the crime bonanza of this or any other century. And nothing is being done to stop it.

The European Union needs an FBI. It does have the embryo in Europol, which is a criminal intelligence-assembling and distribution facility headquartered in The Hague and made up of police and customs forces from the fifteen member states. However, it is virtually unworkable. The eagerness of Germany, which openly refers to it as an FBI with itself at its head, is resented by every European country with memories of the Second World War. Inevitably, the resentment means there is strong resistance to Europol ever being allowed to become fully operational. The interpretation of laws emanating from Brussels also poses such problems that, at the moment, Europol cannot even properly perform the function for which it was established. Each of the fifteen have adopted the EU Directive on data protection in different ways. Thus Europol – dedicated to upholding law – can actually break national legislation by asking for, and disseminating, criminal data in states where it is forbidden to do so by national legislation.

In addition, Europol does not receive any support from the institutions that might be perceived as having similar aims. Interpol, criticised for its great inefficiency and, in any case, simply another intelligence bank without any operational remit or function, is jealous of what it fears to be its eroding position. Consequently it snipes at Europol and does its best to undermine

---
1. This article first appeared in *World Review*, Volume 1, Number 1.
2. Freemantle, Brian. op. cit. (see footnote 1 page 137)

its growth or acceptance. So do the individual police and law enforcement agencies of the member countries. No city, district, county, state, or national force is prepared to surrender one jot of their authority or responsibility to a supranational bureau. They are resentful and suspicious of any organisation empowered to enter their country unhindered to investigate crime that they consider themselves capable of solving, but are not. No national government will countenance such intrusion.

The result? Organised crime is plundering billions from the EU goldmine, and will continue to do so. I have toured every country in the Union and, with level-headed criminologists and legal experts who are not given to sensationalism or exaggeration, have discussed the hold that organised crime has established. Their consensus was that, unless some properly constituted, properly authorised, properly staffed federal organisation is established within two years to fight it, organised crime will be unbreakable, so deeply will it be embedded in the fabric of Europe.

One year of that cataclysmic deadline has now gone by. No federal force is functioning, nor is there any sign that it will be in the years to come. So organised crime has won. And we are talking big crime, crime organised professionally by men and women who operate it as a business, conducting it through structures closely resembling legitimate multinational corporations and conglomerates, their boardroom-like hierarchies serviced by accountants and financial advisers. In certain countries, particularly in Eastern Europe, there is a risk of it becoming so powerful it will 'own' countries just as the Mafia, through the now discredited Christian Democrat Party, once came perilously close to ruling Italy.

Crimes that are included in the catalogue of organised criminal activities are varied, but all involve big money. The crime most worrying world governments – but insufficiently, it would seem, for them to do anything positive about it – is the smuggling of nuclear material and technology, as well as conventional arms, from the former Soviet bloc. The trade is inextricably linked to illegal drug trafficking, each funding the other. The cosmic profits from both require highly sophisticated money-laundering techniques to convert dirty money into clean. Most of the techniques to handle the money-laundering depend on the border-crossing ease of computers. This fosters other entire areas of crime such as computer sex, an innovation to the more traditional prostitution and pornography industry. To feed that industry, men, women and children are taken, often by force, from the enormous business of illegal immigration. It is also fed by the kidnap or purchase of children and young adults from Latin America and Eastern Europe, which then, in turn, services a further, even more horrifying crime: the trafficking in human organs.

Drugs finance the terrorism with which some religiously-dominated Middle East states – eager purchasers of nuclear and conventional weapons –

actively seek to destabilise Europe. In addition, those states have raised further terrorist finances by selling their country's fine art through European auction houses. Those same auction houses also trade in huge amounts of fine art stolen throughout the fifteen countries of the EU, as well as those looted wholesale from the former Soviet empire.

The mafias of Europe are closed societies, ruled by the blood oath of *omertà*, the traditional Mafia code of silence. But they have, literally, donned a further concealing and protective cloak. They have forged links throughout Europe with 'Orient' Freemason lodges, proscribed by the world-governing British Grand Lodge because of their acknowledged criminal connections and because they flout the accepted principles of the Brotherhood. The Masonic/Mafia liaison is particularly strong within the permanent institutions of the European Union. I have met MEPs and officials of those institutions who talk openly of witnessing the hand- and cheek-kissing, that is the respectful Mafia form of greeting, in the corridors of power in Brussels.

The institutions of the European Union, the edicts they pass, and even Brussels itself, are a further gangster's goldmine. Again, despite the efforts of a very few, nothing is done to stop the fraud, deception, and blatant criminality currently milking at least £10 billion a year from the EU exchequer. The institutions of the EU squabble and bicker among themselves like the head-in-the-sand law enforcement bodies of their member states. The Court of Auditors, which is supposed to monitor the EU's £57 billion-a-year budget, considers the non-elected European Commission to be arrogant, and correctly claims that it ignores criticisms, particularly those involving criminality. Meanwhile, the Commission, the permanent bureaucratic machine supposed to run the Community, despises the Court of Auditors as weak and vacillating, which it is. The Commission also considers the Court of Auditors to be unprepared to press its findings forcefully enough, which is also true. The Council of Ministers, for its part, regards both bodies as mere functionaries of the Union, above which it aloofly holds its unreported meetings to decide on policies. At a later date these are then invariably fudged in trade-offs between the various countries and their ministers, which all obey the regulations and directives that suit them and totally ignore those that do not. And finally, the European Parliament considers all three bodies – the Court of Auditors, the European Commission and the Council of Ministers – to be undemocratic, inefficient, sometimes corrupt, and greatly in need of wide-sweeping reforms and redesign. All of which is true, but which, unfortunately, will not be corrected. Not surprisingly, the European Parliament is regarded by the three institutions to be a cosmetic necessity but quite irrelevant figurehead forum. Lip-service is paid for the sake of politeness but no other notice whatsoever is given. This is also the view of the majority of the member states.

The £10-billion-a-year extracted from the EU institutions by organised crime is quite a small nugget from the mother lode of European crime gold. It is, however, one of the few that can be calculated with any reasonable degree of accuracy because it is a privately conceded estimate from auditors who do, at least, have some figures with which to work An estimate of profits made from other criminal activities is much more conjectural because organised crime does not have its books checked and most certainly does not pay tax. However, those estimates – from the few professionals dedicated to maintaining some sort of survey – are still claimed to be right to within a 10% fluctuation. Some of these estimates include £500 billion for drug distribution. It is a toss-up whether that is the league leader or whether nuclear smuggling, with atomic warheads priced at £14 million each, is the top crime earner. The countries of the Middle East – Iraq, Iran, Algeria, and Libya, with Pakistan as a Far East purchaser – are the queuing customers for smuggled atomic material and technology. The concern with this is clear. For instance, I know there have been top-secret discussions between Britain, Italy, France, and Germany about creating a £20 billion 'Star Wars' shield to protect Europe from surprise attack from the South.

The billions lost to computer crime are even more difficult to assess. Almost without exception – I cannot, in fact, quote an instance to the contrary – the financial institutions of Europe prefer to stand the loss themselves rather than admit to the general public, whose money they administer, that hackers and computer fraudsters can enter supposedly secure financial databases and help themselves at will.

Computer crime and the stealing and fraud of fine art are 'clean', white-collar activities. The most obscene crimes that I uncovered during my researches were the sexual exploitation of children. Some even go to the depths of 'snuff' movies, films that climax with the victim being murdered for the sexual gratification of their viewer. In one case, I investigated a man who photographed himself in sexual acts with a 14-month-old girl, whom he intended to murder on video, and whose body he intended disposing of by putting it in an acid bath and then feeding it to piranha fish. I learned of other cases of children as young as ten being shipped from the former Communist Eastern Europe for sexual exploitation in the rest of Europe. It is common for minibuses packed with East European teenagers – boys and girls – to pull up outside Dutch sex clubs, and the teenagers to be then offered for sale for £2 000 each. The clubs whose owners refuse to buy are frequently firebombed. The European sex industry is estimated, in total, to be worth £15 billion a year.

The law enforcement authorities of the EU member states know how bad organised crime has become. They know that its tentacles are gaining an unbreakable stranglehold, but instead of fighting it as it should be fought with an FBI-type agency, they hurry into national legislation with ill-considered and flawed statutes. The British Home Secretary, Michael Howard's Criminal Justice and Public Order Act is a typical example: it does everything for 'tough-on-crime' political soundbites but nothing to solve the problem.

The inability – and lack of political will – of the member countries to confront crime is the best example of why the European Union can never, and will never, become the United States of Europe. No one is united. Except, that is, for the organised crime groups who have formed their interlinked, mutually-beneficial multinationals and laugh all the way to the bank, some of which they are rich enough to own.

F. Our moral evasion

David Selbourne

David Selbourne is the author of The Principle of Duty *which stresses the importance of linking 'rights' and 'duties'. The following is an extract from his booklet "Moral Evasion" (Centre for Policy Studies).*

Many moral conflicts which bear upon public policy – as in matters of education, penal reform, family support and welfare provision – often engage us, and society at large, in candid and truthful exchanges. Varied in tone and content, it is plain that the public debate on ethical issues is as vigorous as ever, however disconcerting (to some) the arguments may often be. That many of those who hold 'traditional' moral positions feel themselves embattled and marginalised, while, paradoxically, those who hold 'advanced' or 'progressive' opinions themselves feel that they are 'up against it' in public debate, perhaps indicates the intensity of the battles that are currently being waged.

Over family and marriage, over moral and religious education in schools, over crime and punishment, over sexual 'rights', over welfare 'dependency', over advances in genetic manipulation and a host of other matters it can hardly be said that silence reigns. In these areas of conflict, there is no shortage of individuals, prominent in the press and other arenas, who have had the courage and resilience to hold their moral ground, whatever that ground may be, with polemics which deserve respect for their integrity and firmness of purpose, and sincerity of opinion.

But there are also many tricks and evasions used – some merely verbal, others of greater substance – by which the protagonists and participants in ethical debates often seek, through the media, to misrepresent the issues before us, or to avoid responsibility for their own conduct, or to discredit by use of falsehood of those whose arguments they disapprove. I give a sample of these devices in the essay that follows.

Some of the stratagems, or 'evasions' as I call them, are intended to paralyse debate itself. They seek to show – and have us believe – that, at one extreme, nothing can any longer be done about our moral condition or, at another extreme, that nothing needs to be done about it, since there is nothing fundamentally at fault in our moral condition in the first place. This essay is addressed to all those who would hesitate over, or disagree with, both propositions – as I do – and who believe that questions about 'the moral order' will deservedly continue to stand at the centre of public and political controversy in the coming period.

It is often argued that there is "no new thing under the sun", as Ecclesiastes puts it. But where, until now, has there been anything like the observation in *The Guardian* by a spokesman for Castle Morpeth council that residents of private care homes are "income-producing raw material" and the dead represent "the waste produced by the business"?

Is it an old moral thing, or a new moral thing, that a lesbian couple practising self-insemination should, before breaking up their partnership, have had two DIY babies using a pickle jar and syringe? Or that another similar couple should purchase the frozen sperm of a stranger via the Internet?

And when, until now, would a distinguished surgeon, describing "the prospect of taking a dead person's face and draping it over the skull of a living man or woman", declare, as *The Times* reported, that "it is simply like changing the cloth of an armchair"?

Is it an old moral thing, or a new moral thing, that there is now an arson attack in at least three schools every day? Or that one in three churches can expect to be the target of an attack of some kind – theft, vandalism, arson – each year? Or that malicious vandalism is now the biggest cause of railway accidents? Or that 86% of alarm calls in the Metropolitan Police area are shown to be false? Or that trees and shrubs planted in memory of the Dunblane victims were stolen within days from the local cemetery?

Has there ever before been such violence directed in the time of peace by youth against the frailest and most elderly, so that even women in their eighties come to be raped? Is it an old or a new thing under the sun that doctors – it is estimated that a thousand of them are assaulted each year – teachers and priests should feel themselves at risk from those for whom they care? When, before, could nursing be regarded as Britain's most 'dangerous profession' with one nurse in three, compared with one policeman in four, suffering an act of violence in accident and emergency units?

The temptation to retreat into the safety of unknowing denial and disbelief is strong. Yet into this moral quagmire the Office for National Statistics and other bodies continue to pour their data on the composition of households, population changes, marriage and divorce rates, drug abuse and much else.

As early as the year 2000, nuclear families could be outnumbered by step-families. By the year 2020, with present trends, one in three people in Britain will be living alone and most women will be single, only 48% of them being wives as such. Married couples will be a minority.

In this whirlpool, the intensifying corruption of our sensibilities, the hubris of technological experiments with the human body, the genetic abuse of the natural order, the disrespect for the carer, the aggression of the impatient, the self-harming of the young, and the accelerating fragmentation and dissolution of the old family bond are all ethically conjoined. They are, in combination, lethal in their effects, each element intricately and sometimes causally, linked to another.

And yet everywhere there are evasions. These seek to show, and have us believe, that nothing can any longer be done about our moral condition, or that nothing *needs* to be done about it, since there is nothing much at fault with it in the first place. The cynicism and amorality with which some address our moral and social confusions are a further cause of our ills.

"The moral issue is dead", declares Hugo Young in *The Guardian*. "The family has had it", says Sara Maitland, again in *The Guardian*, seeming to gloat over its "terminal sickness". "When politicians talk about strengthening the family, liberals reach for their revolvers", says Polly Toynbee, also in *The Guardian*. "Families are by their nature Darwinian units", argues Simon Jenkins demeaningly in *The Times*.

And marriage? The cynic and the amoralists are hard at work on it, once more with women to the fore. Here is Tania Kindersley in *The Times*: "Nobody seems able to tell me why we're still doing it...Surely we have the imagination to come up with something better... than an institution that came in with the Ark?"

This is a mere glimpse into a small part of the moral wasteland being made for us – or, it seems, being in some cases, sedulously striven for – by our fellows, and to which the media give an ever enlarging and unwarranted space.

It is a cynicism which saps commitment by attrition, amorally rearing its head in every field of debate. Are you concerned, for example, about the increasing incidence of violence reported to be committed by young girls? You may well be. But, replies a 'professor of gender relations' in *The Times*, "Young women are much more positive about themselves and are likely to be more assertive...If women are becoming more active in society, their behaviour is more likely to be like men's." And, says a woman academic researcher in *The Guardian*: "If, to prove their equality, they have to punch someone, then so be it."

We are continually being given sight of a cynicism which dwells in moral darkness, and deepens it. The common link with all these commentators is that an important ethical issue generally lies latent within their arguments, and that, seemingly in consequence, a destructive urge is aroused to desecrate a moral truth or civic principle.

"The first thing you notice, as you plead to get out of jury service," noted Catherine Bennett in *The Guardian*, "is how many others are doing the same thing." This is to dump ordure on a civic duty.

There is no shame shown in this denial, or amoral rubbishing, of belief and value. Its reach is now far and wide, even getting at the very core and crux of the idea of principle itself. Consider John Lloyd in *The Times*: "If one does not stand for policies in the old sense...then you are free and can set others free...in these merry, piping times of peace, a Prime Minister (Blair) who stands for nothing is the best leader to have...for that is the way the times must move and 'isms' would stop it." You would be wrong to look for irony in this last sentiment, or for principle. It is a nadir of its kin. It emanates from a moral wasteland made bleaker by the evasion of moral responsibility and *engagement*.

There are many types of such evasion, but eleven arguments recur when a moral problem confronts us. There is the notion that 'there is nothing you can do about it, or not much'; the idea that 'it has never been any different'; the proposition that 'there is no quick fix' for a given ethical dilemma; the excuse that 'this is the price of a free society'; the cliché that 'it is no use turning the clock back'; the insistence that a problem is 'much more complex than you think'; the alibi that a problem is 'beyond the reach of law'; the smear that 'you are focusing on the wrong issue'; the defence that 'people in glass houses shouldn't...' and the base evasion that, since 'everyone does it', how can you object?

The cumulative effect of these evasions is often to paralyse debate itself. And, when all other arguments fail, the objector is dismissed as a 'moral crusader'; a 'moral authoritarian'; a 'puritan' or – the old standby – 'right-wing'. One ends with a situation in which even a Church leader, the Bishop of Edinburgh, can pronounce "moralising" to be "one of the least attractive of human characteristics".

Evasion and falsehood are widely employed to give the slip to the idea that common moral rules can and should exist. There has not been, since the French Revolution, a greater concern for, and insistence upon, the promotion and expansion of individual rights in an already deeply free society. Yet this culture of rights coexists with a cynicism about the distinctions between right and wrong. There seems to be no doubt, assiduously promoted, about the latter. It is a dramatic combination.[1]

---

1. Part of this extract appeared in *The Times* under the title "Our Moral Evasion".

G. REGIONALISM AND WORLD PEACE[1]

Ted Dunn

Ted Dunn is the author of Regional Peace and Development Programmes *(1993)[2] and* Step by Step to World Order *(1998).*

As an enthusiastic supporter of 'regionalism', to the extent that I have just had a book published on the subject,[3] may I take the idea of interlocking circles, as advocated by the *New European*, further, by relating it within the wider concept of world peace?

I raise this question because far too little attention has so far been given to the nature of power, when centralised within a region. Power, as is well known, corrupts, and when concentrated tends to become uncontrollable leading to social unrest and possibly international conflict. The problem that faces us therefore is to learn how to co-operate without creating these problems.

New European's idea of interlocking circles co-operating where interests overlap offers an answer by recognising the need to control power and, implicitly, that we need to give our first priority to nurturing the spiritual nature of man, such as meaning, purpose, belonging and feeling wanted. This is not to deny his or her needs for the material things of life but these are the fruits of peace and follow from, rather than precede, a society living in a state of social cohesion.

Even with the most perfect of societies, however, the problems of power and conflict will remain, albeit on a smaller, manageable scale. Our task, therefore, is to encourage regions to ritualise their conflicts by accepting recognised codes of behaviour, enforceable by law. The law itself must, however, be based on social, economic and natural justice, if it is to gain universal trust and confidence. Fortunately, the UN Universal Declaration of Human Rights provides the ideal reference point which all nations have recognised. Power, in other words, needs to be controlled, not enhanced.

The problem to be resolved, therefore, is to seek a structure of organisation which enables us to obtain the benefits of co-operation without incurring its potential disadvantages. It is a problem that is still unresolved for Europe

---

1. Originally published in the *New European*, Vol. 1, No. 4, 1989-90.
2. Dunn, Ted, *Regional Peace and Development Programmes* (1993) London.
3. Dunn, Ted, *Step by Step to World Order* (1998) Gooday Publishers, London.

with two very different approaches competing for our hearts and minds. On the one hand we have the Council of Europe, and on the other the EEC. Both are considered to be one and the same, but in reality the Council of Europe is primarily concerned with protecting social, economic and political human rights, whereas the EEC is primarily concerned with 'harmonising' and bringing all activity in Europe under one centralised authority. This trend towards a centralised European organisation should be resisted. It is not necessary for creating wealth, as the experience of Switzerland and Sweden for example, both members of the Council of Europe but not of the EEC, testifies. But we do need enforceable European and international law under which all individuals, whether they be politicians, soldiers or terrorists, are accountable. This is not to deny our needs for economic well-being but these needs would be better served (as the New European's first editorial puts it), by "a network of overlapping policies (which would form) a Europe that was pulling together, not a Europe that was pulling itself apart".

The Council of Europe's approach meets this criterion and by doing so protects individual rights. The EEC's approach on the other hand, leads to a mass of directives which threaten in the long term to take away a nation's independence. It is one thing for a nation to sacrifice a small degree of sovereignty to a European or UN authority, in order to ensure human rights and the rule of law, quite another for it to sacrifice its independence and individuality. The first approach protects the individual, the second threatens the very nature of our being by undermining the individual's sense of involvement without which there can be little sense of community upon which so much of our spiritual lives depends.

Clearly, if we encourage the route of harmonisation and centralisation at the expense of individuality, Europe will close in on itself and become more and more a protected zone. Barriers will be erected and others will see Europe as a threat to their economic well-being. Another uncontrollable great power will have been created. If, however, the Council of Europe's ideals are upheld, the idea of interlocking circles overlapping other regions becomes possible. The harmony of opposites, unity without uniformity, and individuality with co-operation could become a reality.

Already the trend towards overlapping circles has gained considerable support and several countries in Eastern Europe are interested in joining the Council of Europe. It is a trend emphasised by the fact that membership of the Council consists of twenty-one nations whereas the EEC only consists of twelve members.[1] This progress towards a universal acceptance of values and ideals needs every encouragement.

---

1. Figures for 1988.

If, however, Europe becomes a more protected, centralised organisation of twelve nations, the other nine in the Council of Europe will feel excluded and their economies threatened. The same practical and psychological problems will also affect most other countries. That is not a recipe for peace. What is needed, therefore, is for Europe to become a more 'open' region, and instead of centralising power we should encourage its devolution by supporting the natural aspirations of small nations, such as Wales and Scotland, to achieve independence. The example of Switzerland's cantons could be followed.

The path that Europe takes could determine the future of other regions of the world, many of whom are seeking to emulate her example. It is therefore important, not only for Europe, but for the other regions of the world that we make the right decisions. If we make the wrong decisions the end result will be many competing regional power blocs. We now have the golden opportunity to encourage world co-operation through regional co-operation as and where interests overlap. Not only would this make for a peaceful world but indirectly would reform the UN by replacing the role of power politics by the rule of law.

A world composed of many regions, with interests overlapping, is a realistic aim for the immediate future, as the example of Western Europe and her neighbours is already demonstrating. We must remember that this example was only made possible through the generosity of the USA providing funds to initiate the Marshall Plan. Britain, as the largest recipient of aid should now accept its moral obligation to repay that debt by helping other regions with similar far-sighted development programmes under the auspices of the UN. There are no shortages of regions urgently in need of help. As an act of enlightened self-interest it would be worthwhile and far more cost effective in achieving good development with peace – based on security – than many ill-conceived development programmes, or defence programmes which can, at best, only deter but not defend.

We are told that we are more prosperous than ever before and that the rich have an obligation to help the poor. This being so we should promote regional peace and development programmes in other parts of the world. Step by step, region by region, with regions overlapping, world peace could become a reality. But it is important we have a clearer understanding of what is meant by regionalism otherwise we may only create yet another problem for ourselves.

H. Nigeria and Europe: not-so-distant cousins

Dele Oguntimoju

Dele Oguntimoju is Director of Publicity for the Movement for National Reformation (UK).

In its Leader for the week ending 18 June 1999 the *Economist* observed of Nigerians that "the name and the football team are about the only things that unite them". This appeared alongside the conclusion it had drawn from the evident voter apathy in the recent European elections, namely that nationhood is not something that can be imposed from on high.

I do not know whether the *Economist* intended a linkage between the Nigerian experience and the European experiment, but someone who is in no doubt about the parallels, and who is principally qualified to speak on the issue, is one Sir Peter Smithers who was the Parliamentary Private Secretary to the Minister of State and the Secretary of State in the Colonial Office from 1952-59. He is also, as fate would have it, a former Secretary General of the Council of Europe.

The letter which is reproduced below from the *Times* is one that Sir Peter wrote in June last year following the sudden death of General Abacha in Nigeria:

> "Sir, during the negotiations for the independence of Nigeria the view of the Secretary of State at that time, with which I agreed, was that in Nigeria we should attempt to put together a large and powerful state with ample material resources, which would play a leading part in the affairs of the continent and the world. This was attractive but it involved forcing several different ethnic and cultural groups into a single political structure.
>
> The negotiations were complex and very difficult, the chief problem as I remember relating, significantly, to the control of the police and the military.
>
> In the retrospect of forty years it is clear that this was a grave mistake which has cost many lives and will probably continue to do so. It would have been better to establish several smaller states in a free-trade area.
>
> In exculpation it must be said that we did not then have the examples of the collapse of Yugoslavia and of the Soviet Union before our eyes. It should now be clear for all but the wilfully blind to see that it is extremely dangerous to force diverse racial and social entities into a single rigid structure, such as that which is being built upon the foundation of the Maastricht Treaty. Recent history suggests that it would

be best to complete the development of the Common Market and to call a halt to political integration in Europe."

The connection that Sir Peter makes is more clearly grasped when the reader realises that 'Nigeria' is not a nation in the classical sense of a people with a common origin, tradition and language: there is no language called 'Nigerian'. The word 'Nigeria' is nothing more than a geographical expression that describes the amalgam of a large number of smaller nations to be found in the surrounds of the area of the River Niger (hence Nigeria) which were put together without regard to the historical integrity of the distinct cultures, borders and languages of these ancient nations.

This reality is normally obscured in popular commentary by references to these robust, proud and wholesome nations as 'tribes'. My people, the Yoruba, with their distinct language and traditions and of which there are close to forty million, are no more a tribe of Nigeria than the English, who number fifty-six million, are a tribe of the British Isles.

Like the nations of Europe, the only thing the nations that make up Nigeria really had in common before their enforced political marriage was skin colour, geographical proximity and trade. The language of the Hausa, the Igbo and the Yoruba (to mention just the three largest of the constituent nations) are as distinct from each other as the language of the English, the French and the Germans within the similar expression 'Europe'. In fact, while the nations of Europe can at least look to the Christian faith as providing a foundation for shared values, the nations of Nigeria had and still have no common faith (as the *Economist* has noted football is the nearest we have come): while the constituent nations in the South have embraced Christianity, most in the North have embraced Islam from the East.

No effort has been spared by the supporters of ever-closer union to get the people to abandon their culturally rich, separate national identities in favour of the synthetic 'Nigerian' identity: They have been cajoled, scolded, bribed and harassed to buy into the designer identity. Those who sing to the One Nigeria hymn sheet are rewarded, while those who prefer the ideal of 'live and let live' are sidelined and condemned as tribalists.

The need to promote the One Nigeria ideal has meant that competence has been forced to take a back seat to equal representation as the selection criteria for filling key posts in government. Similarly, critical economic/industrial policy decisions are taken not on pure commercial considerations but on the basis of the need to allow all regions to feel part of the family. Thus oil refineries are situated in the far North even though the crude oil to be refined is produced in the far South.

Rather than economic policy and development strategies being tailored to the unique resources and competitive strengths of the component nations (which would allow the Igbo, for example, to capitalise on their flair for manufacturing), the different nations have been compelled to march to a 'national' economic goose step. Nothing highlights this push-me-pull-you quality of the Nigerian State more than the field of education. While the Christian half of the country has always placed a great premium on formal education, the Muslim half has not. Rather than each side being allowed to live according to the priorities of its own people, the Muslim half (that has had political control of the country since independence) has imposed its own values by deprioritising education as a result of which the once-respected universities of Ibadan, Lagos and Nsuka are now no better than sixth-form colleges. As well as deliberate underfunding of education, the motivation to pursue the highest standards in education has been undermined by a legislation of positive discrimination that operates against the Christian half.

Far from fostering a shared sense of identity, the result has been to create a welfare-dependent mentality amongst certain of the nations, which has given rise to feelings of resentment and contempt amongst those that have had to stand back to let others through. Not surprisingly, many in the Christian parts have voted with their feet by setting up camp in the West.

The imperative of destroying the original national identities to make room for 'the Nigerian' dictates that local governments cannot be trusted and there must be increasing centralisation of policy. In the immediate aftermath of independence from Britain in 1960, Nigeria had a parliamentary system of government with three strong regional governments (the Northern Region for the predominantly Hausa territories; the Western Region for the predominantly Yoruba territories; and the Eastern Region for the predominantly Igbo areas). The Eastern Region's attempt to secede to form Biafra, and the resultant civil war, provided an excuse for increasing centralisation. Thus, while still wearing the tag of the 'Federal Republic of Nigeria', the country is in fact a unitary and highly centralised state. Thus policies on education, health, the economy, taxation and industry are all centrally planned.

The Nigerian experience is that when different nations are placed into a single political structure, they become preoccupied with their relative internal positioning. Until such time, if ever, as a single identity emerges, the constituent nations' collective performance in relation to external competition will be a secondary concern as they drag each other down into a state of uncompetitiveness. This is the nightmare that Nigerians have been enduring since independence: we have spent our time checkmating each other while more homogenous nations the world over have been pulling further and further ahead.

Given the experiences of the peoples of Nigeria, the nations of Europe are mistaken if they think political union will make them more competitive as a whole. The natural tendency will be for the larger nations to jostle for the leadership position so as to impose their values on the others. In the process the bigger nations who fancy their chances as top dogs will provide all sorts of inducements to the smaller nations, who are only interested in being looked after, in order to secure their support. The seeds of such sentiments were there to be seen in the haggling over the location of the European Central Bank.

At a political meeting in Oxford recently, I was fortunate to hear one of the speakers define democracy as a state of affairs where there is such a degree of homogeneity amongst the people that the minority are able to submit to the will of the majority. William Hague in his recent contribution to this publication[1] said the same thing when he said: "a nation is a group of people who feel enough in common with one another to accept government from each other's hands".

I would venture to say that the vast majority of the British people have no experience of living or working with Germans just as the vast majority of the Yoruba in Nigeria have no experience of living or working with the Hausa. Indeed the Yoruba in Nigeria feel more at home in the Republic of Benin, where their fellow Yoruba (who were cut off by the crude boundaries of Nigeria) live, than they do in Abuja or Enugu. It is this reality that explains why the democratic experience in Nigerian elections as in European elections is a hollow one.

One consequence of such hollow democracies is that candidates and policies that would be unsaleable to the local electorate can be pushed through at the supranational level. The evidence is there to be seen in recent employment law emanating from Europe such as the Working Time Directive. It is also to be seen in the means by which General Olusegun Obasanjo came to become President of Nigeria even though his own people, the Yoruba, (even his townsmen) made it clear through the ballot box that they did not want him. He did not need their support because he was loyal to the One Nigeria cause.

The related problem arises from politicians rendering their account of their stewardship in some far away parliament. The void between trustees and the beneficiaries on whose behalf they act is the breeding ground for corrupt and inefficient practices. Because a man cannot steal from himself, when the governed and the government are in close proximity the chain of accountability is shorter and the scope for corruption is reduced. The problem arises as governors are given charge over larger and larger constituencies: as the chain of accountability becomes longer and intermediaries are

---

1. *European Business Review (New European)* Vol. 99 No. 5, 1996.

interposed, the opportunities for, at best, inefficient allocation of resources and, at worst, corrupt practices becomes greater.

If the political consequences of these synthetic supernations are as unappealing as I have suggested, what drives people towards them?

Part of the answer can be gleaned from Sir Peter Smithers' explanation that the motivation for forcing the diverse nations of Nigeria into a single political structure was to "create a large and powerful state with ample material resources" so as to be a global player. This is also part of the thinking underlying the drive to ever closer union in Europe.

What we often forget is that the priorities and values of the world of business are, more often than not, diametrically contrary to our priorities as social creatures: while 'social man' sees (and wants to see) the world in all its colours and variations, 'business man' sees the world as one – a profit is, after all, a profit, whether it is expressed in pounds, francs or lira and profits are best maximised through standardisation combined with critical mass. The holy grail of business is a mass market, with one currency, one language and uniform laws.

It should therefore be no surprise that supernations like Europe and Nigeria are driven by the consummate desire of the business community for standardised and larger markets. But while growth through mergers and acquisitions may be a valid strategy in the world of business, when you are dealing with man as a social animal, any growth strategy for the social unit which is anything but organic is destined to be demerged in the longer term. The other group of sponsors of supranational states are those politicians who cannot tolerate diversity. Under the guise of promoting the brotherhood of man, they are secretly bent on converting all heathens to their values, beliefs and ways of life. For these people, there can only be peace on earth if we are all Catholic, Christian or Muslim depending on the camp to which they belong.

By 1 October 2000, Nigerians will have spent all of forty years trying in vain, in King Canute-like fashion, to struggle back to the real national feeling that the constituent nations have within themselves. In our efforts to cast out the demon of cherishing the identities and values that our ancestors lived by, we have tried the British parliamentary system and the American presidential system; we have tried multiparty and two-party democracy; we have had no less than six constitutional reviews; from the three regions immediately after independence, we moved successively to four, to twelve, to nineteen, to twenty-one, to thirty and, most recently, to thirty-six; the soldiers have had a go and the civilians have had a turn; we started with Balewa, and then there was Ironsi; Gowan followed him who was then followed by Muhammed and then we had the first coming of Obasanjo; he handed over to Shagari who was shoved aside by Buhari and who in turn was elbowed out by Babangida who, making as if to pass to Shonekan, handed over to Abacha, who died in mysterious circumstances and enabled Abubakar to hold the fort until the second coming of Obasanjo.

All the time, effort and resources that have been spent trying to cheat nature through genetic modification of the human spirit could have been used so much more constructively if only we were prepared to embrace diversity by saying: "to each his own".

The first step towards resolving any problem is to acknowledge it. I content myself with knowing that what goes up must one day come down: Nigeria will, sooner rather than later, have to come to terms with the experience of the Roman Empire, the British Empire, the Soviet Union and Yugoslavia. Nigerians will need help in doing so to ensure a soft landing.

I. Karekin I, Catholicos – obituary[1]

His Holiness Karekin I, Catholicos and Supreme Patriarch of All Armenians, died of cancer on 29 June 1999, aged 66, in Etchmiadzin, the spiritual centre of the Armenian Church. He was born on 27 August 1932.

Catholicos Karekin I was the head of one of the oldest Churches in the world, which will mark its 1700th anniversary in 2001. His death, after only four years as Catholicos of Etchmiadzin, is a major loss – not only to the Armenian Church but to all the Churches. A man of considerable intellect, warm personality, and with a delightful sense of humour, Karekin Sarkissian made an outstanding contribution to the ecumenical movement.

He came to the historic patriarchal seat as the 131st Catholicos, in succession to Catholicos Vazgen who had been Catholicos for almost forty years. He brought with him a sense of the challenge and opportunity to rebuild the Christian life of Armenia following the collapse of Soviet power and subsequent independence.

He had had a close relationship with the Church of England from the time that he studied in Oxford, 1957-59, and was an observer at the Lambeth Conference of 1968. As a research student he wrote a thesis on the Council of Chalcedon and the Armenian Church. In it he examined the historical roots of the Christological issues which divided the Armenian Church, as one of the ancient Oriental Orthodox Churches, from the Greek and Latin Churches which accepted the 'two-nature' Christology of the Chalcedonian Definition.

He strongly supported the theological work in recent times which has endeavoured to reconcile those on opposite sides of this ancient divide, though his joint declaration with Pope John Paul II in December 1996 was criticised by some as he had not agreed the declaration with some of his senior prelates in advance of the meeting. His hope earlier this year for a papal visit to Armenia at the beginning of this month was not universally welcomed for similar reasons. The Pope's unprecedented proposal to visit the dying Catholicos at the end of his recent Polish visit was frustrated only by the Pope's own indisposition.

Karekin's visit to the Archbishop of Canterbury in 1997 was a happy and fruitful visit and he particularly enjoyed a day visiting his old haunts in

---

1. *The Times*, 14 July 1999.

Oxford and was delighted to be made an honorary fellow of St Catherine's College on that occasion. He was the first Oxford graduate to be elected head of an Eastern Church. With characteristic humour he explained that the pointed 'ararat' cowl worn by the Armenian clergy is of that particular shape "so that the Devil cannot dance on your head".

His ecumenical work made him a leading figure in the Middle East Council of Churches and later in the World Council of Churches. He served as Vice-Moderator of the World Council's central committee from 1975 to 1983, having previously sat on its central and executive committees, as well as being a member of the Faith and Order Commission. He was also an observer at the Second Vatican Council.

Born in Kessab, an Armenian village in northern Syria, he was baptised Nishan Sarkissian. In 1946 he was admitted to the Theological Seminary of the Armenian Catholicossate of Cilicia in Antelias, a suburb of Beirut. Ordained deacon in 1949, he graduated with high honours and was ordained as a celibate priest in 1952, taking the name of Karekin.

In 1955 he was raised to the dignity of Vardapet and became a member of the theological faculty at Antelias, becoming dean the following year. In 1963 Khoren I was elected as Catholicos of the Great House of Cilicia, and Karekin became an important and significant aide to the Catholicos.

He was consecrated a bishop in 1964, serving from 1971 to 1973 in the diocese of New Julfa-Isfahan, Iran, where he modernised the museum and library of the historic Armenian community there. For a further four years he served in America before his election as Catholicos-Co-adjutor of Cilicia in 1977, succeeding Catholicos Khoren on his death in 1983. As Catholicos of Cilicia, residing in Beirut during the civil war in Lebanon, Karekin stayed with his people and shared their problems, at times during fighting in the neighbourhood of Antelias being forced to take refuge with his monks underground.

He worked hard to try to overcome the suspicion between the two Catholicossates, representing respectively the Middle Eastern focus of the Armenian diaspora and the historic heartland of Armenia, but under Communist domination.

When Karekin was elected Catholicos of Etchmiadzin in 1995, he inherited a Church which had had to deal with major problems – the devastating earthquake of 1988, the collapse of the Soviet empire and the war with Azerbaijan over the disputed territory of Nagorno-Karabakh.

He saw the need for reconstruction and a renewed teaching of the faith after seventy years of Communist rule. Karekin was helped in this by his close personal friendship with Levon Ter Petrossian, President of Armenia, though the roles of Church and state were kept separate.

Illness prevented him from realising as much of the vision he brought to Etchmiadzin as he would have wished; his inability to delegate also played its part, though he was able to look for financial support to the Armenian diaspora.

Conscious of the endurance of the Armenian people through periods of genocide and dispersion, he spoke of God's gift of Christian faith as enabling his people to overcome trials, past and present. This same faith sustained him through the last two years of his life.

Sales agents for publications of the Council of Europe
Agents de vente des publications du Conseil de l'Europe

AUSTRALIA/AUSTRALIE
Hunter Publications, 58A, Gipps Street
AUS-3066 COLLINGWOOD, Victoria
Fax: (61) 33 9 419 7154
E-mail: Robd@mentis.com.au

AUSTRIA/AUTRICHE
Gerold und Co., Graben 31
A-1011 WIEN 1
Fax: (43) 1512 47 31 29
E-mail: buch@gerold.telecom.at

BELGIUM/BELGIQUE
La Librairie européenne SA
50, avenue A. Jonnart
B-1200 BRUXELLES 20
Fax: (32) 27 35 08 60
E-mail: info@libeurop.be

Jean de Lannoy
202, avenue du Roi
B-1060 BRUXELLES
Fax: (32) 25 38 08 41
E-mail: jean.de.lannoy@euronet.be

CANADA
Renouf Publishing Company Limited
5369 Chemin Canotek Road
CDN-OTTAWA, Ontario, K1J 9J3
Fax: (1) 613 745 76 60

CZECH REPUBLIC/RÉPUBLIQUE TCHÈQUE
USIS, Publication Service
Havelkova 22
CZ-130 00 Praha 3
Fax: (420) 2 242 21 484

DENMARK/DANEMARK
Munksgaard
Østergade 26A – Postbox 173
DK-1005 KØBENHAVN K
Fax: (45) 77 33 33 77
E-mail: direct@munksgaarddirect.dk

FINLAND/FINLANDE
Akateeminen Kirjakauppa
Keskuskatu 1, PO Box 218
FIN-00381 HELSINKI
Fax: (358) 9 121 44 50
E-mail: akatilaus@stockmann.fi

FRANCE
C.I.D.
131 boulevard Saint-Michel
F-75005 Paris
Fax: (33) 01 43 54 80 73
E-mail: lecarrer@msh-paris.fr

GERMANY/ALLEMAGNE
UNO Verlag
Proppelsdorfer Allee 55
D-53115 BONN
Fax: (49) 228 21 74 92
E-mail: unoverlag@aol.com

GREECE/GRÈCE
Librairie Kauffmann
Mavrokordatou 9
GR-ATHINAI 106 78
Fax: (30) 13 23 03 20

HUNGARY/HONGRIE
Euro Info Service/Magyarország
Margitsziget (Európa Ház),
H-1138 BUDAPEST
Fax: (361) 302 50 35
E-mail: euroinfo@mail.matav.hu

IRELAND/IRLANDE
Government Stationery Office
4-5 Harcourt Road
IRL-DUBLIN 2
Fax: (353) 14 75 27 60

ISRAEL/ISRAËL
ROY International
41 Mishmar Hayarden Street
PO Box 13056
IL-69865 TEL AVIV
Fax: (972) 3 648 60 39
E-mail: royil@netvision.net.il

ITALY/ITALIE
Libreria Commissionaria Sansoni
Via Duca di Calabria 1/1, CP 552
I-50125 FIRENZE
Fax: (39) 0 55 64 12 57
E-mail: licosa@ftbcc.it

MALTA/MALTE
L. Sapienza & Sons Ltd
26 Republic Street, PO Box 36
VALLETTA CMR 01
Fax: (356) 233 621

NETHERLANDS/PAYS-BAS
De Lindeboom Internationale Publikaties
PO Box 202
NL-7480 AE HAAKSBERGEN
Fax: (31) 53 572 92 96
E-mail: lindeboo@worldonline.nl

NORWAY/NORVÈGE
Akademika, A/S Universitetsbokhandel
PO Box 84, Blindern
N-0314 OSLO
Fax: (47) 23 12 24 10

POLAND/POLOGNE
Głowna Księgarnia Naukowa im. B. Prusa
Krakowskie Przedmiescie 7
PL-00-068 WARSZAWA
Fax: (48) 22 26 64 49

PORTUGAL
Livraria Portugal
Rua do Carmo, 70
P-1200 LISBOA
Fax: (351) 13 47 02 64

SPAIN/ESPAGNE
Mundi-Prensa Libros SA
Castelló 37
E-28001 MADRID
Fax: (34) 915 75 39 98
E-mail: libreria@mundiprensa.es

SWITZERLAND/SUISSE
Buchhandlung Heinimann & Co.
Kirchgasse 17
CH-8001 ZÜRICH
Fax: (41) 12 51 14 81

BERSY
Route d'Uvrier 15
CH-1958 LIVRIER/SION
Fax: (41) 27 203 73 32

UNITED KINGDOM/ROYAUME-UNI
TSO (formerly HMSO)
51 Nine Elms Lane
GB-LONDON SW8 5DR
Fax: (44) 171 873 82 00
E-mail: denise.perkins@theso.co.uk

**UNITED STATES and CANADA/
ÉTATS-UNIS et CANADA**
Manhattan Publishing Company
468 Albany Post Road, PO Box 850
CROTON-ON-HUDSON, NY 10520, USA
Fax: (1) 914 271 58 56
E-mail: Info@manhattanpublishing.com

STRASBOURG
Librairie Kléber
Palais de l'Europe
F-67075 STRASBOURG Cedex
Fax: +33 (0)3 88 52 91 21

Council of Europe Publishing/Editions du Conseil de l'Europe
F-67075 Strasbourg Cedex
Tel. +33 (0)3 88 41 25 81 – Fax +33 (0)3 88 41 39 10
E-mail: publishing@coe.int – Website: http://book.coe.fr